W9-DFD-427

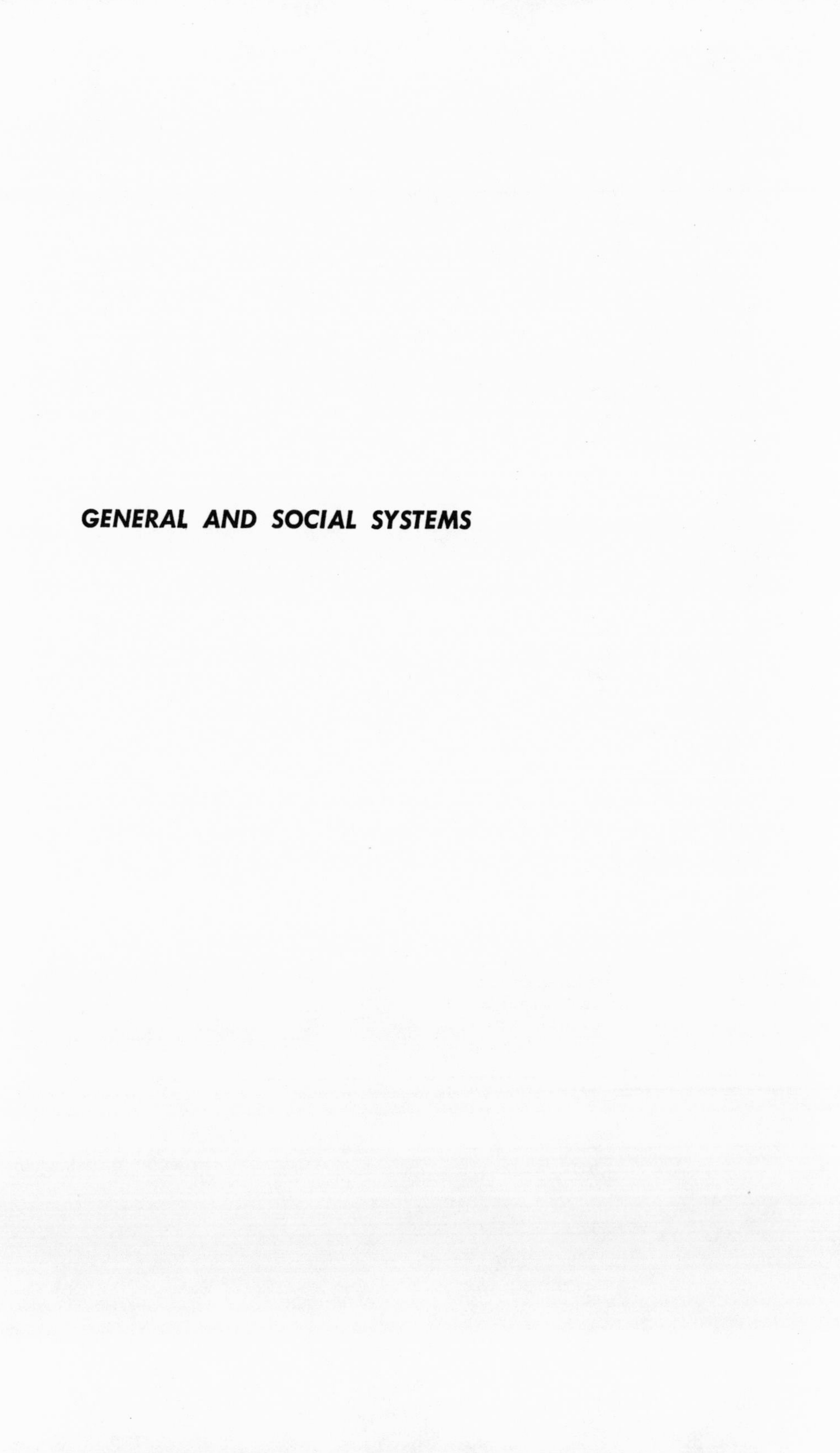

GENERAL AND SOCIAL SYSTEMS

GENERAL AND SOCIAL SYSTEMS

by F. Kenneth Berrien

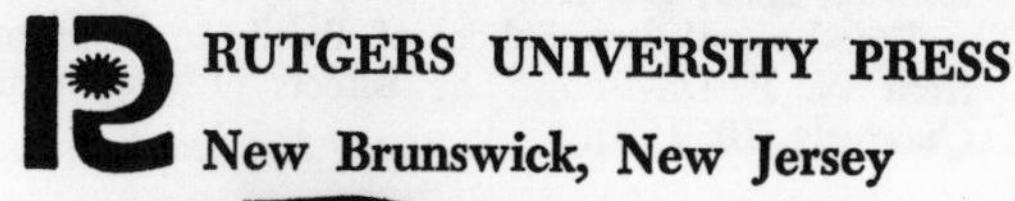

ISBN: 0-8135-0585-2 Cloth
0-8135-0796-0 Paper

Library of Congress Catalogue Number: 68-29552
Manufactured in the United States of America by
Quinn & Boden Company, Inc., Rahway, N.J.

Permission to quote has been kindly granted by the following publishers:

American Psychological Association, Washington—from D. T. Campbell, "Blind Variation and Selective Retention in Creative Thought as in Other Knowledge," in *Psychological Review*, 1960, 7.

Annual Reviews, Inc., Palo Alto—from L. I. O'Kelly, "Psychophysiology of Motivation," in *Annual Review of Psychology*, 1963.

Basic Books, Inc., New York—from *Toward a Unified Theory of Human Behavior*, ed. by Roy R. Grinker, 1956, 1967, Basic Books, Inc., Publishers, New York.

California Institute of Technology, Pasadena—from K. S. Lashley, "The Problem of Serial Order in Behavior," and from J. von Neumann, "The General and Logical Theory of Automata," both in *Cerebral Mechanisms in Behavior*, ed. L. A. Jeffress, 1951.

The Carnegie Corporation, New York—from its *Annual Report*, 1962.

Columbia University Press, New York—from V. Grant, *The Origin of Adaptations*, 1963.

Harcourt, Brace and World, Inc., New York—Nagel, E.: *The Structure of Science*, 1961.

Harvard University Graduate School of Business Administration, Division of Research, Cambridge—from A. Zaleznik, C. R. Christensen, and F. Roethlisberger, *Motivation, Productivity, and Satisfaction of Workers*, 1958; and from H. O. Ronken and P. R. Lawrence, *Administering Changes: a Case Study of Human Relations in a Factory*, 1952.

J. B. Lippincott Co., Philadelphia, and Curtis Brown, Ltd., London—from Stanley Loomis, *Paris in the Terror, June 1793–July 1794*, 1964.

The Macmillan Company, New York—from Robert Frost, "Mending Wall," in *Chief Modern Poets*, Selected and Edited by Gerald DeWitt Sanders and John Herbert Nelson, 3d ed., Copyright © The Macmillan Co., New York, 1943; and L. J. Henderson, *Fitness of the Environment*, Copyright © The Macmillan Company, New York, 1913.

M.I.T. Press, Cambridge—from R. G. H. Sui, *The Tao of Science*, 1957.

W. W. Norton and Co., Inc., New York—from W. B. Cannon, *The Way of an Investigator*, 1945.

Philosophy of Science, St. Louis, Mo.—from M. Bunge, "A General Black Box Theory," 1963, *30*.

Society for General Systems Research, Ann Arbor—from W. R. Ashby, "General Systems Theory in a New Discipline," in *General Systems Yearbook*, 1958, *3*, and K. E. Boulding, "Toward a General Theory of Growth," in *General Systems Yearbook*, 1956, *1*.

Tavistock Publications, Ltd., London—from J. Bronowski, in *Darwinism and the Study of Society*, ed. M. Benton, 1961.

John Wiley and Sons, Inc., New York—from W. R. Garner, *Uncertainty and Structure as Psychological Concepts*, 1962; from C. S. Hall and G. Lindsey, *Theories of Personality*, 1957; and from J. March and H. A. Simon, *Organizations*, 1958.

The Woodrow Wilson School of Public and International Affairs, Princeton, N.J.—from W. P. Davison, "The Effects of Communication," in *The Public Opinion Quarterly*, 1959, 23.

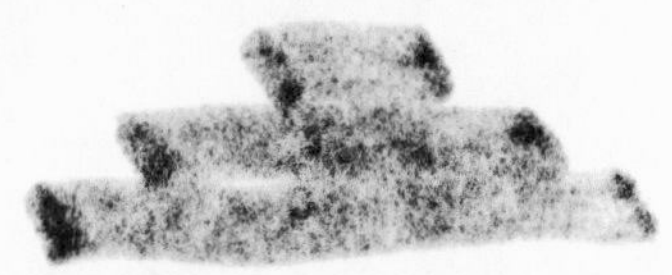

PREFACE

This is an outline of ignorance. Let the readers and reviewers of this effort make what they will of this admission. It is made, however, out of no false modesty but as simple declaration of fact. For today it is not given to any man to master the knowledge even of the discipline in which he has been formally educated, let alone the knowledge of fields apart from his own. I am reminded of Kenneth Boulding's report that, when his visions of general systems integration soar too high, his wife sometimes remarks, "If you are going to be the great integrator, you ought to know something." Nevertheless, the advancement of understanding, I am persuaded, comes about by the clarification of what one does not know as surely as it does by building on what has already been accepted as "true." I am encouraged to present this outline in the hope that my ignorance may stimulate others as well as myself to fill in some of the gaps or revise portions of the framework. The desperate need for a general systems theory I shall not dwell upon here, since this is the burden of Chapter I.

Consistent with the general systems theory proposed, I have adopted the editorial *we* in its exposition. This does not refer to multiple authors, albeit I owe a great debt to those whose ideas and research I have unashamedly and gratefully employed. Instead, the plural pronoun was adopted in the hope that the author and reader could form a system. I have had the image of a dialogue in which reader and author together struggle for clarity and understanding. Unfortunately, the transmission has of necessity been one-way no matter how much I wanted and would have profited from an exchange of views.

One of the great frustrations in writing about general systems comes from the difficulty of finding, not just the right starting point, but the order of presentation even after the exposition has begun to unfold. The concepts are so much of an integrated whole that to talk about one presupposes some acquaintance with others. Even to define a system requires some understanding of a boundary. The latter has no meaning except as it is an aspect of the system. Adaptation is the consequence of certain kinds of system processes, but these processes are not describable unless one first understands adaptation. The theory of general systems is itself a system.

For this reason the exposition is somewhat spiraled with frequent but, I trust, not boring returns to an earlier point. It is my hope, consequently, that the reader will suspend some judgment until at least the total framework—Chapters II, III, and IV—is before him. Perhaps this is a greater charity than any author may legitimately request or expect. While every effort has been made to develop the definitions and propositions as rigorously as our language and logic permit, some may find shady and slippery meanings or logical lacunae in the argument. Where this may be the case, the reader will do himself and others a service to raise objections. On the other hand, I picture this system of concepts as buttressed and trussed by many cross connections so that a weakness in one or two may not be disastrous for the total structure.

As the title indicates, the aim has been to provide a systems foundation for social psychology. The audience I have had in mind is those students and researchers who call themselves sociologists, social psychologists, social anthropologists, organizational theorists, and others who may prefer merely the label "behavior scientists." The focal audience, however, is composed of those psychologists concerned primarily with group phenomena.

One of the side effects of this book, I hope, will be to minimize the vexatious question of whether psychology is a social or a biological science. There are various invidious implications in either answer to this question. If the theory of general systems as outlined here takes root, the distinction between biological and social science will at least be obscured and the controversy over the proper allegiance will become an academic administrative problem rather than a question of which is more trivial or more precise.

The central concept that pervades this book is this: primitive randomness evolves into organized complexity. This is true for the beginnings of life and, before that, in the chemical evolution of the universe. It is equally true of our social evolution. And for those phenomena we label thought, it was John Dewey, perhaps more clearly than anyone else, who saw first that the consequence of thinking was not to mirror nature but to make over nature into something that was organized, integrated, formed. This general theory of systems is such an attempt.

One should not be misled by the order in which the theory is presented.

It did not evolve that way. My thinking has been disorderly, confused, swinging from the picayune and trivial to the broadest of meaningless abstractions. In part I have been amused by observing in myself this example of system organization developing out of nearly random ruminations. I trust that the results of these hunting efforts will be neither meaningless nor mere frivolity for the reader.

No author so rash as to embark on such an expedition as the one that follows could possibly complete the journey without the considerable help of others. Bernard P. Indik has been an invaluable aid over the last five years, reading and discussing large portions of the manuscript, calling attention to sources I would not have consulted otherwise. Wendell R. Garner, Yale University, was good enough to read those chapters in which I referred to his own work, and through his correspondence encouraged me to plunge further. L. Joseph Stone of Vassar read an early but incomplete version, made numerous helpful suggestions, and, likewise, wrote the kind of encouragement I needed at a critical point. George Strauss and Stephen Ulrich, members of my own college faculty, helped on those portions that pertain to physical phenomena.

I owe a special debt to Kenneth Boulding, University of Colorado, a former colleague and friend of long standing. Beyond these personal matters, his cogent writing and provocative ideas on general systems were a major influence from the start. He was gracious enough to read and criticize the semifinal draft, which immeasurably benefited in the final form because of his comments.

Whatever errors may be discovered are, of course, chargeable to me and not to those who have so generously offered their wisdom.

Mrs. Louise Aerstin has often rescued my thoughts and clarified their meaning from the nearly illegible handwriting woven between the lines of my crude typing. With some assistance from Mrs. Hazel Rule, she typed the entire book from early partial drafts to the final copy. I was indeed fortunate to have such a patient and efficient secretary.

Although this book has been germinating for some years, a half year's leave of absence in 1964 and a modest subvention more recently, arranged by the Research Council of Rutgers, The State University, gave me the momentum to carry it through. Finally, the continuous and unfettered support, since 1956, of the Group Psychology Branch, Office of Naval Research, in the persons of Luigi Petrullo and Richard Trumbull, has been a major factor in providing the opportunity to conduct a number of field studies to which references are made in the following pages. Although these studies are not emphasized, my puzzlement about them grew first into an essay, and then suddenly I found it impossible to ignore the more extended questions explored in the following pages.

F. K. B.

October 1967

CONTENTS

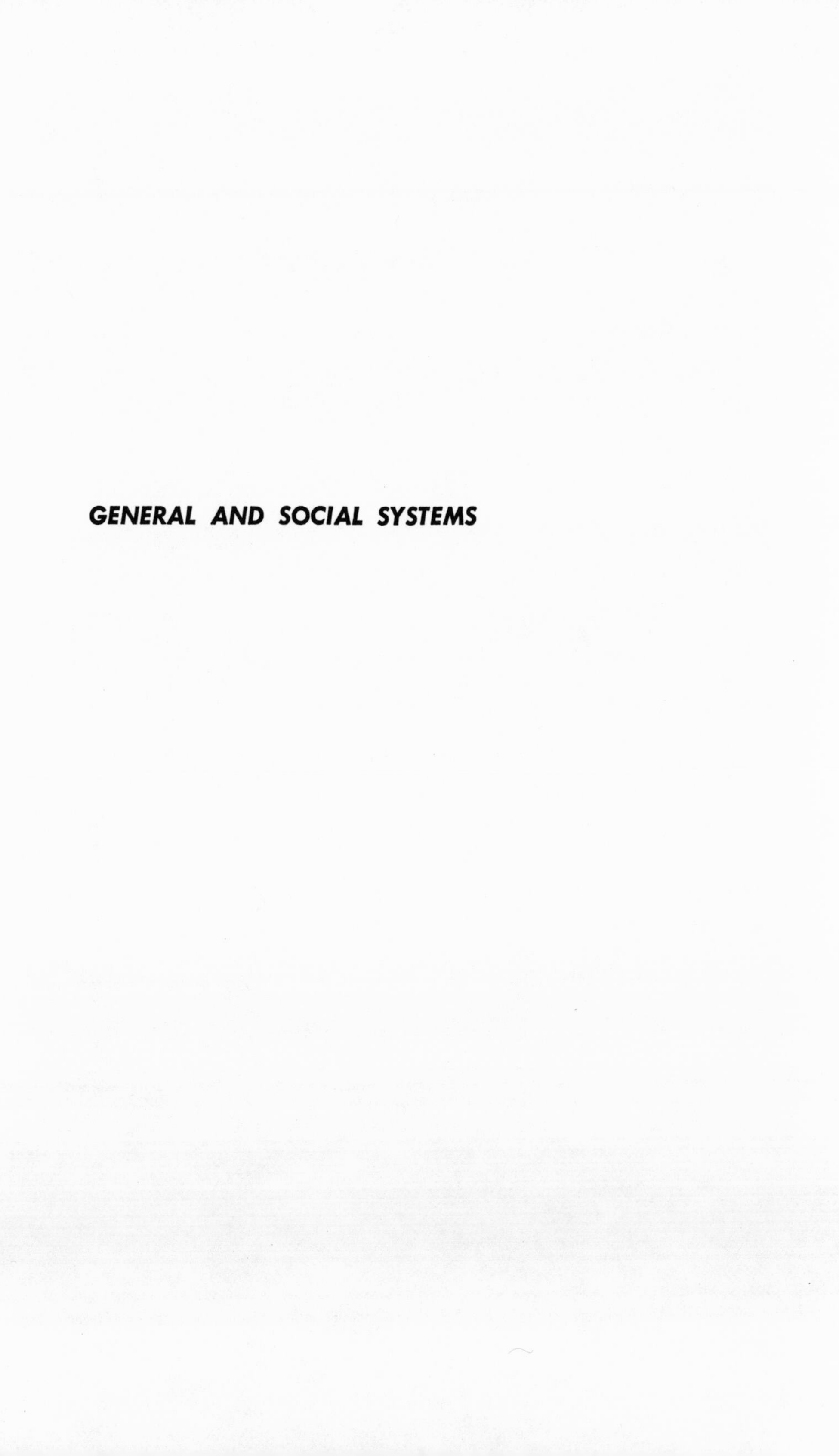

GENERAL AND SOCIAL SYSTEMS

I / THE NEED FOR GENERAL SYSTEMS THEORY

Every scientist, whether physicist or psychologist, astronomer or microbiologist, is overwhelmed by the information explosion. In the twentieth century, scientific research has grown like a jungle, rich, vibrant, branching and interlacing overhead as each investigator tends that little plot which is his own specialty. Journals sprout faster than most libraries can afford to buy them. In an effort to supplement these expanding channels of communication, the academic mails are clogged with a mounting flow of mimeographed preprints whose authors either are too impatient to wait their turn in the appropriate journal or feel obliged to satisfy their supporting patrons with records of progress. This outpouring of data, hypotheses, theories, and considered speculations vie for attention, a place in the sun, choking one another for time and space. The nutrient rain of federal funds has contributed to the lush growth, with the result that the carefully weeded and pruned gardens of a former era have outgrown the gardeners' efforts. The seeds of research have scattered from mathematics to psychology, from thermodynamics to cellular biology, from communications to computers, from sociology to animal behavior, from electronics to neurology. It is nearly impossible to distinguish the "wheat from the tares." Each of our specialties has branched and subdivided, cutting across the prior boundaries of neighbors.

In all this flood of paper reading, writing, and reporting, it is easy to detect a primary emphasis on the analysis of the simple. Enormous progress has been made by reducing the complexity of the world as given, to the "essence of things." Thus Pavlov examined with great care the salivary behavior of dogs, Sherrington isolated the stretch reflex, and Culler studied dogs with functional spinal cords only. The major trend of research in psychophysics, sensation, and even social behavior has been characterized by efforts to refine and purify the dependent and independent variables into their simplest form. This emphasis on reductionism has had the consequence of producing both the constriction of specialties and the necessity for relating visual phenomena, for instance, to the biochemistry of the retina and photoelectronics. Our understanding of chemistry, physics, biology, psychology, and their subdivisions and hybrids has been undoubtedly enhanced by this general approach. Ashby (1958) [1] has pointed out that "these triumphs have been chiefly those of identifying the *units* out of which the complex structures are made."

Given the enormous curiosity of mankind and the greater complexity of the universe, it was perhaps inevitable that intellectual specialization should arise. In a delightful collection of essays, the Chinese scientist-philosopher Sui has this to say (1957, p. 120): "Specialization accorded considerable advantages to the individual. Inasmuch as the horizon of possible knowledge is unlimited, the number of areas open to his selection is very large. Under such a scheme most people, talented or mediocre in native ability, are capable of at least restricted excellence. To gain the esteem of the world as a learned authority one needs only to persevere in a circumscribed field of interest which is carefully selected to fit his temperament and is relatively shorn of competitors. This enables the generally inept but concretely capable, who comprise a goodly number in the world, to contribute significantly to science and at the same time to gain considerable recognition. The universal scholar gradually became a dodo of the past; the narrow specialists rapidly gain ascendancy."

On the other hand, there is an obvious need for a complementary effort that has never been absent but has been muted throughout the recent history of behavioral science. This is the effort to bring about order and synthesis, so that one may make some conceptual connections between the phenomena, for example, of vision and learning, between attitudes and psychophysics, between maturation and political behavior. Even the juxtaposition of these terms no doubt provokes some uneasiness, a vexation caused perhaps by the failure to see how, in any significant terms, they could be related. It is this very failure to perceive immediately the unities in diversity that poses the issues of this book. Without some sense of the interrelatedness of data, the search for new data is blind and unsatisfying. Empiricism without theory is as sterile as theory without data. The first produces a dust heap of facts, the second an ephemeral fog obscuring the subject matter it attempts to

[1] A bibliography, arranged by chapters, follows Chapter X.

integrate. Scientific progress requires the marriage of data and generalizations.

Within the field of psychology, nearly fifty years have passed since anyone has had the temerity to set forth a "grand theory"—and the present effort is not intended to bring an end to the period. Neobehaviorism, represented by Skinner and Spence, and before them Hull, Weiss, and Watson, is such a theory. Gestalt psychology, proposed in the second decade of the twentieth century, is its principal rival. Instead of striking out in new directions on some grand scale, the present-day theoretically oriented psychologists have either spent their efforts on refining the details of their mentors' conceptions or have been content to evolve "miniature" theories encompassing a small range of data. Part of the reluctance to develop broad-scale theories has perhaps come from the segmentation of the field itself, which makes it unfeasible for anyone to integrate the vast array of both miniature theories and multitudinous facts.

Originating outside the mainstream of psychological thought, general systems theory has grown in roughly a decade to a point where its claim on the attention of psychologists is increasingly compelling. It proposes no less than an encompassing set of principles which finds expression at the level of molecules and the solar system, in psychotherapy and communication theory, in the behavior of groups and ecology, in thermodynamics and international relations. The audacity of this effort cannot be underestimated any more than its current status can be ignored. Although it goes without saying that the concepts are still in the formative stages, the main outlines are growing in clarity and precision, particularly as they find useful guides in several applied fields.

The impetus if not the origin of general systems theory came from von Bertalanffy, a theoretical biologist (1950), who was subsequently joined by Boulding, an economist (1956); J. G. Miller, a psychiatrist and psychologist (1955); Ashby, a bacteriologist (1958); Rapoport, a mathematician (1956); and a growing list of persons representing a diversity of formal training and academic affiliations. The development of general systems theory (GST) has profited from concurrent theoretical elaborations in cybernetics, information theory, game theory, graph and network theory in mathematics, to name but a few of the sources from which stimulation has been drawn and to which GST has made some contribution.

Perhaps the main thrust of GST has been in the direction of finding analogies and isomorphisms between chemomechanical and biological systems. The conceptual links with psychological and social-psychological phenomena are certainly more ambiguous. Miller's 1955 article elucidated some nineteen propositions with general application to biological, psychological, and societal systems. He was forced then, as he has been in more recent publications (1965), by the absence of experimentally derived data to employ anecdotal illustrations in showing the relevance of his propositions in the latter two areas.

As one examines in detail a molecular system, say, one of the hydrocarbons, as it interacts with other molecular systems, he is struck by its similarity to the interactions that characterize cell-to-cell, tissue-to-tissue, and organ-to-organ relations. Behavior becomes increasingly complex as one moves to higher-order systems, but a common core of relationships appears to be present at each level. There is a basic similarity among the interactions.

Furthermore, if one were to approach the "big buzzing confusion" that William James described as the world through the eyes of an infant with the eyes of the hypothetical man from Mars, he might organize the world of knowledge along lines quite different from ours. Instead of placing things in categories such as living and nonliving, animal and plant, gaseous, liquid, and solid, he might have categorized in different dimensions such as autonomous or dependent, growing or decaying, self-regulating or "wild." We have come to accept the common distinctions between animals and plants, but every biologist knows that some plants behave in part like animals and vice versa. And the apparently sharp distinction between living and nonliving systems becomes less clear when we look at a common vegetable seed or at the life cycle of viruses. These complex protein shells containing nucleic acids reproduce and consume their host cells, but in isolation are as inert as the grains of sand by the sea.

The categories we normally take for granted are those that man has imposed on nature for his own convenience. (A friend of mine has said that, fortunately for college administrators, knowledge is naturally divided into units that can be taught in forty lectures of fifty minutes each.) Each of these categories has developed its own jargon, its own units of measurement, its special concepts and theoretical formulations, with little attention to what is said in other specialties. But every informed person knows that nature, as well as the social world we have created, is an interwoven fabric of interdependent, connecting strands. Nature is not compartmentalized. Consequently, it is not farfetched to assume that in spite of our current fragmented science, there are generalizations that overarch the conventional categories connecting what is now often unconnected.

Our theories of cosmology and evolution—chemical, biological, and social—stand as testimony to the essential relatedness of phenomena. That is to say, if one assumes that life in all its current manifestations evolved from a single cell in some primordial chemical stew, the processes that generated it may still be manifested in all of its descendants. This is not to say that new processes may not have appeared as organisms grew in complexity, but these also may be understood best as increments in both structure and function that conform with consistent principles at each new level of complexity, spanning the diverging branches of biologic forms. One finds at the chemical level, for instance, a remarkable similarity between the concentrations of sodium, calcium, and potassium in sea water and the blood of Homo sapiens. Taking 100 for Na^{+} as a base, sea water contains 100 Na^{+}, 2.16 K^{+}, and 2.27 Ca^{++}. Human blood contains 100 Na^{+}, 3.51 K^{+}, and 1.73 Ca^{++}. No one could argue that sea water and the fluids of Homo sapiens are alike. The fact that these similar concentrations exist "naturally" in a human being who may never come in contact with sea water may not be pure coincidence. Instead, there exists convincing evidence that the evolutionary process extending over millenniums has preserved the appropriate concentration of chlorides as necessary constituents for the survival and reproduction of all species along that long string of forms that were the progenitors of man.

One of the persistent issues in collegiate education, particularly in the liberal arts, has been the development of a sense of the wholeness of knowledge. Students are exposed to a segment of mathematics, a segment of natural science, a sample of the humanities, portions of philosophy, a foreign language or two, and perhaps a potpourri of sociology, economics, history, and political science. Yet when college faculties are challenged to provide some integration of this mixture, they have almost universally retreated, with the rationalization that it is up to the student to do his own integrating—a task which the faculties feel is too difficult for themselves. Consequently, if some means could be found for conceptually connecting at least larger segments of these subject-matter areas, the educational experience would become more meaningful. It was Ackoff (1960) who succinctly said: "We must stop acting as though nature were organized into disciplines in the same way that universities are."

Andre Lwoff of the Pasteur Institute, Paris, and Nobel laureate in physiology, began his Nobel lecture with these words (1966): "An organism is an integrated system of interdependent structures and functions. An organism is constituted of cells and a cell consists of molecules which must work in harmony. Each molecule must know what the others are doing. Each one must be capable of receiving messages and must be sufficiently disciplined to obey. You are familiar with the laws that control regulation. You know how our ideas have developed and how the most harmonious and sound of them have been fused into a conceptual whole which is the very foundation of biology and confers on it its unity."

If one were to reread this statement, substituting for *organism*, organization; for *cell*, group; and for *molecule*, person, the statement would still have the ring of truth. Moreover, the parallel which Professor Lwoff draws between the harmony of biological units and conceptual integrations again points to the potentials which lie in the general systems approach for spanning the natural and social sciences.

In the chapters that follow, we shall present a version of general systems theory as a set of definitions and postulated relationships. These, we shall argue, are both sufficiently precise and sufficiently abstract to be applicable to systems at various levels of analysis—chemomechanical, electrical, biological, psychological and social. The theory, it should be pointed out, finds its expression in particular models, just as the theory of games as a set of consistent statements is abstracted from particular models (poker, chess, and so on) that are substantively different. And so it is with the various models of general systems theory. The exchanges of information between members of a group, for example, may have a different form from the nutrient and waste exchanges between cells, yet some meaningful and illuminating propositions may be made about the common characteristics of both types of transactions.

It is important, as well, to remember that a model is regarded as a description in generalized terms representing a class of systems. It is literally impossible to describe all systems; hence one can only deal with a "typical" system within a class. Such a phenotypic system in our scheme is a model whose description may omit certain unessential details found in genotypic systems. The task that we have set before us is to construct a systems theory that is a logically consistent set of propositions covering a wide variety of system models. We shall then attempt to show that these models are also faithful representatives of some real systems as evidenced by empirical data.

In the pursuit of these aims, we will encounter places where data are lacking or fail to verify some of the phenomena ascribed to the models. At such points we have to make a choice: Shall we modify the model, or reject the data? Most empiricists would accept the former choice out of hand. But it is not that simple. Good theories have been rejected in favor of poor or incomplete data.

There is the case of Driesch, a German zoologist who, about 1900, shook apart two cells of a fertilized frog egg. Normally, one cell should have become the right side and the other the left side of the frog. Much to Driesch's surprise, each cell developed into a perfectly good frog without defects on either side. This finding so disturbed Driesch that he forsook naturalistic explanations and embraced vitalism. Later Childs demonstrated that Driesch's discovery could be explained by concentration gradients of O_2 and CO_2 centering at the poles of the embryo. (See R. W. Gerard in Fields and Abbott [eds.], 1963.)

There is the further consideration represented at the one extreme by the novelist Arthur Miller (1966), who decries the claim that only through empiricism can one discover "truth," and by Marion J. Levy, Jr. (1966), who takes the position that empirical data should always be regarded merely as hypotheses about facts. Those who have any awareness of the information explosion are also aware that facts, like fallout radiation, have a half-life. Some of what most of us accept now as established facts will prove at best curious half-truths in the future. But, as the campus quips put it, no one knows which facts he ought to forget now. The data which we adduce to support the theory may eventually prove invalid, or, the reverse, what we chose to ignore or discount may prove valid. We can only plead that a conceptual scheme which can encompass facts bearing logical relationships with other facts otherwise unconnected may have a higher probability of enduring than those excluded. As we shall see in subsequent chapters, the developer of a theory must choose, just as the operator of a mechanical system must choose, to respond to some stimuli and reject others. The conceptual structure thus erected is neither true nor false; it is useful or not in promoting additional study and in bringing about understanding, order, and unity to elements otherwise disparate. Finally, whatever the conceptual structure may be, it will bear some distinctive feature of its creators rather than exist as a disembodied, purely "objective" scientific product. We shall return to this later point in the final chapter.

But even if we succeed in finding consistencies that apply to many systems, the question may persist: So what? No doubt the law of falling objects applies to animate and inanimate bodies, but this consistency across the fields of biology and physics is trivial for the former, of major significance to the latter. The biologist, economist, or psychologist addresses himself to problems which may not be illuminated by finding such parallels. It has been argued that the effort to attain some universality of principles may not be superior to the conventional approaches characterizing each of the several disciplines.

There is, of course, the danger of expecting too much from systems theory and of theorizing about issues having only metaphysical consequences, even if cloaked in the metalanguage of mathematics. On the other hand, unless the exploration is attempted, we may not be able to verify even these possibilities. In addition, the long view of scientific advance teaches us that progress is made by efforts to unite what at first may seem to be different. Bronowski has observed (1959) that "all science is the search for unity in hidden likenesses. . . . The scientist looks for order in the appearances of nature by exploring such likenesses. . . . The scientist or the artist takes two facts or experiences which are separate; he finds in them a likeness which had not been before; and he creates a unity by showing the likeness."

These statements by Bronowski not only support the contention that the search for unity is one of the legitimate aims of science but also raise another issue. What is the appropriate function of analogies in the logic of science? Despite Bronowski's repeated emphasis on likenesses, these should not be construed as identities. Two events which are alike are analogous, not identical. In some quarters analogies are looked upon with a jaundiced eye. Two systems that are analogous in characteristics *A, B,* and *C* are not necessarily analogous in features *D, E,* and *F*. The fact of correspondence in some features gives no reason for expecting them to be similar in others. On the other hand, the perception of analogies among systems has been a powerful means for stimulating a search for additional similarities and the formulation of principles having wide generalization. Nagel (1961) observes that "the history of theoretical science supplies plentiful examples of the influence of analogies upon the formation of theoretical ideas; and a number of outstanding scientists have been quite explicit about the important role models play in the construction of new theories. For example, Huygens developed his wave theory of light with the help of suggestions borrowed from the already familiar view of sound as a wave phenomenon; Black's experimental discoveries concerning heat were suggested by his conception of heat as a fluid, and Fourier's theory of heat conduction was constructed on the analogy of the known laws of the flow of liquids; the kinetic theory of gases was modeled on the behavior of an immense number of elastic particles, whose motions conform to the established laws of mechanics. . . . In each of these examples as in many others that could be mentioned, the model served both as a guide for setting up the fundamental assumptions of a theory as well as a source of suggestions for extending the range of their application." Consequently, while it is recognized that analogies cannot be employed as the "proof" of a theory, they can be of significant aid in the formulation of theory, and it is in that respect that we shall unhesitatingly employ them.

The use of the word *proof* in the preceding sentence compels us to clarify our position with respect to the cognitive role of theories generally. We take the position that a general systems theory is fundamentally a description of relationships. It starts with a set of definitions that may be neither true nor false in some final sense, but which at this point are assumed to be true and convenient—useful. It is recognized that other definitions might be constructed which would lead to another kind of general systems theory. Given these definitions, the theory proceeds to a set of logically consistent propositions about the relations between the defined concepts. In the elucidation of these propositions it will be necessary to refer to particular systems or models as illustrations of the propositions, but these illustrations are not offered as the sole verifications. It will be the definitions and logic of the propositions in the first instance that lend plausibility to the theory. Later we will present empirical foundations for the theory as it applies to the analysis of social systems.

Miller's (1965, pp. 211–215) classification of generalizations may help to explicate further the special contribution of general systems theory. He suggests that there are at least two kinds of generalized statements: those that pertain to uniformities across individuals of a given class, and those that pertain to different classes. For example, an ornithologist observing the mating behavior of ringdoves in cages may note certain recurrent uniformities in their mating cycle. These Miller would call *type* statements. They pertain to similarities among a class of individuals. If, however, the observer were to find mating uniformities extending over all species of birds, from eagles to chickadees, these would be, in Miller's terms, *cross-level* statements. These statements are not often made by prudent scientists. Nevertheless it is the bold, but controversial, aim of general systems to develop statements of such generality that they span at least two, and perhaps many more, levels. It was that mathematically trained philosopher, Alfred North Whitehead (1926), who declared, "You cannot think without abstractions; accordingly it is of the greatest importance to be vigilant in critically revising your *modes* of abstractions. . . . A civilization which cannot burst through its current abstractions is doomed to sterility after a very limited period of progress."

Having emphasized the fruitfulness of analogies and the need to search for similarities, it is necessary to point out that in no way does the task before us deny the differences among phenomena. It has certainly been one of the main tenets of psychology that all men are different. The clinician, physician, lawyer, automobile salesman, or clerk who operates on the opposite assumption does so at his own discomfort, as does the theorist about human behavior. The propositions of any broad-scale theory may not explicitly state that differences are coextensive with the similarities, but this should always be understood, just as many "laws" are prefaced by "other things being equal." Many of the quarrels which arise between the proponents of a theory and its critics center on the generality of the similarities; each party ignores the fact that where similarities are perceived and emphasized by one, differences are more important for the other. It is only by discovering where the similarities cease and the differences begin that we can evolve toward a genuine understanding of the area of discourse.

Moreover, the theory will permit a somewhat more orderly organization of empirical observations and may provide leads to testable hypotheses not previously obvious. One of the functions of any theory is to provide a strategy for the fruitful examination of nature. Again, Nagel (1961, p. 133) has pointed out that a precise picture of some segment of nature is a relatively unimportant service which a theory may provide. "It is not a flaw in the molecular theory of gases, for example, that it employs limiting concepts such as the notions of point-particle, instantaneous velocity, or perfect elasticity (none of which 'exist' in nature). For the task of the theory is not to give a faithful portrayal of what transpires within a gas but to provide a method for analyzing and symbolizing certain properties of the gas, so that when information is available about some of these properties in concrete experimental situations, the theory makes it possible to infer information having a required degree of precision about other properties."

It was Dewey's position in the later years of his life that the most fundamental task of thinking was not merely to be a searching spectator of knowledge. The business of thinking and theory building, said Dewey, is not to find a copy of nature, but to reconstruct it in satisfactory terms for humans who, like the rest of nature, are imperfect and fallible.

This is not to say that the theory presented herein is pure fiction. Like all other theories, it has grown out of a multitude of observations, even though at points the chain of evidence may be indirect. It is factually relevant. The advantage of general systems theory lies in its parsimony, its capacity for encompassing a wider variety of phenomena and established observations than is often true of theories limited to a particular discipline.

One final disclaimer. The language of the logic that follows is English rather than the metalanguage of mathematics. Mathematics lends itself best to precision; at this stage of our understanding most of the concepts in general systems theory lack the precision which permits translation into the formal mathematical statements. Once again, this condition exemplifies the stepwise progress of science: qualitative statements first, which become progressively refined and circumscribed until, later, they are amenable to mathematical formulation.

It was von Neumann (1951) who pointed out that the main significance of the McCullock-Pitts theory of formal neural networks was the demonstration "that anything that can be exhaustively and unambiguously described, anything that can be completely and unambiguously put into words, is ipso facto realizable by a suitable finite neural network. Since the converse statement is obvious, we can therefore say that there is no difference between the possibility of describing a real or imagined mode of behavior completely and unambiguously in words, and the possibility of realizing it by a finite formal neural network. . . . A difficulty of principle embodying any mode of behavior in such a network can exist only if we are also unable to describe that behavior completely." Of course, as von Neumann subsequently pointed out, the description of the central nervous system of a human being—complete and unambiguous—might take a lifetime to *read.* It is nevertheless possible with words to reach a level of precision that matches the precision of mathematics. Generally we avoid this laborious task by the shorthand precision of mathematical statements. However, at this stage we are offering statements of approximations as precise as our current understanding permits and as wide in their implications as we believe the logic and empirical information warrant.

After pointing out that advances in the physical and biological sciences brought to the twentieth century not merely techniques but a problem-solving method and point of view, McClelland (1965), professor of international relations, makes this cautious, but in our judgment justified, prediction: "Although we are still at the beginning, general-systems analysis being *general,* being specific to any wanted degree in application, and being indifferent with respect to the dividers usually set up to keep subject matters apart, appears to have good prospects for the study of social systems and such dangerous properties as conflict within and between social systems. Yet, for all that promise, it should be kept in mind that the general-systems approach is neither a formula nor a doctrine, but a cluster of strategies of inquiry; not a theory but an organized space within which many theories may be developed and related." Perhaps our dissent with respect to McClelland's last clause is only semantic, but we would insist that an "organized space" and a "cluster of strategies of inquiry" are inseparable attributes of a theory.

To recapitulate and summarize this introduction, we have called attention to the proliferation of specialties spawned by the information explosion. There is an undeniable urgency for some unifying principles transcending the conventional compartments of research and academia. Kenneth Boulding wryly remarked that if the present trend toward specialization continues unabated, in which communication across specialties becomes increasingly impossible, he could visualize the time when scientists would become so insulated that each could only mumble to himself. The cognitive roles of theories generally, and general systems specifically, have been suggested as a possible approach to meet this need for unification. It is to this task that we shall now turn our attention in the pages that follow.

II / BASIC DEFINITIONS AND ASSUMPTIONS

In this and the next two chapters, we shall establish the groundwork and assumptions of a general systems theory. The theory will consist of assumptions, the definition of concepts, and their associated propositions. We should explain that we are most concerned with those systems which survive.[1] Hence part of our theory must account for the decay and disintegration of systems, but this will be a minor theme. Our primary focus is on systems which function over a time span measured usually in days, months, or perhaps even centuries, rather than seconds, minutes, or a few hours. Before we come to grips with these definitions, it might be well to warn the reader that we must, of necessity, first define some concepts in terms of others initially undefined. Like Whittesey (1949)—who insisted that one could not understand banking without first understanding money, and to understand money one had to have a firm knowledge of banking—we shall jump into the circle of meaning by first of all making statements that may have little meaning.

SYSTEMS DEFINED

A system is defined as a set of *components* interacting with each other and a *boundary* which possesses the property of filtering both the kind

[1] Miller (1965) has distinguished between conceptual, abstract, and concrete systems. The first are those composed of symbols, such as a language. The second are relationships abstracted by an observer in the "light of his interests, theoretical viewpoint or philosophical bias." A concrete system is a "nonrandom accumulation of matter-energy, in a region in physical space-time, nonrandomly organized into coacting, interrelated subsystems or components." We shall deal in this book only

and rate of flow of *inputs* and *outputs* to and from the system. It will be necessary to define each of the terms in this statement as we go along, but for the moment let us try to clarify the concept. This definition specifies the structure (except for the term *filtering*) of a system. One may also superimpose on this a functional definition as follows: A system processes inputs and expels products which are, in some detectable characteristic, different from the inputs. That is to say, given a structure as defined, the system does something to the inputs it accepts so that the products are not merely copies of the inputs but different in some identifiable way. We set as an axiom that the structure of a thing determines its functions and, hence, the structural definition takes primacy over the functional definition. Without structure, function is impossible.

We propose, furthermore, that this definition of a system permits us to conceive of the universe—at least from the solar system at one extreme to atoms at the other—as systems within systems (Miller, 1955). In the simplest conception, the universe may be thought of as a nesting of systems, in which each system (a) is embedded in a larger system (A) whose components consist of $a_1, a_2, \ldots, a_n$. Such a concept can be applied, for instance, to cells within a tissue, to organs within an organism, to companies within an industry, to nations within an alliance. Each of these levels of organization can be conceived as a system composed of subsystems in which relations between the subsystem components result in certain outputs that contribute to the larger system. This latter point we shall deal with at greater length subsequently. It is sufficient now merely to establish the definition in structural terms.

OPEN VS. CLOSED SYSTEMS

It has been customary to distinguish between open and closed systems: open systems are those which accept and respond to inputs (stimuli, energy, information, and so on), and closed systems are those which are assumed to function "within themselves." [2] Equations which represent a chemical reaction of two or more substances that are transformed into a new product are examples of closed systems. For the analysis of certain aspects of a system's behavior, it is sometimes helpful to assume a

with concrete systems, but the definitions and propositions differ in several important ways from those presented by Miller.

[2] Bertalanffy (1932) was the first to emphasize the open-system concept in biology and was impressed, as Cannon was, with the dynamic stability of most living systems which could not be satisfactorily explained by the closed-system principles of physics. Our definiton of an open system does not imply, as Bertalanffy's did, that the system may be stable.

system to be closed. However, every chemist knows that the balanced chemical equation tells only part of the story. For instance, $C_6H_{12}O_6 + 6O_2 = 6CO_2 + 6H_2O$ represents the oxidation of glucose into carbon dioxide and water. The equation says nothing about the heat inputs necessary to cause the reaction, nor does it reveal the energies which are released in the course of the reaction. The closed systems analyzed by the chemist are merely convenient assumptions for a limited analysis of one part of a system's behavior.

Another "closed" system is a watch that maintains a steady level of operation so long as the mainspring tension does not drop below a given point. But periodically, new inputs are necessary to keep the system functioning.

If one examines other examples of systems, such as the thermostat-furnace system, it will become obvious that none operates completely in isolation. The furnace must have a fuel source. The electrical connections between thermostat and furnace must be energized. These energy requirements must come from other systems. Although it is conceivable that such a system could be connected to the total fuel supply, this would be possible only if no other system made any demands on the available supplies. In a world of many systems, this is patently impossible. Miller (1965) has made the assertion that in open systems entropy may increase, remain in a steady state, or decrease; while in closed systems entropy never decreases. "Whatever matter-energy happens to be within the system is all there is going to be, and it gradually becomes disordered. A body in a hermetically sealed casket, for instance, slowly crumbles and its component molecules become intermingled" (p. 203). But even these systems are open to gravitational forces.

We are compelled to view all real systems as open, recognizing that the degree of openness may vary among systems. There may, for example, be an isolated social group which remains out of contact with other social groups for extended periods of time—perhaps for generations—as in the case of the early Hawaiians. Some animals hibernate. A few individuals are hermits. Viruses, germs, seeds may remain dormant for extended periods of time. Yet in all these cases, one is forced to admit that some exchanges occur with the suprasystem. The early Hawaiians, isolated from other cultures, had to respond at least to the physical environment. And if viruses, germs, and seeds remain dormant beyond a given critical period, they die, which is evidence in itself that some slow deterioration process is at work, brought about by some minimal inputs from the environment. One further example is found in the effort to "mothball" equipment of various kinds. These are measures taken to minimize the otherwise normal exchanges that occur between the environment and the equipment. Even when not functioning, systems accept inputs of a kind that is generally, although not necessarily, inimical to their continued existence or efficiency. The main point is that we conceive of all systems as open. Contrariwise, systems stagnate and then disintegrate when appropriate inputs diminish or are eliminated.[3]

COMPONENTS

A component of a system is a unit that in combination with other system units (subsystems) functions to combine, separate, or compare the inputs to produce the outputs. It is conceivable that a system could be composed of all blue-eyed people of age *X* that are lefthanded; however, in order to qualify as components of a system, it would be necessary to show that these people interacted among themselves in some way on stimuli they received to produce certain outputs. In the case cited, this is highly improbable. On the other hand, commercial aircraft pilots within a specified radius of an airport, the traffic controllers in the control tower, and the meteorologists compose a set of components designed to interact so as to produce safe and efficient air traffic. It should be noted that each of these separate components employs highly complex mechanical subsystems in the discharge of his functions. This illustration points up another characteristic of components: they need *not* be homogeneous, although homogeneity is not eliminated as a possibility in some systems. The feature that defines a component of a system is whether or not it interacts with another component within the boundary to produce a product that is distinguishable from the interactions themselves and from the inputs.

THE BLACK-BOX CONCEPT

Moreover the pilot-controller-meteorologist system suggests one of the enormous complications in "completely and unambiguously describing" (von Neumann's phrase; see previous chapter) any system and its components. Fortunately, those who have been working on the theory of automata and communications have offered a useful concept that circumvents to some extent this difficulty. It is the concept of a Black Box. Essentially, this concept proposes that when faced with any system which we cannot describe, either because it is inconvenient and tedious or because the internal structure of a system is unknown, we invoke the Black Box. Let Ashby (1958) present the idea:

[3] We differ with Miller (1965, p. 204) in his distinctions between totipotential and partipotential systems, which under the prèsent definitions are either unnecessary or are equivalent to the distinction between closed and open systems. The concept of an open system clearly implies some dependence upon other systems for survival.

> We imagine that the investigator has before him a Black Box that, for any reason, cannot be opened. It has various inputs–switches that he may move up or down, terminals to which he may apply potentials, photo-electric cells on which he may shine lights and so on. Also available are various outputs–terminals on which a potential may be measured, lights that may flash, pointers that may move over a graduated scale and so on. The investigator's problem is to do what he pleases to the inputs and to make such observations on the outputs as he pleases, and to deduce what he can of the Box's contents. (See also Beer, 1959.)

While Ashby has presented the concept in terms of an electrical model, it can be conceptually generalized to fit any system, biological, mechanical, or social. In fact, Bunge (1963) has presented a generalized mathematical schema worked out for a box with only a single input and output that, however, can be further developed to handle multichannels. He assumes that "the intensity $R(t)$ of the output at time t is determined by the intensity of the input S at times u prior to and up to $u-r$ and that the form of the dependence is

$$R(t) = \int_{-\infty}^{t} du M(t,u) F[S(u-r)], \tag{1}$$

where u is the integration variable and r the time delay (reaction time) of the box for a given channel. . . . The functions M and F, which may be real or complex, sum up the global properties of the box. Notice that the response is not, in general, a function, but a functional of the stimulus; moreover, R need not be a linear functional of S, so that (1) covers both linear and nonlinear systems. The instantaneous response of the box to a stimulus is a function of its entire history unless M (the memory or hereditary functions) vanishes for certain past intervals."

Any subsystem may, for purposes of explication, be considered solely in terms of inputs from, and outputs to, the suprasystem of which it is a component. As one progresses downward from macro- to microlevels, what was accepted as a black box at one level becomes the central concern at a lower level. *We can thus enter the hierarchy of systems at any convenient point.* It is not necessary to build up descriptions of all the subsystems lying below that point or trace through several higher layers the consequences of a given system's outputs as they become the inputs for suprasystems lying above them. On the other hand, the systems definition permits one to follow processes in either direction as far as one's interests, time, and intellectual capabilities permit him.

Without mentioning the Black-Box concept, Herbst (1957) proposed a set of general equations for the analysis of social organizations solely in terms of input-output relations. He was able to draw inference from these equations that pertained to the internal structure of the organization.

The enormous saving which such a concept provides is further revealed if one considers a Black Box with eight inputs and one output—a fairly simple arrangement not far different from a neuron with multiple dendrites and a single axon. Further, let us assume that each input channel can either "fire" or "not fire" and the output may exhibit either response *A* or *B*. It is obvious that there are 2^8 input states. With only two possible outputs, the number of possible internal connecting or not connecting input-output states is 2^n, where n is the number of distinguishable input states. The number is then 2^{2^8} or 2^{256}! Consequently, the variety of states within such a simple Black Box defies the time necessary to describe them (Beer, p. 30). This simple calculation reveals the enormous variety possible even in uncomplicated systems.

It is relevant to point out that Clark Hull, in his efforts to develop a learning theory based solely upon input-output observations, was attempting to deduce from these the intervening variables—of a Black Box. Perhaps the model given above suggests one of the fundamental reasons why his achievements were less than complete and why the systems approach to such problems reveals some of the sources of complication.

MORE ON COMPONENTS

Let us return to the question of components themselves and their definition. In the model of a multiperson system—a group—we have little difficulty in identifying the individual components; they are the separate persons. However, when dealing with some classes of systems, especially at the molecular level, a problem exists in distinguishing between components and subcomponents. We are, therefore, faced with the necessity of providing some criteria for making this distinction. We may approach this problem by an understanding of the nature of chemical bonds. These are of two types—covalent and ionic bonds. The first are those in which electrons are shared by two charged atoms. Ionic bonds are those in which ions of different charge are held together by their mutual attraction. Rarely are bonds exclusively of one type; most often, they are mixed. Organic compounds are usually covalent (shared atoms), and when these bonds are formed, energy is lost. That is, when molecules are formed from atoms, the latter lose energy. This bond (covalent) then represents a less stable condition than ionic bonds, because in order to reverse the process—that is, to separate the atoms—the energy lost during the formation of the molecule must be supplied.

When we consider how molecules are held to other molecules, it becomes clear that they are tied by weak intermolecular bonds, that is, by the mutual attraction of their total charges, and these can be broken quite easily. The ionic bonds are strongest when the molecules barely touch, and weaker as the molecules move apart. Moreover, if the molecules are pressed together beyond the mere touching distance, the electron clouds of the separate atoms begin to overlap and the like charges tend to repel one another. Thus, there is an optimum stable distance between the molecules characteristic of the atoms composing them, brought about by the balance of mutually attracting and repelling charges. (See Blum, 1962.)

This condition at the molecular level suggests the possibility that a similar state of affairs may exist more generally. That is to say, forces of mutual attraction exist among components within a system that are balanced or nearly balanced by repelling forces. The forces of mutual attraction are those which permit the components to function together; the repelling forces are those which preserve the identity of the components. If the repelling forces are absent or are overbalanced by the attractive forces, the separate components merge into a subsystem in which their original identities are lost. This is essentially what happens in the fertilization of an egg, in the assimilation of proteins and carbohydrates by cells, and perhaps even at the level of social assimilation and the intraexchanges of a group.

Simon (1962) has made essentially the same point under what he calls the near decomposability of systems, pointing out that the smaller units of a hierarchic system are the least subject to disintegration. High-energy, high-frequency vibrations are associated with the smaller physical subsystems, low-frequency and lower-energy vibrations with larger systems composed of the subsystems. In a social system, the members of smaller subunits communicate with and influence each other to a greater extent than the units communicate with and influence their superiors.

We may anticipate here some exposition to be included in a later chapter by proposing at this point that, in systems which evolve upward (that is, which grow by the development of successive suprasystems), the subsystems initially possess stronger attractive forces, are less easily disrupted, and function more effectively than the "younger" suprasystems. Contrariwise, systems which evolve downward (by developing specialized subunits among the components) possess greater cohesion and stronger attractive forces than the "younger" subsystems. Consequently, we are able to distinguish between systems and their supra- or subsystems by noting the difference in attracting forces between any given system and its contiguous other systems, and the direction of its growth. However, as we shall see later, evolution upward may proceed to the point where the suprasystem which was initially "weaker" gains sufficient integration so that it may overpower its subsystems. Likewise, for downward-growing systems, subsystems may develop greater attractive forces than their parent systems even to the point of separating themselves from any major dependence upon their suprasystems. It is therefore proposed that *the components of a parent system or systems giving rise to either sub- or suprasystems initially exhibit greater mutual attraction or bonding than the components of the "younger" systems.*

BOUNDARY

The boundary of a system is not conceived in its most general terms as a physical line or a skin surrounding the components, although in particular cases this may be so. The boundary is that region separating one system from another; it can be identified by some differentiation in the relationships existing between the components inside the boundary and those relationships which transcend the boundary. It can be seen that the criteria defining the components are the same as those defining the boundary. The boundary of the telephone system is all the receivers and transmitters that can be linked. The boundary of a cell is the cell membrane. The boundary of a committee is the set of constraints that prevent some of its internal communications from being made available to its parent body. A family also reserves certain kinds of relationships to itself that are different from those the members have with others.

The boundary, in addition, possesses a coding and decoding property. The transfer of information, energy, sustenance, or any other form of exchange between one system and another undergoes some modification which is discriminably different in frequency, phase, amount, or quality from exchanges between components within the system. The construction of any model on the basis of this definition requires that some difference be specified for the relations within, as compared with the relations across, the boundary. The coding and decoding process at the boundary assures these differences.

Boundary coding is found in the most unlikely circumstances and involves some intriguing explorations that run the gamut from cellular chemistry to international communications. As one studies the biochemistry of the cell or the formation of proteins from amino acids or the complex structures of hydrocarbons, it is clear that atoms may arrange themselves in an almost infinite number of ways. How they arrange themselves, we propose, is determined by the systems themselves as the atoms enter through the boundary. If one considers that the fundamental units of proteins are the amino acids, the existence of twenty or more kinds of such units would permit a fabulous number of combinations and permutations *if there were not some restrictions* on their arrangement (Blum, 1962, p. 130). These restrictions, according to our definition, are imposed by the boundary of the system. It is known, for instance, that "if a given protein is fed to a mammal—say a dog—it is hydrolyzed in the digestive tract into amino acids, which are carried to the cells of the body and resynthesized there to protein. The protein thus formed bears no relationship to that from which the amino acids were derived, but is characteristic of the animal whose cells resynthesize it. That is, a dog fed on beef protein synthesizes dog protein from it" (Blum, 1962, p. 132).

We find the same basic phenomenon when light falls on the retina of the eye. It is transformed into neural impulses that are complex electrochemical waves propagated along the dendrites and the axons. A cruder form of this phenomenon is shown in the systematic changes that occur in rumors as they circulate from person to person. *What goes into a system is not what is impressed on it.*

The boundary, in serving as the "exit" for the products produced by the components, can be said to decode what the components have processed so that the product will be in a form useful to the suprasystem. The computer writes out the answers, not in terms of its operations, but in the language which the operator can understand. The telephone or television receiver decodes the impulses which it processes into modulated sound waves and cathode-ray displays intelligible to the human observer. More precisely, the vibrating diaphragm of the telephone and the phosphors of the TV tube are the boundaries. Efferent neural impulses stimulate muscles to contract or glands to secrete that in turn perform some organismic function. Muscular contraction is not brought about by the neural impulses directly but, instead, they release a chemical—acetylcholine—which activates the muscles to contract. What comes out of systems is *not* what went on within them.

It can be seen that the boundary of one system, viewed as an output filter, is also the boundary of its suprasystem to which it is coupled at the interface of the two systems. (The interface may be another system, or it may merely be a region through which the exchanges between systems must pass.) The cell membrane serves as the coding filter for the cell, but it is also the decoding filter for the system of intercellular fluids. The sound waves originated by a speaker are codes of his meanings transmitted over the intervening air space to a listener, where they are decoded into neural impulses in the cochlea (and eventually into meanings). The air is, in this case, the interface of the two systems, the speaker and the listener.

To some extent, this definition of a boundary is comparable to the terminal or pole employed in electronics. Terminals are access points into, or out of, a system. Boundary, as defined, permits the possibility of energy transfers in either direction, depending upon the imbalance of forces on either side of the boundary. Moreover, this definition makes it possible for models to be constructed in which a given locus on the boundary may serve as a filter for both inputs and outputs. At the same time, it preserves the possibility also of specialized input and output channels.

Finally, the boundary—in addition to serving a coding and decoding function—also performs as a *gate*, controlling the rate of input-output flow. We shall not elaborate this point here but, instead, will merely assign the function to the boundary at this time since the problems of rate require an understanding of inputs, outputs, and feedback, to which we shall turn our attention subsequently.

By way of summary, we define the boundary as that region through which inputs and outputs must pass, during which exchanges with the system's environment undergo some modification or transformation.

PROXIMITY AND SYSTEMS

The boundary of a system we have defined as a filter, not a physical constraint like an envelope, holding the components within a given proximity. It is necessary to recognize that the interaction among components may be, and often is, a function of their proximity. The strength of ionic bonds is a function of the distance separating the ions. Atoms must be brought together as a necessary, but not sufficient, condition for the formation of molecules. Van der Waal forces holding molecules together may be increased or decreased by the manipulation of exogenous conditions of pressure or temperature. A man and woman must reach a degree of propinquity before they form a family. The cells of a tissue may not function as a tissue unless they are spaced in a certain way. On the other hand, the ships making up a task force at sea may be spread over a wide expanse of ocean. Nevertheless, some critical distance no doubt could be determined beyond which such a task force could not successfully carry out its mission. Space has a bearing on the possibility of components interacting as a system.

Given these considerations, it is clear that we must posit some exogenous forces, conditions, or fortuitous circumstances derived from other systems that bring components into a necessary proximity before they can be expected to function as a system. Proximity alone is not sufficient to ensure the formation of a system. Prisoners within a compound may not inevitably organize themselves into a group any more than will employees within a given department or section organize themselves effectively to discharge their responsibilities. We therefore offer the following proposition: a critical proximity of components brought about by exogenous forces is a necessary but insufficient condition for system operations.

INTERFACE

The region between the boundaries of two systems we shall define as the interface of the two systems. This may exist in some, but not all, situations. The interface is merely a medium transporting information, energies, and so on from the output boundary to the input boundary of the adjacent systems. An example of an interface is the air that transports oxygen from green plants to animal life and also conveys the carbon dioxide expelled by animals to the green plants for their consumption. Not all interfaces are so extensive. The microscopic region between cells through which various input-output exchanges occur is another example. The feature that distinguishes an interface from a system is the absence of any interaction between the energies, elements, information, and so forth while in transit across the interface. Moreover, the interface is the region which accepts entropy. Figuratively, it is a wastebasket.

THE STATE OF A SYSTEM

It will be necessary from time to time to speak of the state of a system. It is possible to conceive of components of a system being arranged in a given pattern at one moment of time and in another way at another moment. In information theory, the notion of a state enters primarily as a mathematical characterization often expressed by differential equations which define a finite number of relationships between system components. It is thus possible to have many states of a system without declaring that each state represents a different system. Moreover, a system may have the possibility of n states, but, because of circumstances to be discussed in the next chapter, it may usually assume only a fraction of these possible states. One of the most general definitions of a state, given in mathematical terms, which still falls short of being applicable to all systems, has been developed by Zadek (1964, pp. 39–50). It will be sufficient for our purposes herein merely to accept the verbal rather than the mathematical definition.

INPUTS

The inputs to a system are the energies absorbed by the system or the information introduced into it. Before going further, it may be helpful to point out the similarity between energy and information. Wiener (1948), and subsequently Shannon and Weaver (1949), demonstrated that entropy is proportional to the negative of information. That is to say, information is transmitted from one point to another to the extent that the energy in the system of transmission is nonrandom, or organized. Stated in reverse fashion, energy which can do useful work is equivalent to information. This principle is evidenced in numerous everyday experiences. The random noise of several simultaneous conversations going on at the rear of an auditorium tends to block off the platform speaker's words. Or the static on AM radio channels interferes with intelligible transmissions. These are random energies. Entropy has, of course, been independently defined in the second law of thermodynamics as that energy cost that is unrecoverable in any reaction—thermal, chemical, mechanical, biological, social, and psychological (although little has been made of the concept in the last two fields). Miller (1965, pp. 196ff.) has developed this idea in some detail and points out that living systems (and I suspect all functioning systems) clearly require specific kinds of energy for their maintenance, as well as what we shall call *signal energies* or information. "Matter-energy and information always flow together," says Miller.

Maintenance Inputs

Inputs, then, of energies or information are assumed to be of two kinds: *maintenance* and *signal.* Maintenance inputs are those which energize the system and make it ready to function, while signal inputs [4] are those which provide the system with information to be processed. This distinction among inputs has not been emphasized by others, except Miller (1965), and may bear elaboration. A simple example of the distinction can be found in the electronic computer. Once it has been constructed and installed, it must be connected to some power source. This is its maintenance input and it can be either too great or too small. The signal inputs are the program instructions and the data to be processed. For another example, let us turn to neurology. It can be put no better than did K. S. Lashley (1950) in speaking at the Hixon Symposium in 1950: "My principal thesis today will be that the input is never into a quiescent or static system, but always into a system which is already actively excited and organized. In the intact organism, behavior is the result of interaction of this background of excitation with input from any designated stimulus. Only when we can state the general characteristics of this background of excitation can we understand the effects of a given input."

Similar evidence comes from embryological physiology which indicates that the organism is active before any specialized sensorial apparatus is

[4] Cf. Clark and McFarland (1963), and Gibson (1960).

developed or functional. The primary source of action of a living unit arises from an internal energy system having as inputs only nutrients that contribute to, and organize, metabolism. Thus, the embryo is wound up, ready to respond, before exteroceptive functions have developed. In other words, the maintenance inputs in this case, and probably in all cases, must precede signal inputs (Grinker, 1956).

At perhaps a more fundamental level, von Neumann (1951, p. 12) argued that, since neurons as switching components in a system characteristically respond with somewhat greater energy than is impressed upon them, "the energy of the response cannot have been supplied by the original stimulus. It must originate in a different and independent source power. . . . The source in the case of the neuron is the general metabolism of the neuron." The same general conditions hold for vacuum tubes and their successors, transistors. In these system models, maintenance and signal inputs are identifiably separate.

Still other models might be cited from communication, mechanical, or molecular systems. It bears repeating here that we are not attempting to prove the validity of these definitions by an appeal to empirical systems in any general sense, but instead are presenting examples to clarify what is meant by the definitions, and to show their possible utility.

The separation of maintenance and signal inputs permits us to deal with some problems associated with the decay and deterioration of systems, for in these instances it is the absence, or insufficiency, of maintenance inputs which accounts for the decay and final disintegration of the system. The earlier discussion of open and closed systems is also relevant in this connection, particularly with reference to those systems which may, for relatively long periods, appear to be isolated (closed) from their surroundings. On close examination, they are found to be receiving maintenance, but not signal, inputs. Hibernation in animals or plants is such a condition and is distinguishable from death by the presence of maintenance inputs (at least respiration). The definition of open systems and the assumption that all systems interact with suprasystems require that as long as a system is functional (and if it is not functional, it is not a system) it exhibits some interchange with its surroundings. The fact that, for longer or shorter periods, some open systems are impervious to signal inputs or signal inputs are themselves absent demands the further assumption that inputs of a different kind (maintenance) be postulated.

Signal Inputs

Signal inputs are those which the system accepts for processing—comparing, combining, or separating—to produce an output delivered to the suprasystem. Each model of a system accepts those signal and maintenance inputs which are appropriate to itself. The retina of the eye accepts light energy—neither sound energy, nor heat energy, nor the chemical energies that result in taste or smell. The digestive system of an animal accepts amino acids in those combinations appropriate to the already-existing protein molecules of its body. On the other hand, if by some means "foreign" proteins are forced into the tissues, the organism becomes sick. If a rabbit, for instance, is injected with hen's-egg albumin, it shortly goes into anaphylactic shock and dies (Baldwin, 1962, p. 21). When we discuss the growth and modification of systems, it will become evident that systems may be modified so as to accept a greater or lesser range of inputs. Consequently, it would be a mistake to imply from what has been said that *appropriate* inputs are immutable over time.

Although we have formally defined two classes of inputs and have some assurance that these can be distinguished in real systems, this is not to say that one can in every instance tease them apart. Since the distinction has not often been made, there is little information in published research which indicates the separate effects of each type of input. This, however, may be one of the fruitful areas for further examination suggested by general systems theory.

A complicated interrelation may exist in some systems (especially living systems) between maintenance and signal inputs. Even though a system may be maintained, a prolonged deprivation of signal inputs often results in the atrophy and decay of the system. Thus the retinal ganglion cell bodies of rabbits born and raised in complete darkness undergo extreme degeneration. Or chicks, artificially fed for periods beyond seven days, never learned to peck for food and starved in the midst of chicken feed. Their "natural" pecking behavior, evident at hatching, never developed (Bird, 1933). A human group that is well articulated, cohesive, with appropriate division of labor, but does nothing, probably would eventually fall apart. Merely running a machine often is as effective in keeping it in good working order as letting it remain idle, although protected from rust and corrosion. It appears that both signal and maintenance inputs are essential for the continued life of a system.

OUTPUTS

The outputs of a system are those energies, information, or products that the components discharge from the system into the suprasystem. These, like the inputs, are of two classes: products useful to the suprasystem, and wastes or products that are useless. This distinction is also rarely, if ever, made in general systems theory.

In order to clarify the distinction, let us invoke the model of a digital computer again. Its useful product is the print-out of the computational results. The useless waste is the heat (entropy) of the operations. All functional electronic systems exhibit these two kinds of outputs, as do chemical, mechanical, and biological systems. In social and psychological systems, the distinction is less clear, but there is reason to believe that a re-examination of events in these systems from this point of view will confirm the generalization. This will be one of the tasks reserved for Chapter V.

When we say that some of the output must be useful to the suprasystem, we are making an assumption that has wide and fundamental implications. We mean that each system must, if it is to survive, deliver products that are acceptable to its environment. If the products are unacceptable, either the producing system itself takes on a different state (see p. 24) or the environment operates in such a fashion that the system is destroyed.

It is necessary to recall that the inputs to one system may be the outputs of its subsystems. The tags which we hang on the flow of energies between systems are descriptive conveniences. What is tagged as an output is so tagged because we view the system from a certain vantage point. The same transaction may be tagged as an input to a suprasystem. We have previously said also that the input which a system will accept is determined by the structure of the receiving system. The rods and cones of the retina are different structurally from the hairy cells of the cochlea, and it is this difference in structure that determines the appropriate and acceptable inputs. A system does what it does because it is built in a certain way.

Now we come to the crux of the argument. Since the subsystems continually supply the suprasystems with inputs, the inputs have to be of a special restricted kind and not random. If, perchance, subsystem (*a*) produces an output unacceptable to system *A*, the latter rejects it and waits until the appropriate output is produced. Therefore, all surviving systems must exhibit selectivity of inputs and (when viewed as subsystems) process their inputs in such a fashion as to meet the requirements of their suprasystems. In the course of these operations some random errors occur and products are produced that are unacceptable. These are merely discarded by the suprasystem, and become additions to entropy.

This principle is in accord with our current understanding of the biological evolutionary process. The basic notion in evolution is that simple systems create complex systems. We intend to deal with this issue in some detail in the next chapter, but at this point let us merely note that the postulated single cell which was the beginning of life was, according to the above formulation, that one which fed into its primordial surroundings products that permitted that suprasystem to function. More precisely, that original progenitor of all life produced outputs, some of which added to an already existing mixture those crucial products which were necessary to bring about certain functions which would survive. Why did the functions survive? Because they in turn were inputs that assisted the cell itself to survive. L. J. Henderson's *The Fitness of the Environment,* which we shall discuss in the next chapter, essentially proposes that an ecological evolution must be assumed to account fully for biological evolution, with which Darwin was exclusively concerned. There was thus created a loop of input-output sequences that was self-supporting.

At the same time, according to the above formulation, the cell may have also produced outputs not useful to the suprasystem (and received other maintenance inputs). If one were to assume the reverse, namely, that a system only produced products useful to the suprasystem, it would be difficult to account for variability, modification, and adaptability of systems. The latter assumption would result in a perfectly integrated universe—and this is patently false. In the course of evolution, nature has produced many misfits; systems have failed to survive. Since the evolutionary process has not ceased (surely in the biological and social fields), the most general assumption possible is that all systems are capable of outputs that may have no utility to their suprasystems as now constituted.

It is of interest to notice that within the assumptions of the formulation it becomes possible to deduce that as the ratio of useful to useless products increased, the system and its suprasystem grew or lengthened their survival time. If the ratio declined so that useless products overbalanced the useful, the system and its suprasystem disintegrated. This of course assumes a finite limit on available input energy.

SELECTIVITY OF OUTPUTS

The basic principle is that the suprasystems must select from among the outputs of the subsystem outputs. Ashby (1963) has made this same point in a different context:

> Not a single clear counterexample has been given in the last ten years to show that an intelligent system is anything other than one which achieves appropriate selection. This is the touch stone of intelligence. According to this view intelligence is, as intelligence does.
>
> Let me give some examples to make clear what I mean. If a man plays chess we need not judge his powers by listening to his boasting—we simply observe whether the moves he makes are very highly selected out of the totality of legal moves, being selected from just those few moves that bring him rapidly nearer the win.

> Again, the good workshop manager is one who, in spite of all the confusions and difficulties of the day, issues such carefully selected instructions as will steer all the work through by the end of the day. . . . And in the so-called intelligence tests, which do test something of what we mean by intelligence, the operational criterion is simply "did the candidate select the right answers?"
>
> Thus, an intelligent machine can be defined as a system that utilizes information, and processes it with high efficiency, so as to achieve a high intensity of appropriate selection.
>
> In biological processes, appropriate selection and intelligence is shown essentially by regulation; the living organism, when it acts "intelligently," acts so as to keep itself alive.

While Ashby has emphasized *intelligent* systems in the major portion of this quotation, it is evident from the last sentence that he believes the principle of selectivity applies more generally to all surviving systems.

Miller (1955, p. 529) makes the same point from a different angle. He proposes that "the dimensionality of the output of a system is always less than the dimensionality of the input." By this, he means that the outputs include fewer variables than the inputs. Amplifier systems, for instance, even those of "high fidelity," increase the volume of certain frequencies, but they do not amplify the line voltage (maintenance inputs), light, temperature, or other associated features of the inputs. The same may be said of sense organs, each of which selects and responds to only the energies it is designed to accept and discharges, not sound waves over the auditory nerve, nor light along the optic nerve, but impulses indistinguishable in one nerve from the other. In Miller's term, dimensionality is clearly reduced.

We have left unanswered the question, What happens to inappropriate outputs and how are they dissipated? First of all, we need to point out that some wastes are wastes from only one standpoint. Without going into details, the well-known carbon-energy cycle reveals that what is waste for one set of systems is an essential input for another set. Thus photosynthesis produces glucose as a product and oxygen is released to the air (the interface of systems) as a "waste." Animal life depends heavily upon the glucose as a source of energy, and oxygen is necessary to release the energy. These processes do useful work for the animals' systems, but, in turn, release carbon dioxide and water as wastes that are necessary as inputs to plants to carry on photosynthesis. However, it is also known that the intricate photosynthetic process involves many photochemical steps at each of which some energy unavoidably becomes entropy. The same is true of the conversion of glucose (along with the amino acids and fats) into useful energy for the living processes of animals. Heat is released from such organisms into the atmosphere and is generally unrecoverable (Lehinger, 1961). The answer to our question is obviously that wastes or inappropriate outputs are discharged into the interface of systems. In the final form, waste is entropy.

We may anticipate some of the subsequent chapters by speculating at this juncture whether social systems likewise produce wastes, some of which are useful to other systems, and portions lost as "social entropy." As a crude first approximation, is it not possible to conceive of the hard-core unemployed within a society as social entropy—wasted, unproductive man power thrown off by the complexities of societal organization? The various social and relief agencies of an affluent society, which are themselves highly organized, become the counterparts of "antibodies" into which some resources from the mainstream of society's outputs are diverted. Yet there are always the halt, the lame, the old and decrepit, the infirm and incompetent, whose positive inputs to the social processes are nearly nil—sometimes for a lifetime. They represent outputs of a social system, or perhaps of a biosocial system, which are in a very real sense wastes, unrecoverable. They consume more of the system's energies than they contribute. One should not suppose that we are offering the above considerations as anything more than a suggestive social extension of the principle that systems produce useful and useless outputs. Before we can give credence to these suggestions, it will be necessary to define the outlines of the social model more precisely.

A further important deduction follows from the proposition that system outputs are different from the inputs. It carries the logical consequence that as we move up the hierarchy of systems each level will be processing products of a somewhat different kind. Cells accept and process amino acids; receptor tissues accept and process light rays, sound waves, or other physical stimuli; human beings accept and process perceptions. Although in these examples we have not tied the levels together, there can be little doubt that the outputs of one level functionally determine what is processed at the next higher level. Indeed a growing body of data points, for example, to a connection between diet and intelligence mediated by the complexities of metabolism. The important deduction is that basic system mechanisms apply to all levels, even though the substances which are processed may be as different as amino acids and messages. Thus there is no logical barrier to believing that we may yet discover basic relationships among and within systems that are the same for biological, physical, and social systems properly defined.

SUMMARY

It will be most useful by way of summary to list the definitions, assumptions, and their associated propositions which have been presented in this chapter. As we proceed, we shall have frequent occasion to refer to these by their numerical designations. (The first digit refers to the chapter in which the statement is discussed.)

Definitions

2.1. A system is a set of components, interacting with each other, and a boundary which selects both the kind and rate of flow of inputs and outputs to and from the system.

2.2. A component is a unit of a system that in combination with other units functions to combine, separate, or compare the inputs to produce outputs.

2.3. The boundary of a system is that region separating one system from another whose function is to filter or select inputs and outputs. It can be distinguished by some difference in the relationships existing among the components *within* the boundary compared with relationships which occur *across* the boundary.

2.4. Exogenous conditions are those external to the system which bring components to a proximity where interaction is possible.

2.5. Some boundaries are separated by an interface region between systems that merely transports inputs or outputs from one boundary to another.

2.6. A system may exist in various states. A state of the system is a particular pattern of relationships existing among the components and the particular filtering condition of the boundary.

2.7. Inputs are energies absorbed by the system.

a. Maintenance inputs are those which prepare or maintain the system to function.
b. Signal inputs are those which are processed by the system.

2.8. Outputs are those energies which are expelled by the system as a consequence of its operations and are different in some significant way from inputs.

Assumptions

2.9. All systems are open.

a. Open systems are those that exchange energies with their surroundings.

2.10. Systems exist within systems.

2.11. Systems which defy current description, or are inconvenient to describe, may be treated as "Black Boxes" without invalidating the analysis of suprasystems in which they are embedded.

2.12. The functions of a system are dependent upon its structure.

2.13. A critical proximity is necessary for components to interact.

Propositions

2.14. Initially, systems exhibit greater resistance to destruction than the subsystems or suprasystem which evolve subsequently. Later, the reverse may be true; see proposition 5.3.

a. Components are both mutually attractive and repellent.

2.15. The state of a system is one determinant of the output.

2.16. Both signal and maintenance inputs are necessary for long-term survival.

2.17. Systems may produce useful or useless outputs as determined by the suprasystem.

2.18. Suprasystems select the outputs of their subsystems which are useful; contrariwise, the suprasystem rejects useless outputs from its own subsystems.

2.19. Surviving systems are those in which useful outputs exceed useless outputs.

2.20. A critical proximity of components brought about by exogenous forces is a necessary but insufficient condition for system operations.

III / FEEDBACK, STORAGE, AND MEMORY

This chapter will continue to lay the foundations of basic propositions pertaining to general systems which will have subsequent applications to social systems. It begins with a discussion of feedback, first in nonliving systems and then in biological systems. This leads directly to a consideration of response-time, reflexive delays, storage, and memory. It is argued that systems, as a fundamental condition for their survival, must possess storage capacity whose stores are discharged in a controlled manner by feedback mechanisms. The development of Chapter IV depends heavily upon the propositions of this chapter.

FEEDBACK

It has been with great difficulty that we have avoided the use of the concept of feedback in the preceding treatment, for it is one of the central and most important concepts in general systems theory. Without the concept of feedback, it would be nearly impossible to understand how systems manage to survive and function even for short periods.

The conventional prototype model used to exemplify feedback is the twin-balled governor of a steam engine or the house thermostat-furnace system. The latter is perhaps more familiar today than the Watt steam engine, whose near obsolescence has made it a historical curiosity that nevertheless pioneered the feedback concept. The thermostat is a heat-sensitive device which operates in such a manner that when the surrounding temperature drops below a given setting, an electrical contact is made which signals the furnace to go on. As heat is delivered to the space in which the thermostat is located, the temperature is raised to such a point that an electrical contact is broken, thus cutting off the furnace and further heat. It can be seen that the thermostat is the controller of the furnace, maintaining near-constant temperature. The principle underlying this device is that the output of the system is sensed and regulates the input, without the intervention of any system other than an operator who sets the level of the effect (temperature) desired. (Notice that even here there is a suprasystem—the operator.)

The importance of feedback derives from the fact that it is automatic and invariant (provided there is no breakdown internally), and it copes with a wide variety of disturbances that would otherwise upset the steady state of the system. The amazing feature of feedback is that a system so regulated can maintain its steady operation even when the timing and pattern of disturbances are not known to its designers.

Let us look at some systems lacking feedback to see the contrast. A structure, such as a house, if built in Japan, where it is subject to earthquakes, typhoons, heavy snows, plus the other less devastating ravages of wind, rain, and intense sun, must be built to counteract *each* of these disturbances if it is to survive. If some miscalculation occurs in the design, say, to compensate for earth tremor, the structure may be damaged. An ordinary airplane is similarly built to withstand the rapid changes in atmospheric pressure, the jolts, vibrations, and stresses on its structure. Furthermore, it must be flown by a pilot who pays vigilant attention to its altitude and direction, making appropriate adjustments through the controls. In each of these cases, the system is unable, by itself, to adjust to forces that would destroy it unless the forces have been calculated in the designing stage. The unique feature of systems with feedback is that they compensate automatically for disturbing forces whose pattern and timing *need not be known beforehand.* To design such feedback control systems, it is merely necessary to know the parameters of possible disturbances and their possible extreme limits.

If one installs an automatic pilot in the airplane, it will then hold its straight and level course in spite of turbulence and without human intervention once the autopilot is set. This is accomplished by devices which automatically sense any displacement in the roll, pitch, or heading of the plane and immediately, through appropriate mechanical linkages, adjust the control surfaces to bring the plane back to straight and level flight. The simpler thermostat-furnace system illustrates the same principle. No matter how rapidly heat is lost, or how frequently temperatures outside the controlled space fluctuate, the thermostat continues to maintain near-constancy within the capabilities of the furnace to supply the heat. The pattern or magnitude of these ambient-heat changes need not be known so far as the design of the thermostat is concerned.

Sufficient is known about the principles underlying feedback that it is now possible to conceive of and build systems which not only maintain a steady state but which modify their behavior in accord with preplanned patterns in the face of ambient conditions that would otherwise force the system to perform erratically. Thus it is possible to plug into an autopilot a transcontinental flight plan that will follow the fixed airways which require periodic changes in direction. Metal-cutting machines have been programmed which automatically turn out complicated shapes. Tape-recorded messages are fed into a telephone circuit if the dialed number does not answer. In these and many other systems, the essential feature which makes their operation possible is a feedback, or multiple feedback loops. Diagrammatically, we can represent feedback as in Figure 1. *I* represents the input, *B.B.* is a Black Box, *O* is the output,

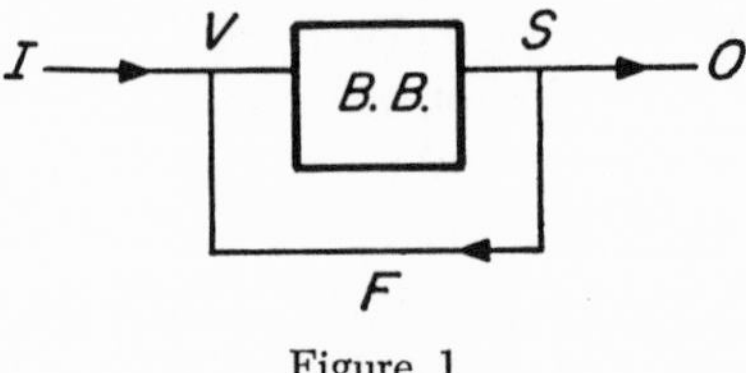

Figure 1

S is some sensing device that "meters" the output and may be adjustable. *F* is the feedback loop and *V* is some valve or other control mechanism permitting more or less of the input to flow into the Black Box. In terms of our previous discussion, notice that *V* and *S* are parts of what we defined earlier as the boundary of the system. They are, in a general sense, filters for the system.

It is convenient to distinguish between negative and positive feedback. The former, negative feedback, refers to the condition when the setting of S is such that the output has reached some predetermined maximum level and the feedback loop conveys the message to the valve to cut off or reduce the inputs. Positive feedback is the reverse situation: the output is less than some maximum and the feedback loop signals the valve to open, allowing more inputs to enter the *B.B.*

FEEDBACK AND THE STEADY STATE

Long before the feedback principle was recognized as having widespread applicability to an understanding of systemic stability, the latter phenomenon had attracted the curiosity of intellectuals. Le Châtelier (1888) proposed the principle (freely translated) that any chemical system in equilibrium if disturbed will change in such a way as to minimize the disturbance. Pareto (1935) declared almost the same principle as it applies to social systems. "At once a reaction will take place tending to restore the changing form to its original state as modified by normal change." Similar statements can be found in Weiss (1925), more recently in Kempf (1958, pp. 894–895), and many others.

It becomes increasingly clear that the stable state, wherever it is found, suggests that some feedback mechanism is at work. Cannon's descriptive principles of homeostasis (1945) are so strikingly in harmony with the concepts presented herein that they bear repeating:

> (1) Our bodies constitute open systems engaged in continuous exchanges with our external environment. They are compounded of highly unstable material. They are subjected frequently to disturbing conditions. The maintenance of a constant state with them is in itself evidence that agencies are acting, or are ready to act, to maintain that constancy. The relative uniformity of blood sugar, body temperature, and a slight alkalinity of the blood may be regarded, in this view, as merely samples of the effect of nice devices at work in the organism. Further research would probably prove that similar devices are effective in maintaining the constancy of other elements in the body fluids.
>
> (2) If a state remains steady, it does so because any tendency toward change is automatically met by increased effectiveness of the factor (or factors) which resist change. . . .
>
> (3) The regulating system which determines homeostasis of a particular feature may comprise a number of cooperating factors brought into action at the same time or successively. . . .
>
> (4) When a factor is known that can shift a homeostatic state in one direction it is reasonable to look for automatic control of that factor or for a factor (or factors) which operate in the opposite direction. This postulate is really implied in the previous postulates and may be regarded as emphasizing the confident belief that homeostasis is not accidental but is the result of organized self government and that research for the governing agencies will be rewarded by their discovery.

When Cannon wrote these words, feedback theory had not reached its present level of development. It is clear that the "organized self government" whose agencies he prophesied would be discovered are found in feedback mechanisms. Perhaps the most convincing evidence that homeostasis is a condition brought about by feedback can be found in the often mentioned homeostat constructed by Ashby (1960). A complete description of this device need not concern us here. Suffice it to say that it consisted of four pivoted magnets electrically connected but each independently controlled by "step switches," each having twenty-five positions. This arrangement provided 390,625 combinations of parameter values. The crucial feature of the device was an arrangement that when a given magnet diverged from its central position, the commutators on the step switches of the other magnets were energized and automatically adjusted the current to the "slave" magnets so that their positions were only momentarily altered. Any single magnet could be disturbed by the operator or, if he chose, two or three magnets might be moved from their central positions. No matter what combination of disturbances one might create, the remaining magnets were only activated for an instant and then returned to their "stable" position. This was accomplished by relatively simple feedback loops far fewer than the 390,625 combinations of input values. The homeostat exhibited adjustive behavior in all respects comparable to that described in Cannon's postulates. This was all the more convincing because the step switches were so constructed that the resistances they tapped were randomized. Thus the step switches were required to "hunt" for the appropriate values which would result in maintaining a zero deflection in the slave magnet.

It can be seen that the homeostat is a purposeful machine in the sense that, regardless of what pattern of disturbances is impressed on it (that is, manual deflection of any combination of magnets), it responds by maintaining stability in the pointer position(s) of the slave magnet(s). The only explanation necessary to account for its behavior is a description of its components and the manner in which they interact with other components. Purpose in terms of some teleological construct is unnecessary.

If we turn to physiological research, there is abundant evidence being uncovered that the feedback concept has empirical validity. Koell and Ferry (1963) found evidence suggesting a negative feedback between the cortex and subcortical areas in cats when stimulated optically. Davis (1958), Davis and Buchwald (1957), and Davis, Lundervold, and Miller (1957) have likewise argued that feedback loops involving pressure-sensitive receptors in arteries and veins, coupled with a yet unidentified control center for the heart rate, account for the narrow fluctuations in both blood pressure and heart rate. When Davis and his colleagues attempted to relate somatic responses to visual stimuli, they found a widespread pattern that involved various measures of cardiovascular, sweat-gland, muscular, and respiratory changes. "Technically put," he says, "we find interaction between response variables, sex groups and stimuli. One pattern of responses is produced by one sort of stimulus, another by a different one and the same stimulus will produce one pattern of response in the male and another in the female. *The pattern is probably also dependent upon the peculiarities of the individual.* . . . The somatic changes produced by our picture stimuli are not 'random overflow' nor yet are they a homogenous pattern of activation or 'general tensions' reaction" (Davis, 1958, p. 52).

In terms of general systems theory and particularly following the homeostat model by Ashby, this means that, as the details of the somatic responses are traced out, we discover that the exact pattern is influenced, if not determined, by the state of the system at the moment some disturbance (stimulus) is impressed on it. On the other hand, Davis pointed out that he could detect what he called a general activation in response to all stimuli that involved an increase in muscular tension and sweat-gland activity with a decrease in all other measures. Thus a kind of average pattern did emerge.

A more general description has been given by Grinker of the enzymatic interrelations that also emphasize the feedback principle. "In the multicellular organism many enzymes are liberated by cells in various tissues for extra-cellular humeral diffusion. They comprise a complicated system of activators with multiple precursors, co-enzymes, and complicated chains of checking and reversing antagonistic enzymes, all of which in health seemingly balance each other to facilitate the conversion of substances for utilizable energy, to store energy, and to mobilize metabolic processes under specific circumstances. Study of these energy systems has disclosed strange and intricate complexities to which there seems no end or beginning. "*Instead the biologist must assume basic circularity of process*" (Grinker, 1956, p. 5, italics added).

The same can be said of the homeostat. The internal adjustments of the step switches "seeking" appropriate values in response to a manual deflection finally reached one of 390,625 possible combinations. However, to trace the time sequence of the unsuccessful adjustments would, no doubt, reveal different patterns depending upon the condition of the step switches at the time of the manual deflection. This would clearly be a difficult, although not an impossible, task. It may turn out that such an approach may be inappropriate. Ashby pointed out that the stability of a system cannot be attributed to any one part or to any one set of responses but, instead, is a characteristic of the system taken as a whole. Stability is achieved by a multitudinal, although finite, number of sequences. Systems analysis does not require that cause and effect relations be traced out in some chainlike fashion, even if that were possible. Instead, the analysis will be sufficient if one empirically defines the system to be studied and identifies the inputs, outputs, and feedback channels, recognizing that the internal operations and some Black Boxes may be more complicated than current techniques can handle.

REFLEX TIME VS. MEMORY

Time is a dimension that we have not considered directly in the discussion so far, yet time is obviously involved in the operation of systems. We start with the innocuous statement that there must be some delay between the input to a system and its output. It is approximately true that this delay will vary directly as a function of the structure and complexity of the system, although this relationship is not always linear (Wiener and Schade, 1963, p. 2). Electrical circuits and mechanical systems can be constructed which delay their outputs for a specified time. Plants transform and fix solar energy that may be released to perform useful work weeks or years later. This latter example, of course, pertains to progressive energy transfers from one system to another, but in principle it is not different from the transfers between components within a system.

One is tempted to equate memory with the time delay between input and output. In the conventional delayed-response studies of both men and animals, how can one account for the results except by invoking the memory concept? If the system is in such a state that S_1 evokes R_1 after a delay of ten minutes, we feel compelled to attribute the delay to a memory "trace." But what is the difference between this delay and one of ten seconds, of one second? What is the dividing line in time between those delayed responses we attribute to memory and those that are reflexive?

As a way of arriving at an answer to this question, it may be helpful to consider various examples that are conventionally considered memory. The data cards or tape fed into a computer are memories. The magnetic cores or tapes in the computer itself are memory reservoirs. The genetic code in the DNA macromolecule—a particular arrangement of submolecules—is referred to as a memory. Although our knowledge of the neurological basis for memory is paradoxically very limited, it is the general view that nerve cells involved in memories are in some fashion different from those that are not, and that the difference persists over a time span. An inventory of raw materials or finished products in a factory may also be considered examples of memories. It appears that *any relatively permanent record of inputs to a system that subsequently affects the processing of other inputs is a memory* (Gerard, 1953). This definition permits a distinction between memory and the necessary delays in the straight processing of inputs to outputs. Those inputs that leave no record behind them, like fish swimming in the sea, produce no memories.

Necessity for Storage

The definition requires an assumption that at least some, but not necessarily all, systems possess the property of storing inputs or their derivatives. A number of questions arise from this assumption. First, why is storage necessary? Second, what is the mechanism whereby storage is accomplished? Third, how does the stored record affect later inputs?

Let us approach an answer to the first of these questions by recalling a fundamental assumption, namely, that systems exist within systems.

It is a further proposition (to be developed in the next chapter) that the evolutionary process can be described as a gradual improvement in the matching of systems to their suprasystems. More explicitly, the outputs at one level initially only approximate the requirements of the larger, encompassing systems. Mismatching is the "natural" condition; matching is the "evolved" condition. Mismatched subsystems are those which produce too much, too little, or the unacceptable kind of output for the suprasystem.

If the subsystem produces too much, storage of the excess may be a possible adjustment. (Unacceptable outputs are relevant to adaptation.) The finished products of a factory that are not immediately sold are such a memory. The water in reservoirs of a city's water system is another example of excess output from the meteorological system that is stored for subsequent use. The rate of chemical reactions is a function not only of the concentrations of reactants but also of the accumulation of a product. It is possible for excess outputs to be dissipated and destroyed. On the other hand, given mismatching in this sense, those systems will most likely survive that have the capacity to store when the demands of the suprasystem are light, and to draw upon those stores when the requirements are heavy. Hence, while storage is not a necessary feature of all systems, those which are so constructed that storage is possible are thereby better equipped to survive. Probably, although not certainly, storage arising from surpluses is limited to maintenance rather than signal functions.

Storage as Structural Change

A second circumstance under which systems store energies, information, and so on, occurs when the components assume and hold a particular state as a consequence of their internal operations. Gerard (1963) and others have applied the term "irreversible change" to designate this condition. They refer to the fact that, in the propagation of a neural impulse, the neuron undergoes a *reversible* change. This is evidenced by the fact that the pulses coursing along a neuron are separated by a finite time interval. The neural "current" is really a wave of electrochemical changes that are reversible. Memory, however, is a change that is irreversible—or, more precisely, is only reversible over a long time span. Precisely what that change is in the neurons is not firmly established, although it is possible that there are many changes, some of a molecular sort in the end bulbs and others involving the growth of fibrils at the extremities of the neurons. However, nerve cells are not the only systems that record traces of inputs. Light-sensitive chemicals are similarly changed in structure by inputs. The streamlining of trees and shrubs subjected to strong winds is a gross example of inputs being recorded in some structural modification. These storage effects are more characteristic of signal than maintenance inputs.

Storage and Dynamically Maintained Change

A third and dynamic way in which storage may occur is by means of some sort of continuing input that maintains a given state among the components. Some neurological theories of memory have taken this form. Gutherie's (1952) explanation of delayed responses in classical conditioning studies assumes a series of stimulus response cycles that continued during the interval between the conditioned stimulus and the response. Lorente de No (1938) provided the neurological basis for Gutherie's position in his well-known discovery of circular networks of neurons so connected that the excitation of one would lead through a number of intermediate neurons to the re-excitation of the first. Thus a circuit could be repeated almost indefinitely so long as the cortex remained alive. Outlying neurons may bring impulses into the circuit and other efferent neurons may carry impulses away. Such networks provide for both regenerative loops as well as input-output possibilities.

Von Foerster (1950) developed a mathematical model of memory based on this assumption of nearly continuous feedback. Making use of the conventional decay processes of chemistry, he initially assumed that the rate at which any set of neural impressions would decay is proportional to the number impressed originally on the system. The theoretical forgetting curve derived from this formulation dropped more precipitously than most empirical forgetting curves. However, by introducing into the equation a negative coefficient, the theoretical curve could be made to conform more closely to empirical results. The negative coefficient that worked best was one which operated under the rule that the "free space" left by normal decay was reimpressed, but not with the same efficiency as the original learning. Thus, von Foerster argued that the necessity for assuming memory was dynamic and could only be maintained by some sort of periodic reactivation of the appropriate components. The background assumption of this point of view is that whatever the residual effects from processing inputs are, they are transitory and must be re-established. Little or no storage capacity is postulated. In this respect the dynamic theory of memory stands in opposition to the previous notions that assume an enduring residual change.

On the other hand, there may be no essential conflict between the dynamic and static views. All memories in any form decay, some at an infinitesimal rate. The print on books fades, IBM cards deteriorate, magnetic patterns dissipate, and, evidently, whatever the neural traces may be, they vanish. Even if we conceive of storage as any *potential* energy, the second law of thermodynamics carries with it the increase in entropy as an inevitable degradation of all energies. It is here that the earlier distinction between signal and maintenance inputs helps to resolve a conflict. *Memory can be conceived to be a stored change in a system as a consequence of signal inputs that are maintained longer by appropriate maintenance inputs.* At the neural or more general biological level, this appears obvious: the metabolism of the cells must be maintained to permit the traces to endure. In the case of punched, magnetic, written, or printed memories, appropriate protections—"mothballing"—serve to prolong the change. These are not maintenance inputs, but instead may be considered barriers to entropic changes in the absence of maintenance inputs. In extreme cases the memories may be renewed by repunching, reprinting, or by relearning in the case of neurologically based memories.[1] These latter are clearly new maintenance inputs.

In part we have already answered the second question: What is the mechanism of storage? It must be some change in morphology or structure as the consequence of inputs. The blank sheet of paper becomes a memory when some symbol is written on it. The computer card becomes a reservoir for data only when appropriate holes are punched in it. The rings in the cross section of a tree trunk are memories of annual variations in environmental conditions. Storage is accomplished in all these and other examples by some structural alteration in the pristine condition of the system.

Storage as It Affects Later Inputs

Third, how does the stored record become integrated with later inputs? As long as one thinks of memories being somehow set off to one side within a system as either semifinished or finished products, this question provides some challenge. In the factory example, the inventory memory is physically set off. However, if we had the space here to develop a systems model of a productive enterprise, it could be shown that the existence of inventories influences the processing activities through subsystem feedback channels. (See Beer, 1959, Chap. XVI.) The question of integration provides no difficulty as long as we remember that a structural change within the system, either enduring or transitory, must result in some change in function. Hence, as a consequence of a change in structure, new inputs will be processed in a way that they once were not. The influence of memory with new inputs comes about necessarily.

To summarize this section: Delay between input and output is a neces-

[1] Evidence that memories in men and animals are not strictly localized but may involve widespread alterations in the nerve net does not invalidate the general principle given above. The possibility of redundancy in complex networks is moreover not limited to neural, "wet" systems but also has been built into many "dry" systems, such as computers.

sary phenomenon. Neither storage nor memory is necessary for all systems. Storage (and hence memory) occurs when (a) subsystems are so mismatched with their suprasystems that the former process faster than necessary; (b) components assume an enduring state as a consequence of accepting and processing inputs. Either or both types of storage require maintenance inputs to extend the life of the stored change. If new inputs (subsequent to storage) involve components whose relationships or structures have been modified, the new inputs must be processed in a way different from the way they would have been processed had the components not been changed.

INPUT-OUTPUT CONTROLS

The previous section has presented the propositions pertaining to storage within systems and has given the logic for its existence. We may now consider the relations between systems which further account for the flow of stored energies in some controlled fashion. Up to this point we have provided no explanation of the controls by which one system may discharge energy, information, or signals to its suprasystem.

Let us first consider the fact that all energy is ultimately derived from the sun. It has been estimated that not more than a very small percentage of that energy reaching the earth is captured by green plants and converted to glucose. Some additional solar energy is transformed into the potential energy of water vapor, creating rains and water power. The excess is dissipated as entropy. Second, the conversion of solar energy to glucose involves storage phenomena, and this stored energy always exceeds the requirements of systems that depend on glucose for their energies (Lehninger, 1961). If this were not so, the supply of stored energy would be exhausted as rapidly or more rapidly than it could be accumulated. In the world as a whole, the available foodstuffs exceed consumption, although within regions the vegetation clearly limits the density of animal life. Desert and arctic areas or other food-importing regions are examples of the latter. Notwithstanding these exceptions, it is evident that the potential input of solar energy exceeds the systems' energy outputs.

Let us now concentrate attention on green plants as the first level at which solar energy is stored. It has been demonstrated that photosynthesis is a complex biochemical series of processes at each stage of which there is degradation of energy transferred to the next stage. Through successive transformations, portions of this energy are stored and portions are converted to useful work. We can only account for the fact that successive systems store energies by postulating that the output constraints of one system are greater than the input potential. Stated differently, maintenance storage occurs when *input exceeds output.* This proposition is illustrated by a hydraulic model (Figure 2).

Figure 2A represents a tank with a larger input than output, and Figure 2B has a larger output than input. Given a constant flow of water in both cases, it is evident that A will store water while B will not.

Figure 2

A number of deductions follow from the above proposition. We shall mention only two. First, if the rate of input exceeds the output rate by a certain degree, the storage capacity will be exceeded and thereafter additional input will not be accepted by the system. Clearly, the tolerable input-output difference depends upon the storage capacity.

We can express these relationships by a simple equation. Let I_c = input capacity, O_c = output capacity, and S_c = storage capacity; then $S_c = I_c - O_c$. It can be seen that we can thus define each of the capacities in terms of the other two. Moreover, it is evident that if I_c is less than O_c, S_c will be a negative number, which means that storage capacity is less than nonexistent. Also, if $I_c = O_c$, then S_c is zero.

A second deduction from the general proposition pertains to feedback and the means whereby a near-constant output might be achieved. In what has just been presented, we have assumed mere coupling of systems in which the inputs and outputs are relatively constant or at least one is directly controlled by the other. Now we assume a more general case in which there is variability in the input rate and some possible variability also in the amount stored (less than the system's maximum capacity). How can such a system maintain a near-constant flow?

Let us look at the hydraulic model. The output capacity is clearly established by the structural limitations (boundary control); but if the outflow were to be controlled at some rate less than this maximum, it would require some control over the amount stored. This could be established either by decreasing the input or output flow. Thus:

$$(1)\quad S_c - X = (I_c - X) - O_c, \quad \text{or} \quad (2)\quad S_c - X = I_c - (O_c + X).$$

Where $I_c > O_c$ (Figure 2A), equation (2) would be impossible to achieve because it requires exceeding the output capacity established by the system's structure. On the other hand, equation (1) is possible. In Figure

2B where $I_c < O_c$ and S_c is less than zero, a reduction in I_c would result in even less storage. Consequently, if $S_c - X$ is to be a positive number, the quantity $(I_c - X)$ must be greater than O_c. To achieve this, it is necessary to reduce O_c to a point where $O_c < I_c$. This amounts to saying that *to control storage at a level less than maximum, thus achieving a more nearly constant output, the control must be located in the larger of the input or output capacities.*

Moreover, if this control is to be automatic, i.e., achieved by means of feedback, the mechanism for sensing the rate of system processing must be inserted in the opposite (smaller) channel or within the storage itself.

How broadly can these deductions be generalized? And of what significance are they? First, if we recall the earlier statements of this section pertaining to storage of solar energy at the first level of green plants, with its progressive transformations and degradations to lower levels, it is manifestly helpful to know where to search for sensing and control mechanisms that prevent the sudden and complete discharge of energy throughout the chain of related systems. In such "natural" systems, we should find the control on the input side, but the sensing mechanisms on the output side.

A very crude example may be found in the satiation phenomenon of man and animals respecting food intake. The physiological details need not concern us now. The organism is an energy storing and expending system in which ingestion is clearly controlled by appetite variations even in the presence of unlimited food supplies. This is a sensing mechanism that signals the control of food-getting behavior.

In the often-mentioned thermostat-furnace system, to take a nonliving system, the fuel input capacity is usually in excess of the output capacity. That is to say, the maximum rate at which fuel could be delivered to the furnace is greater than the furnace's capacity to burn it and transmit the heat to the space being heated. Again, the input channel rather than the output is the control locus.

It is of some interest that Garner, in a book to be discussed in Chapter IV, concluded (although he protests that the data are not definitive) that human beings, considered as information processors in relatively simple psychophysical discriminations, probably exhibit greater constraints (smaller channel capacity) on the response (output) side than on the stimulus (input) side. To the extent that the conclusion is valid, it is consonant with the deductions presented above.

Other examples might be cited, but the generality of the proposition does not rest on a marshalling of specific systems. Instead, the generality is limited by the assumptions from which the deductions were drawn. Any system—and we believe there are uncounted hundreds or thousands—which stores maintenance energies that operate automatically in the near-constant processing of inputs will be found to possess control devices in those channels we have specified. Moreover, if we are to create social, economic, or political systems and have the opportunity to design them with the objective of having them operate as we have just described—smoothly and automatically—and can specify the input-output capacities, these deductions tell us where to place the controls.

SUMMARY

The following definitions and propositions are embedded in Chapter III, although not in the order in which they are presented below.

Definitions

3.1. Feedback is the control of inputs as a function of output.

3.2. Storage is that property of systems which permits the delay of outputs beyond the minimal response time of the system.

3.3. Memory is the storage of signal inputs.

Propositions

3.4. The near-steady functioning of systems is evidence of feedback.

3.5. Time is required in processing inputs to produce outputs.

3.6. Storage may result from:

a. Excess maintenance.
b. Relatively irreversible structural modifications caused by processing inputs. The latter persist longer if appropriate maintenance inputs are available.

3.7. Stored energies subsequently affect the processing of inputs.

3.8. Both stored maintenance and memories are necessary because of the imperfect matching of input-output flow from system to system.

3.9. The control locus of memory or maintenance is to be found in the larger of the input or output capacities.

IV / VARIABILITY AND ADAPTATION

The previous two chapters have presented basic definitions, assumptions, and propositions for general systems and have given a few glimpses of how these definitions may apply to a variety of special systems. This chapter is designed to deduce from these definitions the manner in which systems grow and interrelate with each other. We now want to apply these definitions in certain concepts that are the common coin of various sciences.

THE PROBABILISTIC NATURE OF SYSTEMS

We have said that the outputs of a system may be either useful or useless. This statement implies that the outputs may show some variability. In order to understand the implications of this statement, we need to go back to Werner Heisenberg's principle of uncertainty (1930). It will be recalled that he arrived at his concept of uncertainty by approaching the problem of measurement precision. He argued that the moment we attempt to measure a phenomenon, we distort it.[1] Therefore, he reasoned, we can never precisely know, for example, the path and the velocity of an electron no matter how finely calibrated the instruments of observation are. For us, the more important outcome from Heisenberg's ideal thought experiment (*Gedankenexperiment*) was the conclusion that the electron on its flight from some ideal atomic gun *could*

[1] The principle has recently been verified in psychological experiments that will be discussed in a later chapter.

not follow a smooth parabolic trajectory because of the presence of photons in the space through which the electron under observation must pass. These photons, possessing energy, would cause the electron to bounce first in one direction and then another. If the photons were reduced in energy, the electrons could not be observed. Heisenberg concluded that at the atomic level the notion of the trajectory of an object as a mathematical line had to be abandoned. Perfect trajectories might be satisfactorily plotted, he thought, for supra-atomic phenomena, but even here small variations in the path of bullets and similar objects do not follow the mathematically ideal path, *because of the interference of other systems.* Instead, as Heisenberg concluded, the path, velocity, and momentary position of any object in flight can only be specified probabilistically.

That is to say, the path can be calculated within a certain range of limits, and the most probable path for any particular electron would be some average that could be calculated from empirical observations under conditions short of his ideal experiment. The same may be said of freely falling bodies or projectiles shot through an atmosphere. Only if we eliminate all other systems can we precisely specify the body's motion. The assumption that all systems are open rules out the possibilities, even in our conceptualizing, of any considerations which presuppose the opposite. Heisenberg's ideal experiment furthermore had to postulate an electron flight through a space containing photons—without which the electron could not be detected but whose presence contaminated his observations. His ideal electron system had to be open to a photon system. Hence open systems must be probabilistic systems.

How is this emphasis on probability related to the initial statement of this section? We have said that systems produce outputs that may either be useful or useless. It is evident that the outputs are not strictly determined by the inputs and the internal operations of the system, which may take a finite number of patterns (the parameters being the number of components and the number of different kinds of relations each component can assume with each other). We cannot determine precisely at any given instant, armed with knowledge of the inputs and components, what the internal arrangements will be, or what the outputs will be except within certain limits.

This fundamental feature of systems needs to be qualified to deal with some systems which *appear* to be strictly determined. The path of a billiard ball struck by another with a given force, rebounding from a cushion of given elasticity, and rolling over a table having a known coefficient of friction, can be determined with high, but not perfect, precision. For the practical purposes of playing a game, the behavior of the ball is determined, and we can predict the path of the ball for such ends.[2]

This latter point may be made explicit: *all system outputs are basically probabilistic, although some are more rigidly determined by their inputs and components than are others.*

The reason we have gone into so much detail in establishing the logic of this proposition is because we need to lay this groundwork to account for the adaptability and modification of system outputs. If outputs were strictly determined in a mathematical sense by inputs and the relations between components, there would be no variability and no logical way of developing a theory of adaptability. *If systems are to be adaptable, they must first be variable.*

Garner's Uncertainty Principle

Before pursuing the implications of the preceding statement, it would be well to buttress the thesis by looking briefly at Garner's (1962) mathematical model of uncertainty. This is somewhat different from Heisenberg's concept and also more directly related to psychological problems.

The uncertainty of a stimulus (input) or a response (output) depends on the probability *range*, says Garner, within which the event (S or R) may occur. Stated differently, if we know the total range of possible inputs to a system, we can then specify the uncertainty of any single input. For instance, the probability of drawing a red card from an ordinary shuffled deck is 1/2. We know there are only two possibilities: red or black. The range is two. Similarly, the probabilities of drawing an ace of either color is 4/52, or 1/13.

It is at this point that Heisenberg's uncertainty and Garner's uncertainty are different. The former concept is nonstatistical. Heisenberg's *Gedankenexperiment* led him to conclude that the velocity and position of an electron could not be determined simultaneously. However, if we cannot determine the velocity and position of an electron, can we any more easily establish the velocity and position of photons that deflect the electron? Obviously not. Hence the initial probabilities of a photon hitting an electron cannot be established precisely and we cannot determine the number that is equivalent to fifty-two in our deck-of-cards example. Heisenberg's uncertainty was therefore a mathematically indeterminate concept; Garner's uncertainty is dependent on the known or assumed finite limits of possibilities.

Because it is somewhat awkward mathematically to handle simple

[2] Notice again, however, that we have an "operator" system whose needs are met by a subsystem which, for his purposes, is *determined well enough.*

probabilities, especially when dealing with more complex bivariate or multivariate problems, Garner employed as his mathematical definition of uncertainty the following: $U = \log_2 k$, in which k is the number of possible categories and the logarithm is to the base 2. If a given event, like the drawing of a card, can be either black or red, the definition gives a quantitative label for such a situation. U in this case would be $\log_2 2 = 1$. If a given event could occur within a range of 32 possibilities the uncertainty, would be $\log_2 32 = 5$. With a little thought it can be seen that doubling the range of possibilities increases the unit of uncertainty by 1. Thus:

Uncertainty	*Total Categories*
0	1
1	2
2	4
3	8
4	16
5	32
6	64

And so on. It is possible and convenient to employ uncertainty to designate the stimulus or the response, or both. In simple psychophysical studies of loudness discrimination, for instance, one may have a range of stimulus tones from 1,000 to 1,070 cycles per second in steps of 10 cps, in which case the uncertainty of the stimulus would be 3 (eight categories). If the subject were required to respond by saying "louder," "not so loud," or "equal," his response uncertainty would be 1.585.

It is interesting that Garner and his colleagues have conceived of human beings in such a situation as essentially a Black Box accepting inputs of a specified uncertainty and giving responses that can be evaluated in precisely the same terms. The subject in a simple discrimination task is conceived as an information processor, translating stimuli into, for him, the best possible response. Moreover, it has been shown that if one increases the uncertainty of the inputs beyond about 2.3, there is no increase in the information processed; that is, the discriminatory responses to the inputs do not also increase. Between 1 and 2.3 levels of stimulus uncertainty, human systems process inputs accurately and monotonically with increasing stimulus uncertainty, provided the differences between the stimuli are greater than threshold values. This is not to say that individuals cannot discriminate more than about five or six categories in more complex situations, but, for simple sensory discriminations of loudness, pitch, brightness, length, and the like, there is clearly an upper limit on the uncertainty of the system. We cannot go into the evidence here, but Garner proposes that (although the data are somewhat equivocal) the restriction lies more on the response side than on the input side of the system. This fits with the general proposition given in Chapter II that the boundary of any system filters both the inputs and outputs, imposing limits on both the kind and rate of intake and outflow.

In dealing with complex situations involving more than a single sensory dimension, simple probabilities become, in Garner's terms, contingent probabilities. It is because of these contingent uncertainties (computed from the probabilities) that we are able to make a greater variety of discriminations in more complex situations. But we are getting ahead of the story. What is the meaning of contingent uncertainty? Let us start with an example. Suppose, with eyes closed, we wanted to select a person of a given height from a collection of people. The probability that an individual drawn from a sample population is of a particular height is affected by the average age and age distribution of the sample. To illustrate, if the sample has an average age of six years, the probability that one individual drawn from it is four feet tall is fairly high—certainly higher than if the sample population was composed of adults. Hence the probability that an event may occur which may be categorized within two or more imperfectly correlated variables is contingent on the uncertainty of both. That is, each person has an age and a height, and these are correlated. Moreover, Garner has shown that the uncertainties computed from the separate probabilities are additive.

Garner defines the structure of any *system* of variables as their contingent uncertainty. This means that if a particular event x_f (which is one possible event in an array $x_1, x_2, \ldots, x_n$) occurs often when condition Y_c is present, the system of two variables is structured. Furthermore the condition Y_c of the array of $Y_1, Y_2, \ldots, Y_n$ can be conceived as being made up of several variables. Pursuing the example of age and height, height as one condition is the consequence of many variables other than age, including nutritional, hereditary, metabolic, and perhaps ecological variables. Contingent uncertainty therefore may be computed for multivariate, not just bivariate, data.

Furthermore, it is possible to conceive of these contingent variables such as x and Y as being features, one of the suprasystem, and the other of the subsystem. From this conception one may derive, in Garner's terms again, the uncertainty of the external (supra-) system [3] and the other, the uncertainty of the internal (sub-) system. The sum of these

[3] Garner, however, does not conceive of the external system as having a structure separate from its relation to another system. When Garner's external system relates to another system, it then achieves its structure, which may be measured by the contingent uncertainty between the external and internal systems.

uncertainties again becomes the uncertainty of the total system made up of supra- and subsystems. This approach gives a mathematical definition of what we have heretofore merely labeled the increasing complexity of systems as they develop more functional relationships (contingencies) and an increasing number of emergent characteristics. Structure conceived as contingent probabilities, however, does not reduce uncertainty; uncertainty (the range of possibilities) is increased. The point that Garner has made is a crucial one, which we will also develop subsequently in the discussion of evolutionary development.

Those outputs which either do not couple with other systems (are not contingent) or are uncontrolled via feedback represent, in Garner's terms, unstructured uncertainty. This is the uncertainty that is uncorrelated with any other variable either within the system or in the suprasystem(s). "Unstructured uncertainty is equivocation, or noise, or error, whichever term you prefer" (Garner, 1962, p. 339). We might generalize and call it entropy.

On the other hand, structured uncertainty, which increases with additional emergent suprasystems having characteristics not found in subsystems, increases the range of possible functions and thus uncertainty increases. This is another way of saying that as systems grow they become capable of performing new functions that are more complex than the systems from which they were derived.

The explication of Garner's uncertainty concepts has necessarily been abbreviated. They are presented at this point only to demonstrate that there does exist a concurrence in final outline of two approaches to some common problems in conceptualizing the nature of systems. Garner called his starting point uncertainty; we called it probabilistic in a nonquantitative sense. He has found filtering in amount and increased discrimination of inputs through learning, demonstrating that human subjects are capable of discriminating in precisely the way the model for uncertainty predicts, up to a certain capacity of the Black Box. His mathematical definition of capacity is not inconsistent with our nonquantitative definition. Humans cannot exceed a given "channel capacity" any more than can electrical, telephonic, computer, manufacturing, or other systems exceed their respective capacities. Garner has been much more rigorous than we in applying his model only to extant data and has carefully limited his interpretations to a restricted (low uncertainty) range of psychological problems.

However, he has said,

> There is just one last comment I would like to make, and that concerns the extent to which some of the concepts and principles discussed in this book have a greater generality than I have tried to show. Some of the

> ideas expressed here can be used in a verbal, and thus less exact, form to describe other psychological problems. For example, we can think of all the behavior of a particular individual as a closed system of variables. The total variability, or uncertainty, of this behavior will then determine the maximum constraint which can exist for this system of variables and the totality of the external system of variables to which the person must relate. Now this total constraint can be divided into internal and external constraint, but the amount available for external relating is limited by the amount of internal constraint. Thus, any given individual can be considered to face a decision concerning the extent to which he becomes structured internally (thus having his own integrated personality) and the extent to which he chooses to relate to the external world. The problem of balance between these two kinds of structure must be a real one.
>
> In a similar vein, any group of persons can relate to itself or to individuals and groups outside itself. Once again, however, the total structure is limited by the uncertainty within the group, and the greater the amount of internal structuring, the less must be the external structuring (Garner, 1962, p. 344).

In this Garner foreshadows the possibility of extending his model from perceptual phenomena to social systems.

We shall return to the special issues of social and psychological constraints, but we need at this point to face the propositions dealing with the conditions that limit variability generally.

THE LIMITS OF VARIABILITY

Structures

Assumption 2.12 (p. 33) declares that the functions of a system are dependent upon its structure. This means that a given structure may serve one or more ends. A hammer can be used to drive nails, pull nails, hold papers in place, keep a door open, and so on. In each of these illustrations the hammer is a component serving a different function in different systems, but its structure remains the same in each. There are, however, a finite number of functions which the hammer may serve, limited by its structure. If we look at a more complicated system, say, Ashby's homeostat, it is obvious that the components (like the hammer) remain the same, but the interrelations among the components may change, depending upon the particular disturbance applied to it. Hence this system may take on a finite number of states (Zadek, 1964, pp. 39ff.). We have said also of components that they function with each other to combine, separate, or compare inputs to produce the outputs. We may now add to this definition the further qualification, coming from assumption 2.12, that the relations they have with other components are dependent upon their structure. The hammer cannot be used as a wrench, nor can the magnets of the homeostat be employed as components of a radio receiver.

The point of this discussion is that *the variability of a system's outputs is limited by a finite number of functions which a given component may perform and a limited number of states which the total system may assume.* The limits, even within a relatively simple system, are wide. (The homeostat had 390,625 such states.) These limitations nevertheless begin to provide us with an understanding of the probability parameters inherent in the outputs of systems.

Another way of thinking about limited variability is to conceive of it as the capacity of the system. The capacity, then, of the components is the number of states these are capable of assuming. The capacity of the boundary is the range or bandwidth of variable inputs—outputs it will transmit.

Boundary Limits

The functional definition of a boundary places further restrictions on the limits of variability. It will be recalled that we have said the boundary accepts only a limited class of inputs—not the full range of energy forms. Furthermore, the same structure-function assumption applies, namely, that what is accepted and coded by the boundary is dependent upon its structure. Rods and cones of the retina accept one form of energy; hairy cells of the cochlea accept another form. However, even with these restrictions, systems may still possess a wide range of possible outputs.

How then is it possible for systems to relate effectively to each other, co-ordinating themselves in the very complicated manner that we see in the grand cycle, for instance, for the production of glucose by photosynthesis, the breakdown of glucose by animals producing CO_2 and water that are reconstituted again by green plants? This is such a complicated, beautifully co-ordinated cycle of phenomena that it is hard to reject the idea of some cosmic control beyond the ken of mankind that arranged the whole organization. We can best approach the issue via the evolutionary route. The question that we face is, basically, how may one account for the subsequent organization of components given the variability of their outputs?

THE EVOLUTION OF ORGANIZATION

Darwin: Biological Evolution

The basic proposition developed in what follows is that organization developed initially by a chance symbiotic relationship between collateral systems or, in other and perhaps later cases, between sub- and supra-systems. Darwin's *The Origin of Species* was a brilliant but only partial explanation of biological evolution. Bronowski (1961) gives a capsule account of this contribution in terms relevant to our question.

> Darwin saw that there must be certain fundamental variants, what he called "sports," on which natural selection works. How does it work? By jostling and shuffling them about until some arrangement which they form branches off in an evolutionary direction of its own. But if natural selection works in this way, at random on a random set of variants, then evolution is at bottom a process of chance—and this even if some random arrangements turn out to be stable and others unstable. The selection of stable sets of heritable variants to form species which are adapted to their environment (and to its fluctuations) is a gigantic wheel of chance. There is no guide to evolution, there is no direction to life, there is no drive other than the hazard of probabilities which happens to throw up one among many possible adaptations. The growth and progress of life, its more and more subtle organization and complexity, all the way from the amoeba to the human brain, is the work of chance.

The Darwinian notion was, in a phrase made famous by Einstein, that of God playing dice. Clearly, the survival-of-the-fit principle was only a partial answer. What accounted for the "stable sets of heritable variants"?

Mutual Evolution: Environmental and Biological

It was L. J. Henderson, in a somewhat controversial extended essay, who offered a companion explanation. His *Fitness of the Environment* (1913) was an argument in defense of the over-all interdependence of systems with other systems. Although his notions were variously received by biologists and others, its essential point was the orderliness and ecological intermeshing of environmental and biological systems. He said in his Preface: "Darwinian fitness is compounded of a mutual relationship between the organism and the environment. Of this, fitness of the environment is quite as essential a component as the fitness which arises in the process of organic evolution, and in fundamental characteristics the actual environment is the fittest possible abode of life." Henderson's thesis was that the Darwinian adjustments to the environment were only part of the story. The environment also went through an evolution such that it was influenced by biological systems and in turn modified them. Many other arrangements of relationships were possible, or could be imagined. Henderson argued that all planets of the solar system, having been born from the sun, must contain the same basic chemicals (and our recent space probes have not so far upset this conclusion). Yet each of the planets has a different atmosphere, which suggests that other patterns than our own are plausible. Why did earth evolve its unique environment? Let Henderson's words convey the issue.

> There is, in truth, not one chance in countless millions of millions that unique properties of carbon, hydrogen and oxygen and especially of their stable compounds, water and carbonic acid, which chiefly make up the atmosphere of a new planet, should simultaneously occur in the three elements otherwise than through the operation of a natural law which somehow connects them together. There is no greater probability that these unique properties should be without due cause uniquely favorable to the organic mechanism. These are no mere accidents (Henderson, 1913, p. 276).

The chemical nature of the atmosphere and the interdependence of plant and animal life must have evolved by the following steps. Most cosmologists agree that the earth was at one time as barren of an atmosphere as the moon is today, but volcanoes poured out gases including water vapor, methane, ammonia, and hydrogen. Harada and Fox (1964, 1965) have demonstrated in the laboratory that thermal energy, when applied to such postulated primitive atmospheres, is sufficient to synthesize some natural amino acids that are the building blocks for proteins which in turn are the constitutents for living cells. The water vapor condensed, forming pools and eventually oceans. Fossil records indicate that for two or three billion years primitive forms of algae, fungi, and bacteria lived precariously in these pools. How these forms came into being no one can be sure. The random scattering of their constituent parts within a liquid over such a long, almost incomprehensible span could permit the occurrence of many highly improbable but possible events, such as the sudden collision of just the right combination of particles under the proper ambient conditions to form a cell. However the initial cells were formed, it is agreed that these were oxygen generators which eventually raised the oxygen content of the pools and the atmosphere to such a level as to support another kind of cell—one without the photochemical property which fixed solar energy. These in turn consumed the plant cells but discharged CO_2, which was a necessary input for the solar-energy-fixing cells. Both of these great systems initially occurred by chance, but once they intermeshed (and it required something like 400 million years) the grand symbiotic cycle was established, which permitted each to augment the other. The randomness of some 400 million years during which only slight changes occurred was reduced when the animal cell systems were integrated with the plant systems. From this era forward, variability was more constrained and the wheel of chance that Bronowski referred to, or God's dice in Einstein's phrase, were far from balanced. Each system was limited by the other and each contributed to the evolution of the other (cf. Grant, 1963, Part 1).

Conceptual Evolution

The basic assumption underlying this account bears further examination at the psychological level. Does the variability of outputs also account for the evolution of new ideas, new concepts? Campbell (1960) argues eloquently and with impressive documentation for the view that blind variation of outputs must be the fundamental condition for the subsequent selection and retention of creative ideas. Beginning at the most primitive level of locomoting protozoa, he points out that the organism proceeds in a given direction until blocked, then varies its direction until it "discovers" that the environment is discontinuous, some but not all regions being impenetrable. The evolution of distance receptors in higher organisms makes it unnecessary (after a period of learning) to contact the environmental constraints directly. And the further development of conceptual capacities in mankind makes possible nonovert "trials" of behavior alternatives to test whether or not they "fit"; that is, whether or not the concepts or ideas meet some previously established criteria of "appropriateness." [4]

Campbell (1960, p. 381) agrees that blind variation of outputs does not guarantee the solution of all problems "or the development of new knowledge, but neither has biological evolution produced the perfect organism, free of disease and perpetual life. Moreover the evolution of ideas is an exceedingly extravagant process. The tremendous number of non-productive thought trials on the part of the intellectual community must not be underestimated. Think of what a small proportion of thought becomes conscious, and of conscious thought what a small proportion gets uttered; what a still smaller fragment gets published, and what a small proportion of what is published is used by the next intellectual generation."

Campbell has some difficulty in accounting for the retention of innovations generated out of "blind variation." On the other hand, if one extends the Henderson principle to the phenomena of which Campbell speaks, retention is the consequence of having found that idea, concept, "knowledge" which serves to complete the conceptual organization of other ideas, concepts, or knowledge otherwise unconnected. Creative thought in this sense is the search for the missing links. Thus initial randomness even at this level brings about organization, and the or-

[4] See also London (1949) for an earlier statement of the probabilistic view.

ganized system of thoughts has a higher probability of survival than do the components taken separately.[5]

Surely, when we move from the early stages of biological evolution to social evolution, Henderson's principle takes on clarity. The organizations we have developed that systematize and regulate relations between persons are the products of man's ingenuity. We created the typical pyramidal shape of an organizational structure, the system of regulations and codes for behavior. But note that these in turn influence mankind. It is the complaint of William H. Whyte, Jr. (1956), that our business organizations have exerted too much influence. Clearly the social milieu, constructed with more or less rationality, feeds back to influence its architects.

Coupling of Systems

This excursion into evolution has been made for the purpose of illustrating that the variability of system outputs may be controlled by coupling the useful outputs of one system to the needed inputs of another, as well as by the other conditions already mentioned. That is to say, given the essential probabilistic nature of a system's processing, the outputs will be limited not alone by the nature of its components but also by the extent to which its outputs serve to provide another system with those constituents necessary for the latter's maintenance, *provided there is reciprocation of maintenance inputs.* Without reciprocation, first one and then the other system must disintegrate. Thus *coupling* of systems is one way by which structural organization may occur.

We may illustrate this reciprocation principle by reference to the experimental studies reported by Rosenblatt and Lehrman (1963) on the changes which may be induced in the maternal behavior of rats. It has been widely assumed that such behavior (nursing, nest building, retrieving the offspring) is instinctive and occurs "automatically" after parturition. Rosenblatt and Lehrman removed the young of rats giving birth for the first time and subsequently observed and tested their maternal behavior. Reintroducing five- to ten-day-old rats in the cages to the postparturition rats after intervals of six to twenty-four days without young showed that the females failed to retrieve or nurse the young with anything approaching the frequency found under normal circumstances. Nest-building behavior was also disturbed. Although physiological hormonal changes occur at parturition that are initially independent of the stimulation by the young, it is clear that the persistence of these condi-

[5] For a further development of the similarities between evolutionary principles and retention as evidenced in human and animal learning, see Russell (1962, pp. 157–193).

tions is the consequence of purely external inputs to the rat. Even nest building is disrupted by the failure to "couple" the rat with her offspring. These and similar studies of instinctual behavior have demonstrated a reciprocal interdependence between behavior patterns and ecological conditions.[6] Instincts have been somewhat romantically described as "nature taking no chances." It would perhaps be more accurate to say now that instincts are the accidental interdependence of nature.

Feedback between Systems

Notice in the "coupled" model that we have not made use of the negative feedback principle. In the earlier case of the animal-plant system, the balance of CO_2 and O_2 in the atmosphere is not controlled except by the populations of plants on the one hand and of the animals on the other. The atmosphere in this respect is an interface between systems transporting the gases from one major system to the other. It would take us too far afield from our present topic to describe the controls which operate within each of these large domains. Suffice it to say that ecological research has revealed negative feedback channels accounting for stable populations of predators and prey, and of a stable density of plant life within a given area. Moreover there are negative feedback channels between, say, the available vegetation and the population of grazing animals (Grant, 1963, Chap. 14). The point is that coupling should not be confused with feedback. Each relationship may contribute to organization, the first by mutually supportive outputs from systems that are themselves internally controlled by negative feedback, and the second by suppressing the flow of inputs to subsystems when they exceed a given level established by the suprasystem. In the grand evolutionary model we described, the animal and plant systems do not stand in a sub- and suprarelationship, but are collateral systems. Feedback need not necessarily exist under these circumstances.[7]

It is important to remember that a system has two classes of relationships: coupling with other collateral systems, and subordinate-superor-

[6] Gerard (1963) refers to a number of other studies of the same sort. A newborn kid taken from its mother only a half-hour after birth may no longer be accepted by the ewe as her offspring. If it survives at all, it grows into an undersized animal clearly deviant in behavior as well.

[7] One may wonder why collateral systems, by reason of their mutual reinforcement, do not escalate to some level that exceeds their capacity to process inputs. The answer is that they may. The arms race between the U.S.A. and the U.S.S.R. has been modeled in just these terms. In the case of the atmosphere's balance of CO_2 and O_2, feedback loops operating at subsystem levels apparently have dampened population growths in both domains with crossover loops in channels not directly involving the atmosphere, such as the example of grazing in areas of adequate vegetation or, lacking these, the reduction of the animal population by predators or by environmental effects which reduce mating behavior.

dinate relations. In the first there is mutual reciprocation of inputs and outputs whose rate of exchange is limited by the channel capacities of each (see p. 45). The maintenance of subsystems is first provided in this fashion, but as subsystems become integrated into suprasystems their dependence on collateral coupling declines and maintenance depends more heavily upon supplies and resources from the suprasystem, controlled by feedback loops. This does not mean that the collateral source of maintenance must necessarily cease when the system joins up with a suprasystem.

The earliest and most primitive of living things could hardly have possessed the complicated feedback devices found in plants or animals as we know them today. It follows that the early environments must have been more stable than they are today. Feedback mechanisms must have evolved from some more primitive type of control. Moreover, they must have evolved because they were required. Why were they required? Because the evolution toward greater complexity carried with it a concomitant increase in variability and inconstancy in the chemophysical sense. Our environments—including the environment of the cell, the tissue, the organ, and on to the total physical and social environments that surround the total plant-animal system—show a progressive instability. On the other hand, viable subsystems within this total complex, because of their structures, can only operate in fairly constant environments. Hence the regulatory mechanisms had to evolve even at the level of the cell and below to ensure their survival.

We are only gradually learning how to build our social organizations so they can deal automatically with disturbances. Indeed, the systems approach to social organizations immediately suggests the search for, and invention of, feedback mechanisms which may bring about the integration of social subsystems into a larger complex, making use of the same principles that account for biological integration. However, we are getting ahead of our development and must reserve these social models for a later chapter.

Emergent Characteristics

It is a logical deduction from the definition of system outputs, and the proposition that outputs must contribute to the functioning of suprasystems, that the suprasystem will function in some fashion differently from the subsystem. In the past some mystery has surrounded the notion of emergent qualities as one moves from one level of organization to more complex levels. Thus intelligence is ascribed to some systems, but not to the components of the systems. Or, the properties of hydrogen and oxygen, taken in their molecular forms, bear no correspondence to their combination as water. These emergent qualities are not mysterious, provided we hold to the principle that each system has a special organization that must be different in some respect from the organization of the components taken separately. Different structures must produce different outputs, and thus be characterized by different properties.

Although the Gestalt psychologists did not use the term "emergent characteristics," their basic proposition was the notion that experience is not given by an analysis of its constituent elements. The classical experiments of Wertheimer (1912) in apparent movement were only the first of a long series of empirical studies which gave force and substance to the undeniable fact that particular stimulus combinations in time and space yield experiences that are unpredictable from a knowledge of the separate stimuli. These are emergent experiences.

Empirically, the emergent-quality principle appears to be borne out in the evolution of biological systems, embryological development, the growth of small groups, the formation of frontier communities in hostile surroundings, the growth of nations, and the creation of international alliances. We cannot now stop to deal with these social models in detail except to say that in each case suprasystems are formed from subsystems and each has its distinctive emergent property. We shall deal further with this question in the discussion of growth.

In summary, organization between collateral sub- and suprasystems evolves first when two or more systems interact in a mutually supportive way which we have called coupling. As organizations come to include more subsystems, variability between systems, or Garner's uncertainty, increases. Such a condition requires another mechanism, feedback, to maintain both the stability of the constituent components and the appropriate relations between the components. As subsystems form suprasystems, new properties appear in the outputs which are called emergent qualities not found in the inputs. These principles appear to be true of biological, conceptual, and probably social evolution.

THE ADAPTATION OF SYSTEMS

The model drawn so far is more idealized than is necessary. It has assumed that by the operation of chance over many aeons, a neat intermeshing of systems has occurred. Nothing has been said about the disposition of errors and very little about the significance of feedback. We have proposed that only the useful outputs make contributions to the suprasystem, aiding its function. What happens to error outputs? If our complex biological and social evolution had occurred only by the procedures outlined so far, we would not need to discuss adaptation at all. However, if we scrutinize the chain of events stemming from the production of system errors, we will see another aspect to the evolution of organizations. It is this chain of events to which the term adaptation more properly applies.

Adaptation has most often been employed in connection with living systems to refer to some feature of their behavior or structure that seems to extend the life of the system. Grant (1963, p. 93) puts the matter as follows: "The reason why each kind of organism is restricted in nature to its own habitat and is not normally found elsewhere is that it is specialized or adapted for making a living under one particular set of conditions. . . . Earthworms are well fitted to live on the organic materials in the soil. No other kind of organism can compete with them in their own territory. But conversely, earthworms are unable to live in the habitats of ducks or sponges and if they are accidentally dispersed to such places they soon die." At a relatively simple level, adaptation has referred to protective coloration and form in animals, to phenotypic modifications of plants in response to variations of moisture and sunlight, to the selection of benign environments among locomoting animals. At more complex levels, adaptation refers to the modification of an individual's values and beliefs, to the avoidance of cognitive dissonance, to the change in thresholds of receptors, to the modification of one's behavior in response to social norms and standards. This is surely a wide and varied collection of phenomena to be included under a single rubric. Is it possible to express in systems terms the common feature that connects all these events that run from protective coloration to cognitive dissonance?

The common feature that distinguishes adaptation is an appropriate response to some input that would jeopardize the symbiotic relationships of the system with its collateral or suprasystem. Putting it somewhat more simply, adaptations are responses to disturbances that may upset "normal" relations. Adaptive systems are those which maintain their essential variables within those limits necessary for survival within the environments in which they exist. (Cf. Marney and Smith, 1964, p. 113.)

What could upset the established relations between systems except some "error" whose origin is outside the system? The "error" may be one of kind, or one of amount of input. A virus enters a cell and interferes with the cell's normal functioning with respect to its suprasystem. An extremely cold wave envelops a house whose interior temperature drops precipitously. Prolonged physical exertion raises the body temperature of a distance runner and may destroy tissue. An intensely bright light falls on the retina of an eye, bleaching the visual purple faster than it can be reconstituted. A dearly loved friend becomes enamored of a person toward whom you have hostile feelings. In each of these instances and many more, an adaptation is called for, and in each an ongoing integrated pattern of relationships between systems is threatened or disrupted.

In the previous chapter we defined the feedback mechanism as one which copes with a wide variety of disturbances that would otherwise upset the steady state of the system. It is the mechanism that accounts for the automatic maintenance of homeostasis. The steady state of a system is one in which it is relating to other systems in a mutually supportive way. Therefore, when we find systems that deal automatically with "error" (disturbance) inputs, we can conclude that a feedback mechanism must be operative because this is the functional definition of feedback. We have come full circle to our first question: What happens to error outputs? The answer is that, as inputs to other systems, the disturbances stimulate feedback loops in such a manner as to block off the errors (iris of eye constricts to bright light) or dissipate and neutralize them in other ways (perspiration and dilation of surface blood vessels in the runner), resulting in an adaptation. If an effective feedback loop does not exist, the disturbed system may integrate. (Your beautiful friendship will cease when you learn of your friend's enemy.)

Protective coloration and selective diets of certain species are sometimes thought to be solely the consequence of the evolutionary process carried over many generations. However, it is possible to find evidence that these developments fit the proposition that adaptations are the consequence of encounters with inappropriate maintenance inputs, even within a single generation. As is well known, toads feed on insects. Cott (1940, pp. 281–289) placed honeybees in a cage with eighteen common toads. For the first couple of days the toads snapped up the bees, but within six days, after evidently being stung a number of times, they ignored the bees, as shown below. The toads, however, ate other insects during this period.

Day	1	2	3	4	5	6	7	22	23	24	25	26	27	28
Number eaten	24	33	14	8	5	3	0	12	9	4	6	3	2	0

An interval of two weeks elapsed, during which the toads were denied food and bees were again introduced into the cage. The table shows some forgetting of the previous adaptive aversion to bees, but quicker readaptation.[8]

The psychologist will interpret these results and perhaps dismiss them

[8] Similar results have been obtained with other toads and other insects by Brower, Brower, and Wescott (1960).

as merely a classical conditioning response. Their significance goes beyond identifying the feedback mechanism, although this is unquestioned. The input (coloration of a bee) is protective for the bee and is recognized as an error input to be avoided for the toad. This view clearly places the selective food-getting behavior of the toad and the coloration of the bee within the domain of adaptation that extends the survival of both.

Genetic Adaptation

It is not possible to discuss adaptation without some reference to genetically determined adaptations. The discussion so far seems to have implied that all adaptations are those which occur within the lifetime of a system—and this is patently at variance with a vast body of data. It has been said that the single most important contribution of Charles Darwin was to force biologists to find the unit of inheritance—the gene or, more recently, the DNA and RNA molecules. The multitude of living forms each adapted more or less well to their environments, but procreating and reproducing themselves required some mechanism of heredity to account for at least the successive duplication of forms (structure). But as Bronowski (1961, p. xiv) has said, what a surviving species inherits is not a set of adaptations, but the *capacity to adapt*. He continues, "The most striking evidence for this is indeed the evolution of the human race itself. For the instrument which has driven our headlong success is the human brain; and the brain is not an adaptation, but a wonderfully complex store of adaptability. In particular because the brain goes on working well after the body does not, it has been able to act as a store for adaptations which cannot be passed on by heredity."

Furthermore, the studies of rats by Rosenblatt and Lehrman (1963) and Cott's study (1940) of the toads and the bees, like others which could be presented, argue for a concept of genetics in which under normal circumstances the environment elicits behavior from a structure that has the capacity to perform a variety of functions, only some of which are adaptive. At the same time, mutations may provide inherited structures so arranged that their possible ranges of functions are more or less adaptive than their progenitors. If the mutation's range of possible functions is more adaptive, a beginning may be made on a new species; if the reverse is true, the new species will survive with a lower probability. It is well to bear in mind that what is inherited is the template for a structure. The play of nurturent and inhibitory circumstances of the environment not alone influences the degree to which the template is fully developed as a *structure* but also requires of the system that it function within certain limits in order to survive.

Adaptations and the Steady State

If we return to the main line of discussion, namely, the proposition that adaptations operate to maintain a steady state, it follows logically that adapting systems should progress toward greater, rather than less, stability. This does not mean that adapting systems are inflexible—just the reverse. If the toads had not been flexible in their selection of prey, they would have survived less well. If the warm-blooded organism is incapable of changing its internal processes to dissipate the more than usual heat from exercise, its tissues will distintegrate. This was one of the paradoxes in Cannon's (1945) homeostasis principle: a complicated pattern of changes had to take place to preserve the stability of certain essential parameters.

The validity of this proposition can only be demonstrated by the examination of all genotypic systems—a task that is clearly beyond us. However, the logic of the definitions leads us to conclude that adaptations are survival-extending mechanisms that deal with system errors via feedback loops. The feedback, furthermore, interacts with disturbance inputs either to reduce or block their flow or to dissipate or neutralize the error.

Adaptation and Instrumental Behavior

Without being explicit about it, the above discussion has been limited to maintenance inputs and their outputs. Adaptation is defined as a survival-extending process. Without maintenance inputs, a system dies; hence adaptation pertains to maintenance inputs. It is in this respect that stability of the system's relation with its suprasystem is of first importance. But is adaptation involved in signal inputs as well? If we hold resolutely to the "survival-extending criterion," behavior in response to signal inputs will be adaptive only if it aids survival, but much of such behavior is not. *Unless we make this distinction, every response is an adaptation and the term loses any distinctive meaning.*

Simple forms of life are "hard, brutish, and short" and nearly all energies of simple systems are consumed by the struggle to live. Whatever modifications in behavior occur at this level are "pure" adaptations.

At somewhat higher, more complex system levels, evidences of instrumental behavior emerge. This is behavior that has only indirect relevance to maintaining the system's life. Skinner's (1953) bar-pressing rats are the familiar examples of instrumental behavior stimulated by certain signal inputs which trigger off behavior that may, or may not in every instance, lead to maintenance inputs. More behavior at this stage has no relevance to maintaining the system. At the very minimum, play, exploration, and similar behavior are evident. It is quite clear that learning is involved in both the earlier forms of pure adaptations and these instrumental forms. But it is also clear that the system is capable at this level of responding to stimuli that have no immediate or "natural" relevance to maintenance.

If we move a broad step higher in system complexity, the distinction becomes even clearer. Signal inputs generate behavior of a sort that has *no* relevance to maintenance. Much of the behavior of men and the higher mammals is of this sort. Puzzle-solving and aesthetic productions are examples. This behavior is engaged in for its own sake or for other rewards, and may even be inimical to survival. These learned behaviors cannot fit the definition of adaptation. They have nothing to do with extending the survival period, and hence there is good reason for distinguishing between those that serve survival and those that do not.

At the human, infrahuman, and social levels of analysis, maintenance inputs, however, take on an additional characteristic which goes beyond mere physical survival. Dogs, porpoises, monkeys, cats, and men, evidently require, or learn to require, social contact with others of their kind as a condition of their well-being, if not survival. If removed from their schools and kept in isolation, porpoises decline in health and may even starve. They are known to solicit stroking from humans in much the same fashion as dogs, cats, or other pets (Norris, 1965). Monkeys deprived of contact with other monkeys during their early life do not develop later the social behavior necessary for procreation (Harlow and Harlow, 1962). We shall deal at some length with this aspect of maintenance in a subsequent chapter, but at this point it will be sufficient to emphasize that such modifications in behavior which enhance these social inputs are included within the adaptation definition.

Adaptation Over Time

Selye (1950) has shown that a pattern of response to generalized stimuli (i.e., cold, fatigue, infections) can be described by the following idealized curve (Figure 3), which he claims characterizes an adaptive response. Initially, the systems show a decline in function followed by

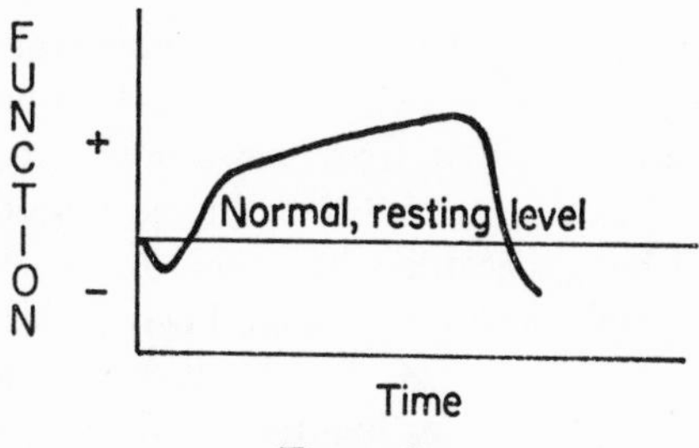

Figure 3

an overreaction that continues until the stress either reaches such a high degree of intensity or is extended for such a long period that the system reaches a point of collapse. The first phase Selye refers to as an alarm reaction, characterized among other things by a decrease in muscular tone, hypotension, depression of nerve activity, deranged capillary and cell membrane permeability, or acidosis. The counteralarm reaction is a transition in which the features found in the initial alarm reaction are reversed, carrying the system into the resistance phase that shows a rise in blood pressure, hypochoremia, alkalosis, and so on. The latter defend the system from stresses greater in magnitude than the initial disturbance. Thus the adaptation response, provided it is not pressed to the point of collapse, permits the system to accept, at a higher than normal rate, those inputs which sustain it.

Much the same sort of response occurs in community systems subjected to sudden disasters such as floods, earthquakes, tornadoes, and major fires. Initially, most, but not all, people flee from the source of danger. The disaster itself disrupts normal routines, communication channels, and the usual patterns of relationships. But in addition to these effects, the alarm reaction, characterized by less than normal rate of functioning, is shown in the apathy, shock, and emotional flatness of persons who have just survived an unexpected disaster.

In a series of Middle Western tornadoes, with almost monotonous regularity the survivors in the zone of destruction were described as appearing "stunned," "dazed," or "shocked" (Wolfenstein, 1957). A witness at Hiroshima was struck by the near silence among those who gathered in a park area. "The hurt ones were quiet; no one wept, much less screamed in pain; no one complained; none of the many who died did so noisily; not even the children cried; very few people even spoke" (Hersey, 1946). A considerable collection of anecdotal data of this kind can be interpreted to mean that the ordinary communicative exchanges at their most primitive level are slowed, retarded; the system as a whole is psychologically depressed. (Cf. various reports by National Research Council, Committee on Disaster Studies, 1952–1961.)

The alarm reaction is quickly followed by the steep gradient in the recovery phase that shows itself in disasters in several ways. The suprasystem mobilizes its resources which flow, often in prodigious quantities, into the stricken area. The Red Cross repeatedly experiences such an influx of clothing and other contributions in the period just following a major disaster that it has great difficulty in merely handling the offerings. The return flow of people—those that have been displaced, the rescuers, and the merely curious—presents a difficult traffic problem. This, of course, would not be true in cases like the Alaskan earthquake and tidal waves of 1964 and flood in 1967, where the surrounding area is sparsely populated, but in these cases resources flowed from points thousands of miles away. At a more personal level, the rush of the recovery phase appears in a sudden upsurge of altruistic feelings and eagerness for social contact. One woman who had survived a tornado exclaimed, "It seemed that when you met anyone that had life in 'em, black or white, you just wanted to grab 'em and love 'em" (Powell, 1954). Or an adolescent girl, following the same tornado said, "Everytime you saw anybody you just hugged them. Even your best enemies were good friends now." While we could take some time to speculate on the underlying reasons for the self-sacrifice and outpouring of socially positive feelings, it would distract us from a simple point. The recovery phase following a disaster seems to have the general features, at both the personal and gross social levels, which conform to the Selye curve.

On the other hand, we are certainly not in a position to say that the Selye curve describes responses to disturbances at the subbiological level or to all disturbances at the psychological or social levels. Nevertheless the data presented above suggest that it need not be limited to biochemical responses in an intact organism. How far it may be generalized remains an intriguing field for empirical research.

Perhaps one of the gravest challenges to general systems theory lies in its application to individual psychological phenomena. Is it possible to find veridical support for the concept of adaptation just presented in a psychological system? We shall later deal with several psychological systems, but at this point it will be helpful to consider adaptation in at least one.[9]

Before we can attack this question directly, it is necessary to define a psychological model. In our view there are many psychological systems (perceptual, cognitive, attitudinal, affective, and so on), just as there are many social systems (family, community, club, business enterprise, and the like) or biological systems (such as insect, mammal, and plant). These systems are of course interrelated. For analysis we must therefore

[9] Miller (1955) has taken the view that any attempt to analyze the subsystems of the individual between the input-output relations of the peripheral sensory and motor apparatus is fraught with unsolvable problems. He points out that if one places test electrodes at the input and output of a given electrical system, 100 per cent of the variance in the readings can be attributed to the system between these two points. If, on the other hand, the system is composed of two or more subsystems none of which may be separately tested, the variance in the overall readings may be in any one of the systems or distributed in an unknown fashion among all of them. In addressing ourselves to the adjustment process in the ego, Miller's strictures would apply if we were engaged in precise, quantitative measurement. It is not our intention to do that even if it were possible. Instead we merely wish to illustrate how adjustive processes are limited to the maintenance channels making use of descriptive data—which are all that are available.

select a psychological system to discover whether adaptation does extend the survival period of that system.

THE SELF AS AN ADAPTING SYSTEM

We select the self as a psychological model for analysis partly because it represents a system less mechanistic than many other systems employed as illustrations up to this point. If the systems approach to this psychological concept is feasible, we have an additional reason to believe in its general applicability to mechanistic as well as nonmechanistic systems. Moreover, one of the major controversies in modern psychological theory pertains to the schism between the behaviorists and the cognitive psychologists. Since most of what has been presented so far appears to give support to the former, the following treatment may help to redress the balance.

The *boundary* of the self is the discrimination one makes between *me* or *mine* and events "out there" (Snygg and Coombs, 1949; Sherif and Cantril, 1947), other people, things not mine. Abundant evidence shows that the boundary of the self is less clear in early life and becomes progressively sharper as the individual matures. Even in maturity the boundary may be modified to include more or less of one's surroundings, yet the criterion for inclusion or exclusion remains relatively stable.

The *components*[10] of the self are both conceptual objects and processes, consisting of those perceptions, evaluations, cognitions, affections, and acts of which one is aware as his own. Except for the last, these are the substance of private experience, available to the public only through the familiar behavioristic verbal report. In making this distinction, it is necessary to deny that we are postulating the "little man within." Hall and Lindsey (1957, p. 468) put it this way: "The self, whether it be conceived as object or as process or both, is not an homunculus or a 'man within the breast' or soul; rather it refers to the object of psychological processes or to those processes themselves, and these processes are assumed to be governed by the principle of causality. In other words, the self is not a metaphysical or religious concept; it is a concept that falls within the domain of a scientific psychology."

Moreover, we are not embracing the position taken by some early behaviorists that the verbal report of private experience is in any sense the same as private experience—a point that has been made explicit by Skinner (1953, p. 282). The self is a separate system which accepts as inputs both exteroceptive and interoceptive stimuli, processing these and,

[10] One need not at this point be concerned about the distinction between the components. We may legitimately declare each a Black Box to be examined later.

along with the other systems of the individual, emitting acts or behavior as outputs. As indicated above, the awareness of these acts is also one of the components of the self.

The self is furthermore characterized by a degree of stability and integration. This does not mean that the self is rigid over a given period of time, but at least one of its properties is a kind of stability which prevents an individual from regarding himself as worthless at one moment and worthy at another. Coleman (1960, p. 69) puts the matter admirably: "Because the ongoing activities of the human system are organized and integrated in relation to self, each individual tends to establish a relatively consistent life style. He has a characteristic way of doing, thinking, reacting, and growing that tends to distinguish him from everyone else. He puts his personal stamp on every role he plays and every situation he encounters. He is fairly consistent in regarding people as honest or as untrustworthy, in regarding life as exciting or threatening or perhaps as a constant struggle, in seeking certain experiences and avoiding others. These typical patterns of behavior are always [*sic*] consistent with his self concept."

When confronted with situations or experiences that are not in accord with one's self-system, the well-known defense mechanisms—rationalization, compensation, projection, displacement, denial, and others—not infrequently come into play. The net result of these mechanisms is to permit the system of self-perceptions, beliefs, and evaluations to survive.

The evidence for survival goes deeper. It is one of the most difficult problems of psychotherapy to modify an individual's self-system, to lower his defense, and to open the self to perceptions which accord more closely with "what is out there." This is offered as evidence that, once established, the self adapts to retain its structure and survive (even one which is, in some larger context, maladaptive). Being a system within other systems, it has greater resistance to modification than its suprasystems. Here we come upon one of the fascinating features derived from systems theory. If the self-system is markedly out of accord with the individual's environment and rejects, rationalizes, or projects inputs, the total set of systems that is the individual produces behavior that may conflict with other systems. Thus the possibilities of the individual surviving even as a biological organization are reduced, *but the self-system survives.*

Having alluded to problem people, it is necessary to call attention to the probability proposition again; namely, that systems operate to produce useful and useless outputs, the criterion of usefulness being established by the suprasystem. At the self level, this is a denial of the position taken by Rogers, Snygg and Coombs, Maslow, and others that the self has a basic tendency toward optimal adjustments, self-actualization, enhancement. It is obvious that problem people—persons poorly adapted to their milieu in one respect or another—become so through the operation of the basic developmental principles that apply with equal force to nonproblem people. It is indeed the position of the mental hygienists and psychotherapists that none of us has attained a perfectly satisfactory or optimal adaptation to the exigencies of living in all its ramifications. In computer or communications theory terms, we all produce some error, some noise. What has been called the drive for self-actualization, self-enhancement, the tendency toward health and away from disease, is a unique organization of the self that is as probable as the reverse (Ashby, 1962).

Ashby makes the point that organizations are neither inherently "good" or "bad." Some are so constructed that they stabilize around an assigned level or value—assigned by some other system. For that assigning system, and in terms of the assignment, the system may be judged good or bad, but only under those circumstances. In more general terms, psychological maturity is not a condition that is the mere automatic unfolding of a predestined pattern of development, but instead is an achievement. It is an achievement that comes about through a certain organization of the self and other psychological systems such that the behavior outputs serve the larger system in a way that it can also operate to produce outputs that serve its suprasystem, and so on. This intermeshing of appropriate outputs at each level is but one of many possibilities. When the intermeshing of self with its suprasystem occurs with only tolerable error, the systems can be said to be reasonably well adjusted. In this view, the therapist merely arranges the individual's psychological environment so that the intermeshing may be more probable. Rogers (1951) seems to have been most explicit on this point, but also appears not to have recognized the needless postulate of a drive toward adjustment.

Where is feedback in this adaptation of self to disturbance? One cannot point to an electrical circuit, a neural pathway, a mechanical linkage, a valve, or a sensor. Feedback is as much a function as it is a structure and can be legitimately discussed in either set of terms.

The fundamental feature of feedback is a measuring or assessment of the system's output, followed by the utilization or input of that assessment for subsequent operations. The self, in this sense, may "look at itself." That is, it is possible for an individual *to assess in retrospect his own overt behavior and covert feelings, intentions, attitudes, and then make use of the assessment in subsequent situations.* Feedback applied in this sense removes some of the mystery that has arisen over the question, "How may the self see itself?" Minsky (1963) has presented an argument justifying the self in terms not unlike those we have used. He says, "If a creature can answer a question about a hypothetical experiment without actually performing that experiment, then the answer must have been obtained from some sub-machine [we would say subsystem] inside the creature. The output of that sub-machine (representing a correct answer) as well as the input (representing the question) must be coded descriptions of the corresponding external events or event classes." In other words, Minsky's justification for postulating the self rests on the functions performed that cannot be ascribed merely to the total "creature" but must logically be referred to some subsystems of that "creature."

How can one deny a threat without first having admitted the data to the self-system and compared it with what is already there? One answer to this question offered by Rogers (1951) suggests that there are levels of discrimination below awareness in which the threat is differentiated from nonthreatening inputs. Some experimental evidence exists which indicates a perceptual defense for tabooed words, for instance, which are not so readily perceived as others.

These considerations give us some confidence that the propositions of general system theory can be applied even to a system that is nonmechanical and purely psychological. The feedback principle, moreover, appears to stand up when used to conceptualize the automatic, almost natural, way in which the self adapts to a variety of disturbances that would otherwise modify it. In its essential outline and fundamental functional characteristics, the self behaves very like Ashby's homeostat.

In the preceding discussion of the self and its defense, we have used terms like rationalization, projection, and so on, rather than feedback channels, electrons, molecules. Some may object that these "mentalistic" terms are not sufficiently precise to warrant their use in this connection. In response to this objection it is our position that the referents for these terms are as substantial and real as are the referents for terms like energy, information, entropy. At base, a projection must be the result of a set of neural discharges whose total energy is small. Even if at the moment we cannot locate or describe the structures with precision, it is legitimate to deal with the phenomena in system terms just as we deal with signals in a computer, or the bonds of chemical compounds.

Let us summarize the discussion of adaptation. Maintenance-error outputs at one level have the possibility of disturbing systems at higher levels. To minimize this possibility, feedback loops, in various ways depending upon the particular model and particular errors, either dissipate, neutralize, or block these error outputs from entering other systems. There is no reason for assuming vitalism in such a formulation, since a more parsimonious assumption that function depends on structure appears to be sufficient, especially when set beside a companion proposition that emergent qualities are a necessary consequence of the processing of inputs to produce something different in the outputs. This set of statements appears to fit living as well as nonliving systems, although many systems have not so far been analyzed in these terms. An extended program of empirical research therefore lies before us.

SUMMARY

In Chapter IV we have developed the following propositions and definitions:

4.1. Open-system outputs are probabilistic. This is true because open systems by definition interact with other systems and the referent system, for any system is itself probabilistic; no system can be observed without the observing system having some effect on the observed system (Heisenberg uncertainty principle).

4.2. Garner's uncertainty concept is a special mathematical statement of 4.1.

4.3. The variability or limits of outputs is controlled by:

a. The structure of system components and boundary.
b. A finite number of states the system can assume because of a, above.

4.4. The capacity of a system is the range of its variability limited by 4.3, above.

4.5. Organizations evolve among components or between "natural" systems initially by accident when:

a. Two or more systems fall into a coupled symbiotic relationship.
b. Feedback relationships develop between complex systems consisting of more than two components.

4.6. Organizations of systems develop toward greater complexity and emergent characteristics.

4.7. Adaptation refers to those behavioral and structural modifications within the life span of a system or across generations which are survival-extending.

a. Adaptation is accomplished by blocking, dissipating, or neutralizing potentially harmful maintenance inputs.

4.8. Adapting systems develop toward greater rather than less stability.

V / THE GROWTH OF SYSTEMS

In the previous chapter, we attempted to account for the adaptation of systems and their integration. Obliquely, we have dealt with growth, but from the standpoint of the evolving integration of one system with another. Growth obviously requires integration, but there are other aspects of growth, and it is to these that we now address ourselves.

Before becoming immersed in the principles of growth, we had better define the concept as we shall use it in this chapter. By growth, we mean the expansion of a system in size in which all parts are functionally articulated. An embryo grows into a mature organism; a book grows as meaningful words and chapters are added; a business organization grows as it employs more productive people. Growth may occur in three ways: by the addition of individual components, by the "merger" of one system with another, and by the self-generation of new components. In all these instances, it is the addition of components that characterizes the change we label growth.

GROWTH PRINCIPLES

Nucleation

Boulding (1956) has proposed a series of five principles which appear to be involved in what he calls structural growth, as opposed to mere accretion. The first of these is the principle of nucleation, which holds that growth is initiated by some core item that sets the process in motion. For instance, a microscopic crystal dropped in a solution will start the crystal growth process; sometimes a small speck of a foreign substance or even a gas bubble is sufficient. In sexual reproduction, the sperm is the necessary addition to the egg before growth occurs. Raindrops form around specks of dust. Auxins, those complex hormone catalysts, have been shown to be the necessary stimuli for initiating fruit growth, and, once started, the process continues to maturity. Luckwill (1959), a pomologist, says, "In other words, we have what appears to be a trigger mechanism that, once released, sets in motion certain growth processes which then continue to completion, even in the absence of any further stimulation." The role of hormones in animal growth has similarly been shown to be essential, although in the more complex systems there appears to be a requirement for a continuing supply of these catalysts. Torrey (1958) has described a method for microscopic observation of single isolated root cells. These can be rendered viable and undergo division for several weeks if a small segment of callus tissue is placed in the center of the agar and peripheral to the cell. The *nurse tissue* (Torrey's term for the callus material) is essential, for without it the cell shortly dies, even when bathed with nutrients. A slightly different example of the "foreign" input principle is found in the propagation of the eggs of both sea urchins and frogs. These develop faster in clusters than in isolation (Allee and Evans, 1937; Merwin, 1945) for the reason that the concentration of CO_2 and other metabolic gases is higher in the clusters. Why should the presence of noxious, nonnutrient gases promote growth? It has been established that these stimulate the cells to ingest the appropriate nutrients, provided the pressure of CO_2 does not exceed an optimal point.

It is not too farfetched to see the analogy of the nucleation principle in the social situations at the conference or breakfast table. One's ideas have an appropriate timeliness about them determined by the situation. Presented at the right time, they serve to bring together into a unity elements that were disconnected.

The growth of a system—nonliving, biological, or social—appears to be initiated by the introduction at the critical time of some especially unique input that permits a semiorganized system to organize itself, whereas previously the elements of the system were nonfunctional. It is worth pointing out that these "growth-producing inputs" are not the same as maintenance or signal inputs. The hormones of biological systems are truly catalysts; they are not "consumed" by the cells or transformed into new chemical forms to become a part of the cells any more than are the dust particles of raindrops transformed into water. (Fertilization of an egg, however, appears to be an exception.) It is possible that "nuclear people" forming new sects, new types of business ventures, new welfare organizations are integrated (consumed) as subsystems within their own creations. On the other hand, if we take a longer time perspective, the seminal individual may disappear from the organization that grew up around him and the organization may persist long beyond his lifetime. He becomes no longer essential to its life. The founder has an existence apart from his organization. His concepts, influence, fundamental values, points of view are the critical inputs. Although they may be identified with the founder, they may also be conceived as disembodied and merely a set of propositions like Marx's *Das Kapital.* The main point is that the seminal idea, the crucial element, or that special substance which triggers the system for growth is not to be confused with either maintenance inputs, which nourish and energize the system, or signal inputs that are the main materials on which the system works.

Given the "foreign" nucleus, why should the system begin the growth process? We have no clear answer to this question. One may observe, however, that living systems, so long as they have adequate maintenance inputs (we shall deal with this issue shortly), tend to function in such a way as to complicate their exchanges with their surroundings. Rats seem to prefer complex environments over simple ones (Dember, Earl, and Paradise, 1957). The spate of sensory-deprivation studies in humans can be interpreted as meaning that the individual prefers—and when deprived, seeks—an optimal level of signal inputs. A large number of animal studies have indicated strong tendencies variously labeled exploration, manipulation, and curiosity (Butler, 1953; Berlyne, 1955; Harlow, Harlow, and Meyer, 1950). Although these studies have related the "drives" to learning, there is no logical reason for denying that they *may* also be the inherent properties of the systems which account for their expansion. In other words, systems grow, once stimulated by a "foreign" agent, because it is one of the properties of living systems to complicate themselves when brought into contact with signal and maintenance sources. Admittedly, this is not a very satisfactory answer, but at the present state of our knowledge it appears to be the best available.

Emergent Characteristics and Growth

We have said before that suprasystems have characteristics not found in their subsystems by reason of the proposition that inputs are not the same as outputs (proposition 2.8). Growth consequences also contribute to these new characteristics. If one, for instance, merely halves, then quarters, and further divides a system—such as a cell—into smaller segments in the way that a fertilized egg develops, at one point an interesting new condition occurs. On the sixth "split" of the cells, some in the center will have no surface in contact with the surroundings of the total system. Their sole environment will be made up of other daughter cells. This is brought about alone by the geometry of the situation. If those at the center are to maintain their structure, either, or both, of two things must happen: the surrounding cells must somehow "feed" them, or the shape of the total system must be modified to bring the center cells in contact with the surroundings. A third possibility is for the center cells to develop a somewhat different structure with different requirements. In any case, mere size requires a change in structure somewhere in the system. Weiss (in Grinker, 1956) has described a situation of this sort:

> Some slime molds consist of separate amoebae which to all practical purposes are each a single individual moving and living as separate entities. At certain times, however, the amoebae aggregate into solid masses, uniting into a multi-cellular organism consisting of tens of thousands of such amoebae. These now move as a coherent multi-cellular organism, and soon differentiate by organized division of labor into beautiful fruiting bodies with a cellulose stalk in the center, a disc at the base, and spores at the top.
>
> Here you have a real synthesis of a higher-order form from combinations of equivalent unit parts. Morphologically, this shows all the properties of an organism, an egg, or any such thing where the cells had never been completely dispersed and secondarily brought together.

Boulding (1956, p. 71) refers to this phenomenon as the principle of nonproportional change, pointing out that it is impossible for models of different size to possess identical characteristics. In particular, functions that depend upon surface areas, linear dimensions, or volumetric dimensions will be differentially favored with increases in size. Surface increases as the square, while volume increases as the cube, of the linear dimensions. Hence, a uniform increase in length, width, and thickness of a system will necessarily require components to assume different functions and will force the development, as in the case of the cellulose stalk in the slime molds, of specialized structures. Boulding (1956, pp. 71–72) presents the situation as follows:

> Architecture and biology—two sciences which are much more closely related than might appear at first sight—provide admirable examples. A one-room schoolhouse, like a bacterium, can afford to be roughly globular and can still maintain effective contact with its environment—getting enough light and nutrition (children) into its interior through its walls. Larger schools, like worms, become long in relation to their volume in order to give every room at least one outside wall. Still larger schools develop wings and courtyards, following the general principle that a structure cannot be more than two rooms thick if it is to have adequate breathing facilities. This is the insect level of architecture (skin breathing). The invention of artificial ventilation (lungs) and illumination (optic nerves) makes theoretically possible, at any rate, much larger structures of a "glob-

> ular" or cubic type, with inside rooms artificially ventilated and lit, just as the development of lungs, bowels, nerves, and brains (all involving extensive convolutions to get more area per unit of volume) enabled living matter to transcend the approximately three-inch limit set by the insect (skin-breathing) pattern. In the absence of such devices, further growth of the structures involves splitting up into separate buildings (the campus) of which the biological analogy is the termite or bee colony.

It is important to recognize in Boulding's examples that they pertain to maintenance inputs and hence, according to our earlier discussion, the changes required by increasing size are *adaptations*.

Determinants of Form

Why is it that as systems grow, they tend to assume particular forms? If we assume—as we have—that systems initially are relatively undifferentiated, why is it that a frog's fertilized egg, for instance, which is outwardly indistinguishable from that of a fish, nevertheless develops into a frog that is easily distinguished from a fish? In other words, mere replication of cells does not account for their differentiation and the eventual production of adult forms that are species-specific.

At the biological level, this is a question that is far from completely understood. Without becoming enmeshed in genetics and the biochemistry of amino acids, proteins, ribose nucleic acids (RNA's), and deoxyribose nucleic acids (DNA's), it can be said that the current theory assumes that the RNA molecules found in all replicating cells provide a "template" against which, or on which, the simpler amino acids cling, taking their pattern from the template as they synthesize into new protein molecules. The DNA molecules, which always are found bounded by a membrane, provide the "master template" of the cells to be formed. The RNA and DNA molecules are themselves made up of components (sometimes called codes) that may be arranged in different patterns. The protein molecules of one species are different from those of other species. Assuming that the template notions are valid, it follows that the RNA and DNA molecules are also species-specific.

The important principle for general systems theory is that a plan of development is carried from cell to cell. Perhaps it would be more to the point to emphasize that, from the very start of the embryological development, structures are contained within the growing system that help to determine its eventual form. This holds true, of course, barring disruptions of the agents responsible for transmitting the plan.

However, as we have already indicated, the mere accretion of more components in a system forces some to take on specialized functions. Consequently, the initial plan as carried at the molecular level in the

DNA's is amenable to some modification. As we shall see in the next section, the modifications are somewhat easier when the cells are at an early stage of specialization.

The general proposition that we wish to emphasize is that the general form that the mature system will take is partly determined by some of the substructures of the initial system (cf. Russell, 1958). While we have developed this proposition on the basis of biochemical considerations, there is reason to believe that it will have wider application at the level of social systems as presented in Chapter VI.

LIMITATIONS ON GROWTH

As we have noted before, systems are both variable in outputs and also limited in their variability; hence, adaptations also are limited. It is not possible for a system to adapt to everything. It is this limitation in adaptability that prevents a system from growing to infinite size. Thus, institutions as they grow, face, among other problems, one of internal communication. Various administrative devices invented to meet this requirement eventually reach an asymptote in effectiveness. Beyond this point the cost of maintaining effective integration and communication outruns whatever benefits may accrue from large size. The system ceases to grow, partly because it is unable to adapt to the internal integrative problems of further growth.

Miller (1965) has hypothesized that the larger (but less than 100 per cent) the total input to a system devoted to information (what we have called signals), the more likely the system will survive. He quotes Best and Marschak (1956), who contend that the more complex the species, the higher is the percentage of total cell mass devoted to information processing. "No one," says Miller, "has yet discovered a species which failed to survive because too large a percentage of its body was neural tissue." Certainly there are examples of animals which failed to survive because the neural tissues were insufficient. On the other hand, Miller's hypothesis appears to overemphasize the signal requirements at the expense of maintenance inputs. Our view is that *an optimum balance must be struck between maintenance and signal inputs, for without an adequate supply of the former, the latter cannot be processed.*

A second limitation on growth is the storage capacity for maintenance energies. It will be recalled that we previously established that input must exceed output if storage is to occur. We may now add that *growth is possible only if some storage of energies occurs within a system over and above that required for the processing of signal inputs.* (In economic systems, capital formation is possible only from savings or profits. Biological systems grow only if nutrients ingested exceed the energy requirements of the mere survival level. Crystals grow in supersaturated solutions.) One limitation on growth is, therefore, a function of the storage capacity of the system. If storage capacity of maintenance energies is severely limited, the requisite energies for new components may not be available.

A third limitation on system growth—especially in living systems, but not limited to them—arises from the storage and memory phenomena already discussed. In the early life of a system, what is stored is relatively small compared with its memory later in life. Stored information, or energy, integrates, we said, with inputs. At the human and higher animal levels, we label these memories "habits." At the institutional level, they are the policy statements and regulations. These conditions—habits in animals and their counterpart, regulations in institutions—create limitations on the system's ability to process some inputs which, without these conditions, it would have accepted. One of the favorite witticisms of foreign-language teachers is to say that it is not difficult for adults to learn to speak Japanese, Russian, or Swahili, because little children learn to speak in these languages. This is an example of the respected, if not entirely understood, principle of habit interference; old memories interfere with the acquisition of new ones. A tree that is bent by the prevailing winds to the east will snap off if forced in the opposite direction. An organization developed to sell automobiles is not likely to grow by gradually taking on the sale of roadmaking machinery.[1]

Another facet of memory that limits growth pertains to the development of specialized functions within certain components to such a degree that the components are unable to modify their functions in response to further growth. For instance, in a series of studies extending over several years, Detwiler, Coghill, and others (Detwiler, 1929; Coghill, 1926) have shown that transplantations in early-embryo amblystoma of one portion of the embryo to another site will result in the transplant assuming the features normal to that site. At later stages of growth, the transplants fail to integrate with the new site. If a forelimb bud is replaced by a tail bud from another animal, the animal grows with a second tail protruding where the foreleg would normally be. At earlier stages, however, the transplantation of cells proliferating slowly into sites where proliferation is much faster results in the transplants adopting the proliferation rate characteristic of the site. It appears, therefore, that at this early stage cells are highly malleable and responsive to the growth

[1] Large industrial complexes manufacturing a wide variety of unrelated products have been built up in recent years by the acquisition or merger of already functioning, but smaller, organizations. This is comparable to a grafting process in botany and is not growth through the gradual development of new structures out of parent structures.

processes which determine their ultimate functions. On the other hand, once specialization has reached a certain point—and specialization is another term for memories of a special kind—the cells are less responsive to a new and different kind of input. Consequently, the system, because of age, becomes less adaptable and restricts its range of sensitivity to inputs.

It might be argued in opposition to the conclusion above that the effect of memories is to widen, rather than narrow, the filters of the system. Logically, this is an equally possible change. Surely, there are numerous examples in which this appears to be the case. Fetuses are first insensitive to exteroceptive stimuli and then mature to a point where they are sensitive. During the early stages of training animals and man in skill, there is a progressive increase in sensitivity to first gross, then minor, cues guiding behavior. This happens in piano playing, flying an airplane, riding a bicycle, applying cosmetics, making photographs, or dancing. As we learn a language, the words we perceive take on nuances and sharpen their differences. In general, growth viewed from this vantage point is characterized by greater differentiation and finer discriminations.

Growth vs. Learning

Notice that in the above paragraph we have slipped into an identification of learning with growth. This is particularly easy to do, and we need, therefore, to make a distinction between them. The improvement in a skill, in intelligence, in ability to perform new tasks is not itself growth, although it is sometimes referred to as such. As we are conceiving of growth, it is that process which, once begun, results in structural modifications solely traceable to maintenance inputs. It has been customary and useful to make the distinction between maturation and learning in explanations of behavioral changes early in life. This is the distinction we wish to preserve, recognizing, however, that both learning (memory from signal inputs) and growth are accompanied by structural changes. Growth and the articulation of systems is always prerequisite to signal inputs or learning.

A possible resolution of the issue presented above is the tentative proposition that those structural changes brought about by maintenance inputs tend to filter out all but a relatively narrow spectrum of inputs, while those modifications resulting from signal inputs *may* result in greater differentiation of inputs. Obviously, these two types of changes may be easily confused, and empirical evidence not yet available may not support the hypothesis. The review and analysis of molecular theories of memory by Dingman and Sporn (1964) indicate a complicated set of relationships between cell bodies, their peripheral synaptic structures, RNA, DNA, and the protein-synthesizing metabolism. Without going into the details here (the article is a tightly reasoned integration of the principal findings from more than a score of studies), Dingman and Sporn strongly suggest that both signal and maintenance inputs are involved, although in a more complex fashion than we have indicated. One brief quotation will not do justice to this article, but at least gives an indication of the emphasis. "We may perhaps more adequately investigate the structural basis of the permanent memory trace if we seek to answer the following questions: What permanent changes in neuronal structure and function result from stimulation of the neuron and what is the mechanism of production of these changes? . . . It is now apparent that the molecular and the cytological approaches to the problem of memory are by no means mutually exclusive, especially if one postulates that a major function of the synthetic mechanisms of the cell body is to provide molecules necessary for the growth and maintenance of axonal and dendritic connections" (p. 27). The article suggests that to date it has not been possible to separate (a) the structural prerequisites for memory from (b) the more or less permanent structural changes as a *consequence* of neural stimulation. The first, we would call growth and the second, learning. Moreover, we are suggesting as a hypothesis that learning is characterized by those structural changes which increase the differential filtering at the boundary of the system, while growth narrows the range of inputs acceptable by the system.

Although the mechanisms and consequences of growth have not been exhausted in the preceding discussion, it may be well to recapitulate the points made so far. Growth appears to be initiated when a "nearly organized" system accepts either a catalytic or a foreign input. The system must be "ripe" and the foreign input must be appropriate. Structural growth with accompanying increases in size requires specialization of some components. Thus, emergent characteristics must occur. These characteristics fit the previous definition of adaptations. Growth is limited by the limits on variability of systems and their adaptations discussed previously. In addition, the relatively permanent memories of systems also impose limitations on what a specialized subsystem will accept as inputs. Although both learning and growth result in structural modifications that are not, as yet, clearly identified empirically, they can be differentiated conceptually. Growth is defined as those modifications and additions (memories) brought about by maintenance inputs, while learning is the consequence of signal inputs. It is hypothesized, finally, that growth changes serve to narrow the range of inputs, while the memories from learning result in greater differentiation of inputs. This hypothesis, though plausible, is in need of additional empirical support.

THE EVOLUTION OF DOMINANT SUPRASYSTEMS

In the previous chapter, we presented a picture of the evolutionary development of suprasystems from simpler subsystems. From that description one might infer that suprasystems are entirely dependent upon subsystems for their survival; that is to say, the outputs of the subsystems become the nutrient sources for the suprasystems, without which the latter would not survive. From the preceding discussion of growth it now becomes possible to introduce some refinement that accounts for the frequently observed fact that the suprasystem often controls the subsystem rather than the other way around. For instance, the management of an organization exerts some control over its various subunits. The federal government of the United States exerts some control over the several states. The organism as a totality influences and modulates the activities of the organs and subsystems. This is not to say that the reverse direction of influence does not exist as well, but this upward- or outward-directed influence we have accounted for previously. Starting from the propositions already developed, how can we account for control from the suprasystem downward to its components?

We start from the proposition that growth in structural size requires modification in some component structures—and consequently functions. Stated somewhat explicitly, growth requires some specialization of functions as exemplified in the slime molds composed of amoebae. Even at this point, without going further one must conclude that the suprasystem, taken as a whole, has gained an ascendancy over the components, "dictating," if you will, the structure they must assume if the total system is to function as a unity. This comes about as the mere consequence of the special form assumed by the system. Spherical forms must have some interior components not in touch with the environment of the total system and therefore must be of a different structure. Long, narrow forms solve this problem, but then most possess stronger than usual connective tissues in their longitudinal directions. Star or octopus forms must have both types of specialization at different parts of the system. No matter what form the system takes, some specialization of structure, and hence function, must occur in some, if not all, of the components.

Second, specialization of structure carries with it a cost in restricting the system's capacity to survive independently. Once embedded in a system, the component to some degree becomes dependent upon the total system for its existence. The greater that specialization, the greater is the dependence of the component on the total system. Hence the restrictions placed on the independence of a component by reason of its specialization further augment the dominance of the total system over its components.

Third, a system composed of specialized subsystems performing functions that in concert contribute to the total system's survival is thereby better equipped as a totality to perform a wider range of functions than any component taken separately. This is the essence of specialization and is its *raison d'être*. It is another way of expressing the Gestalt principle that the whole is more than the sum of its parts. One of the further consequences of this increasing range of function is that the total system may be capable of accepting inputs and engaging in processes that none of the separate components could accept or perform. The total system, when composed as indicated, has somewhat greater probability than any of its components of successfully dealing with the variability in its environment. Hence again, the suprasystem, if it can slough off some noncontributing subsystems and encapsulate or generate replacements, may have a longer life than the components. This latter process is precisely what happens in many multicellular-growing biological systems.

If one thinks about a manufacturing corporation, the same principles hold. The integration of specialized man-power skills permits the organization to do more than the sum of the individuals if they all worked as separate entrepreneurs. As members of the organization their skills are more limited and their dependence on the totality is correspondingly greater. The diesel-locomotive engineer may operate his train efficiently and safely, yet his economic well-being depends upon the efficiency of an entire railroad. Without a railroad system, his skills are virtually useless. One consequence is that the system then exerts control over the engineers. (A counteracting control is, of course, the railway unions, but even here the individual becomes dependent upon a different suprasystem.)

One can conceptualize the findings of embryonic studies of the amblystoma in terms of increasing dependence on, and control by, the suprasystem. The early stages of embryonic development may be characterized as a system in which the cells were more uniformly structured than later. The early parent cells of what would normally become the cranial pole of the spinal cord are so unspecialized at one point in development that they may be transplanted successfully to the caudal pole of the embryo with no subsequent malformations (Detwiler, 1929). In our terms, the boundary filter for these cells is sufficiently wide to accept the nutrients and other suprasystem inputs of either its original or the transplant site. With increasing maturity and specialization, the cell assembly that would normally become the cranial end of the spinal cord fails to accept the metabolic and growth inputs of the transplant site, but, instead, develops as it would if it had not been transplanted. The amblystoma survives, although deformed. Looking at these same data from the standpoint of the suprasystem influence, it seems clear that it is the system of cells surrounding a given locus that determines how the cells within that domain will specialize, provided they have not already developed a high degree of specialization incommensurate with the suprasystem's requirements. One surely cannot argue that the structural destiny of the cells is carried immutably in the early cells and is independent of the influences of the immediate surroundings. The observations on the amblystoma are, therefore, wholly consistent with the proposed increasing dominance of the suprasystem over its subsystems and the counterpart dependence of specialized subsystems upon the suprasystem.

We have argued that in the early life of a system its components are more tightly integrated and more resistant to destruction than the system itself. The power to control survival, or in Thibaut and Kelley's (1959) terms *fate control,* resides in the subsystems. As the relationships between sub- and suprasystems mature, a point is reached in which they are equally balanced. At this time, the integration of the sub- and suprasystems are most vulnerable to disruption. Once this critical period is passed, further adjustments may continue internally, but the suprasystem is destined to survive these disturbances. The major adjustment problems are centered at another level or in another direction—the relation of the suprasystem to its counterparts elsewhere.

The history of the United States exemplifies this deduction. Immediately after the Revolutionary War, the colonies reluctantly and tentatively delegated a few powers to the Confederation. The subsequent federal system grew in strength as the powers of the states declined. The mid-1800's were the critical years. The War Between the States tested "whether that nation, or any nation, so conceived and so dedicated can long endure." While the exponents of states' rights are still to be heard and the appropriate domains for local determination are still unsettled, the dominance of the suprasystem can no longer be in doubt.

We shall leave for a later chapter an analysis of the development of an empire with its colonies making use of the same principles. Virus infections can also be modeled in the same terms. It would be almost a trivial exercise to deal in these terms with the major data of group pressures on individuals—especially deviants—toward conformity to group norms.

It appears, therefore, that it is possible purely on logical grounds to account for the control of suprasystems over their components, given the initial proposition that growth involves structural modifications and specialization of component functions.

The Dependence-Independence Conflict

The discussion above leads to one of the most intriguing deductions of GST. If the subsystems are to serve their functions in the suprasystem, they must retain their identities and a degree of autonomy. This identity is manifested in the retention of the subsystem's capacity for variability, even to the point where it may on occasion produce some outputs unacceptable to its suprasystem. Otherwise the boundaries disappear with their specialized filtering functions. This requirement for continued identity is especially evident in social systems whose individuals complain when their special needs are ignored, when their names are forgotten, or when the organization's hierarchy fails to recognize the uniqueness of persons in the lower echelons.

It is therefore inescapable that in all growing systems a conflict will exist between the supra- and subsystems. The suprasystem requires specialized functions of the subsystems for its own existence. The subsystems are capable of performing those functions only if they are not so completely absorbed that their constituent components scatter beyond the limits of the boundary. We shall see in a later chapter the special implications of this principle for social systems.

SUMMARY

In Chapter V, we have attempted to establish the following propositions:

5.1. Growth may be viewed as structural modifications initiated by some "foreign" input permitting the acceptance of maintenance inputs.

a. Emergent characteristics of systems are the necessary consequences of growth and attendant modifications.
b. Because growth modifications are such as to permit the system to be maintained more efficiently, they can be viewed as adaptations.
c. Growth is limited by adaptation limits and memories.
d. Growth follows a "plan" embedded in substructures of the initial system modified by localized specialization.

5.2. Learning may be viewed as structural modifications (memories) resulting from signal inputs.

5.3. Suprasystems, although evolving out of their subsystems and hence dependent upon them, gradually gain control over the subsystems. This is the consequence of the necessary specialization of structure and function in subsystems by reason of growth requirements.

5.4. Some conflict is inescapable between the requirements of the suprasystem and the continued identity of the subsystems.

VI / SOCIAL SYSTEMS: COMPONENTS, STRUCTURE, AND BOUNDARY

In the preceding chapters, we have made many allusions to social systems as examples of the various propositions and definitions that form the framework of this general systems theory. In part, we have already begun the main task of this chapter, which is to fit social groups into GST. The present chapter addresses itself directly to the relevant definitions and propositions, developing a social model that corroborates the general theory and is empirically grounded.

It will be obvious shortly, if it is not already evident, that when we deal with social systems, we must at times speak with less precision for the sake of generality than is possible when dealing with molecular, biological, or engineered systems. Although both social and engineered systems are the products of man's ingenuity, our ability to conceptualize the former in rigorous terms is handicapped by at least two limitations: the lack of basic mensuration units comparable to grams, centimeters, and seconds; and the imprecision of operationally defined input-output criteria distinguishing error from utility. On the other hand, nonparametric statistics have provided tools of considerable power, and we can also identify, in crude ways, useful and useless outputs for social systems.

One may take as an example of these two limitations the institutions of higher education being expanded throughout the United States. In one state, a new university is being developed from the top down—establishing a graduate school first, and later building an undergraduate school beneath it. Another institution is deliberately growing in the reverse direction, from undergraduate to graduate school. Granted that there may be more than one way to achieve a given result in engineered systems, the educational plans of these two institutions include neither a measure of their educational output nor an evaluation of internal operations which approach in precision the familiar Just Noticeable Difference of psychophysical studies or the calories per mole of chemistry. We are, therefore, handicapped in efforts to determine whether one pattern of development is more advantageous than the other. Parenthetically, it may be added that those responsible for these and other new institutions appear to be uninterested in finding out.

A further precaution must be mentioned preliminary to coming to grips with the main issues of this chapter. We assume that the components of social systems—people performing roles—possess characteristics such as expectations, beliefs, values, perceptions, and cognitions that influence their behavior. In making the assumption that cognitions are one class of behavior determinants, we are not introducing gratuitous concepts that originate outside the system theory. On the contrary, proposition 5.1a says that emergent characteristics must show themselves as systems progressively increase in complexity. It is our contention, first, that cognitions are undeniable in the experience of humans (and to a lesser degree in infrahumans) and, second, that they are the consequence of the greater neurophysiological complexity of humans. These are private phenomena available for analysis only to the extent that they are expressly revealed by the individual.[1]

From one standpoint, the ability of components to reveal—via language symbols—what is going on within their respective Black Boxes is an advantage. Nonliving and most living systems are sterile in this respect, and their internal machinations are consequently harder to discover. Nevertheless, this new source of data provides additional complications when it is recognized that the verbal report may be subject to distortion from some unidentified, although potentially identifiable, sources. Consequently, it is not an easy matter to decide when the verbal report of one's private experience is to be accepted, rejected, or qualified.

A further difference needs to be borne in mind in raising the focus of analysis to the social level. Although in Chapter II the discussion of inputs and outputs drew on the similarities between energy and information, we must recognize in what follows that we shall be speaking mostly about information, rather than energy, flow. Du Brul (1958) made the interesting, if somewhat inaccurate, observation that "speech is the spark that spans the synapse between two nervous systems." If we

[1] Our position at this point is different from Miller's (1955), in which he expressly confined himself to "public" data.

bear in mind that the information transmitted from person to person may set off patterns of behavior whose energy expenditure is generally unrelated to the *bits* of information received, we can avoid some logical difficulties. Energy is analogous to information either at the input or output side. It would be a mistake, however, to suppose that we could analyze inputs in energy terms and outputs as information, or vice versa, without encountering complicated transformations within the Black Box.

Finally, humans as individuals and social systems composed of humans represent unquestionably a higher degree of system complexity than molecules, tissues, or organs. And with this greater complexity goes a higher degree of uncertainty in Garner's sense. We should not be surprised, therefore, if there is an apparently lower degree of lawfulness in the arrangements between men. We cannot agree with Mason (1960), however, that *in principle* the interrelationships of mankind partake more of error than is true of natural systems. The appearance of "error" merely reflects our current ignorance of the relevant variables and the contingencies of their interconnections.

In spite of these caveats, the interpretation of social groups in terms of GST is a rewarding task, to which we may now turn our attention.

THE SOCIAL GROUP DEFINED

A group is a set of two or more individuals interacting with each other in a manner different from their interactions with other individuals. This is a minimal definition of a group that conforms with the system definition 2.1 on page 32. The exchanges taking place within the group are of a kind that distinguishes them from exchanges taking place between the group and its surroundings. If one compares even in a cursory manner the communications, say, within a committee with the communications between the committee and its parent body, the former will show somewhat greater confidence, greater intimacy, greater detail. Family relationships are surely different in many respects from the behavioral relationships existing between these individuals and nonrelatives. Where this is not so, one can, with both theoretical and commonsense justification, claim that the family group has disintegrated.

When we say that the individuals of the system interact differently from their interactions with individuals not in the group, we imply that their group-related behavior is constrained. This is one way of defining what many have called a role (cf. Biddle and Thomas, 1966). We can accept the statement of Parsons and Shils (1951, p. 190) that "the conceptual unit of the social system is the role. The role is a sector of the individual actor's total system of action. . . . The individual then becomes a unity in the sense that he is a composite of various action units which in turn are roles in the relationships (systems) in which he is involved. But this composite of roles is *not* the same abstraction as personality."

Miller (1965) has defined seventeen critical subsystems which are proposed as essential to the life of any living system, whether cell or society. He divides these into two classes (matter-energy and information-processing), which bear a strong similarity to maintenance and signal inputs proposed herein. In the first class he places the ingestor, distributor, decomposer, producer, matter-energy storage, extruder, motor, and supporter. In the second, or information-processing subsystems, are input transducer, channel and net, decoder, associator, memory, decider, encoder, and output transducer. The boundary of a system, Miller proposes, processes both matter-energy as well as information. Finally, most, but not all, living systems possess a reproducing subsystem, but this is not essential for the life of the system itself.

When considering social systems, it is not necessary to posit a separate individual for each of these subsystems. Instead, we may conceive of Miller's subsystem as functional roles, many of which may be performed by a single individual; or, in large social systems, special roles may be assigned to separate persons or to specialized divisions of the organization. Thus the input transducer on the information (signal) side for a large commercial firm could be the market research office; for a church, it could be the flow (with filtering) of information that bears on its activities which is carried by all its members about the surrounding community or its "worldwide" parish. In similar fashion, as Miller has illustrated, an analysis of social systems will reveal that they possess specialized roles, instrumental devices, or subunits that perform each of the functions listed.

Moreover, groups exist within other groups (assumption 2.10). The nuclear family exists within an extended family that, in turn, exists within a clan or community, which is a component within some larger societal unit, the state or nation. A work group in a factory is a component within a department that is part of the manufacturing division of a corporation, existing within a competitive industry making up a segment of the economic system within a nation having political, economic, military, and other relationships with other nations, some of which may be bound together by treaty ties in opposition to other nations similarly bound. Exchanges occur among each of these levels. Subject to the qualification given in the next paragraph, if one compares adjacent sub- and suprasystem levels in such a hierarchy of systems, the subsystem will exhibit greater resistance to destruction or, contrariwise, will be more cohesive than its immediately higher suprasystem. This is in harmony with proposition 2.14. (See also Ramsöy, 1963.)

Somewhat in opposition to this proposition, we have argued that as organizations grow, forming a hierarchy of the sort just delineated, the suprasystems may gain dominance over the subsystems. (See Proposition 5.3.) More exactly stated, sub- and suprasystems become interdependent, each supplying appropriate signal and maintenance inputs for the other. In the early stages of such a symbiotic relation between sub- and suprasystems, it is the older subsystem that retains the power to determine whether the suprasystem survives and has a greater resistance to destruction. Later, for two reasons, the suprasystem gains the upper hand. First, the growth of the suprasystem is accomplished by capturing within it addtional subsystems that become increasingly specialized, and each is less able to survive independently. Second, the suprasystem, taken as a whole, thereby becomes a major source of maintenance inputs for its components. If this condition does not develop, we have argued, the organizational input-output arrangements are mismatched, resulting in less than optimal integration. Numerous evidences of this principle in operation can be cited from labor-management disputes, state and federal governmental relationships, supervisor-subordinate conflicts, and issues arising between informal groups and their formal organizations.

Let us take a generalized union-management dispute for explication. The main thrust of the union movement has been to obtain returns from the economic process in the form of wages, fringe benefits, and interpersonal considerations, which, in the perception of the union, are their just due. We will not argue here whether or not these perceptions are legitimate. We take them as given. It is also obvious that both capital and managerial contributions, on the one hand, and labor, on the other, are necessary inputs to the organization's functions. If, in the extreme case, either withholds its contributions, the organization will fail to function. Equally important, if the maintenance feedback from the enterprise to the management-capital side (profit) *or* to those who provide the labor (wages, and the like) is less than a certain critical level, some disruption in the organization will occur. The bargaining which occurs between union and management can be understood as a trial-and-error process in which each subsystem is searching for that arrangement of maintenance inputs which will give maximum support to the survival of each system. At one stage of development, neither party is much concerned about the survival of the other. Later, maturity in management-labor negotiations is characterized by increasing awareness that each may contribute to the survival of the other to their mutual advantage (cf. Schelling, 1963, and Harbison and Coleman, 1951). This is not to say that the end result is always one that ensures the survival of the organization, any more than the biological evolutionary process ensured the survival of dinosaurs. We are saying that the evolution of social organizations depends upon the output of maintenance products which enable both sub- and suprasystems to continue their relationship, and this is not different in principle from biological evolution. The only way in which the bargaining process just described differs from proposition 4.5 is in the possibility that the components involved possess the capability of assessing, with some error, the future consequences of their choices.

THE PROBABILISTIC NATURE OF SOCIAL BEHAVIOR

The introduction of the term *choice* in the preceding sentence compels us to return to a fundamental proposition (4.1) that all systems are probabilistic in their outputs. The choice behavior in human systems is evidence of this probabilistic feature. Any choice is a response selected from among a range of alternatives. Given identical inputs to an individual or a group on two different occasions, the choice that is selected is a function of the internal state of the system. For individuals as well as groups, the number of these states is very large. The number of cells in a human body is of the order of 10^{15} and the number of neurons alone is about 10^{10}. The number of neuronal combinations, assuming the all-or-none law of neural activity, would be $2^{10^{10}}$. Of course, not all of these states would be equally probable at any instant, but it is because of this vast complexity of states that we have so far been unable empirically and rigorously to specify the limits of choices in social situations. Conceptually, however, we may assume for humans, as we have for lesser systems, that there exists a finite limit of alternative responses; and the most probable of these could be determined if the state of the system were completely known (cf. von Neumann, 1951, and Garner, 1962).

At this point we are impinging upon what has come to be known as decision theory. Without taking a side excursion into this burgeoning field (Goldman, 1962; Edwards, 1954), it is sufficient for our purposes here that a number of input and system aspects have been identified as interacting on the decision-making process, such as the set of behavior alternatives, the subset of these considered by the decision maker, the outcome of each choice, the "payoff" value or utility of each alternative, the risk or probability of "success," the emotional or crisis features of the situation and the decision maker. Decision theory has thus provided at least some of the input and system parameters within which contingent probabilities of choosing action A over $B, \ldots, n$ may be determined.

However, there exists another feature of probabilistic behavior that has developed out of Heisenberg's uncertainty principle and Garner's contingency-uncertainty concept. Essentially, these same principles find expression at the social level. That is to say, it is almost a truism—perhaps more often neglected in psychological research than in physics—that, in measuring the dependent variables, the experimenter, by his presence and instructions, inevitably distorts what he seeks to record. Although Sells (1965) has made a strong case for an ecological approach to human behavior, there can be no doubt that the mere presence of an observer in a playground (Barker, 1963) or in an industrial work area (Berrien and Angoff, 1960) disturbs what goes on "naturally." At the very minimum the observer is selective in what he records and in that sense distorts the totality of exhibited behavior. Back and others (Back, Hood, and Brehm, 1964; Back, 1962; Orne, 1962) have demonstrated on theoretical and empirical grounds that the psychological experiment using human subjects can be modeled as a two-component system in which the experimenter (and there always must be one) is the "operator" and the subject or group is a processor of instructions (signal inputs). However, rather than being an inert object manipulated by instructions, the subject is in fact perceiving not merely the instructions but a host of other subtle and uncontrolled inputs. It has been long known that what a person perceives is not just what he receives. The effective inputs are an amalgamation of stimuli coded into terms affected by the subject's state.[2]

Even the recruitment of naïve subjects on a voluntary basis is a self-selecting process. Back has shown in a series of experiments that self-selection is related to the potential subjects' sex, their scores on an inventory of self-disclosure, and their interest in the expected experimental situation. (This is a crude, but useful, description of their state.) The manner in which they are recruited is also a factor. "Thus if volunteers are used in an experiment, we will get male subjects, if they are willing to tell something about themselves; while we get women subjects who are interested because of the situation either at the time of volunteering or what they expect the experiment to be like. If we do not use volunteers, we get some resistance in the male subjects according to the amount of self-disclosure they are willing to make, and in the female subjects we get ones who are not interested in the situation and may react against a particular experiment. In both cases we see that a variable irrelevant to the experiment, like sex of the subject, is bound to make a difference in experimental results" (Back, Hood, and Brehm, 1964, p. 185; see also Hood, 1964, and Ora, 1965).

Essentially in agreement with Back, Mills (1962) argues that the subject's orientation toward the experimenter may often explain some otherwise inexplicable results. The results of a study by Indik (1963), involving small groups of college girls, gave dramatic confirmation of

[2] State is here used in its broadest definition as given in proposition 2.6.

Mills's argument because the subjects expressed hostility toward one of the observers to such a degree that the planned study had to be revised. Orne (1962) has shown that subjects sometimes engage in activities which they would not undertake in other circumstances because they wish to help the experimenter confirm the hypothesis they think is under investigation. It is abundantly obvious that the moment a subject is placed in an experimental situation, the variables under study are contaminated by the subject's uncontrolled expectations and the experimenter's presence, even if he is represented by a disembodied tape recorder or a sheet of written instructions. When we embark upon a psychological experiment with humans, it is naïve to suppose that we are dealing with naïve behavior. The mere intrusion of an experimenter, even without the sophisticated controls of the laboratory, disturbs the behavior we wish to record. This is the Heisenberg principle in social garb. However, at the social level, the principle may have greater significance, because the disturbance may be a much larger proportion of the observation measurement than is true of atomic measurements.[3]

The relevance of this principle in our present discussion lies not so much in the magnitude of the behavioral disturbance, but rather in the subtlety of the system's selectivity (proposition 2.18) and the boundary coding process. Some persons choose to avoid contact with certain types of innocuous (to the experimenter) experiments; others choose to be exposed, but interpret the "controlling" input instructions in ways not always intended by the experimenter. If we place these considerations against the rationale of the controlled experiment, it becomes clear that we face some exceedingly complex issues. The classical definition of an experiment assumes that it is possible to control all variables affecting a given kind of behavior, keeping all but one constant and systematically manipulating the independent variable. (Of course, more complex designs are possible, but logically they all reduce to this formula.) Translated into systems terms, this means that for purposes of experimentation the individual is conceived as a closed system except for one input channel—the independent variable. The data of Back, Orne, Mills, Indik, and others stand as challenges to this conception. We are forced to conclude that, discounting biological exchanges, humans, at least, remain psychological open systems even in "controlled" experiments, and this conclusion is in harmony with assumption 2.9. The choices they make when responding are not merely outputs determined by the independent variable but, instead, are a complex function of this and other partially controlled inputs interacting with the already existing state of the system

[3] The development of unobtrusive measures by Webb and others (1966) circumvents these difficulties to a large extent, but are so far applicable to a very limited range of social behavior.

(cf. Bunge, 1963). This is a restatement in social terms of proposition 2.15.

Let us now refer to Helson's (1959) adaptation level theory, for in this he speaks of essentially the same probabilistic features of human behavior that we have been discussing. His theory proposes that all judgments are made with respect to a neutral point which, in turn, is approximately a weighted log mean of (a) the immediate focal inputs, (b) the coexisting background stimuli (or at least those stimuli that have very recently occurred), and (c) the residual effects of one's total experience (in our terminology, memories). Helson's equation is:

$$\text{Adaptation level} = \bar{S}^p B^q R^r,$$

in which $\bar{S}$ is the geometric mean of the stimuli being judged, B is the background stimulus, R is the residual, and the exponents p, q, and r are weighted coefficients whose sum is 1.

Within this framework, Helson has been able to show with remarkable ingenuity that a wide variety of judgments can be understood involving psychophysical judgments, affective behavior, personality appraisals, and social relations. Schulman (1964) has shown that the adaptation level theory helps to identify the sources of variance in scaling attitude measures. On the other hand, at this writing, no one has been able to obtain measures of S, B, and R in units which permit their being simultaneously inserted in the equation. The studies cited by Helson and others have manipulated one or the other of the three parameters, assuming the remaining ones to be constant. Looking at a number of such studies, we get an impression of their relative weights, but neither all the variables themselves nor the weights have been generated from a single set of data which permits an empirical test of the equation.

One of the reasons for this lacuna lies in our currently inadequate scaling techniques. However, a more serious theoretical limitation also exists. Schulman found that a person's own attitudes on disarmament, as revealed by responses to a Thurstone-type scale, influenced the scaling of the items in ways predicted by the adaptation level theory when that person was used as the standardization judge. Since all attitude measures must, by their nature, be dependent upon some body of judgmental data, and since these judgments have been shown both empirically and theoretically to be influenced by Helson's S, B, and R with undetermined weights, one is faced with an indefinite regress of uncertainty in establishing any judgmental measures. That is to say, if one were to set up a standardization sample of judges to scale a set of attitude statements, this sample already would have some net, or average, attitude toward the issue under examination which would contaminate the scale values. If they had no attitude, they could not make discriminatory judgments.

But the determination of their average or net attitude must be measured by some other device whose scale values have been determined by another sample, subject to the same deficiencies. Thus there is no final referent sample whose biases can be precisely described.

To summarize, we have made two points: (1) Choice is the human equivalent of probabilistic outputs in the more general systems theory. (2) Although some of the determining parameters of choice have been specified by Helson, their precise measurement is subject in principle to an uncertainty of the same general kind as originally indicated by Heisenberg.

Simple Dyadic Relations

Having established the essential probabilistic nature of choice in the components of a social system, we may now proceed to an analysis of the manner in which choice operates in the formation of groups. We start with the simplest case, a dyadic relationship whose dimensions have been explicated perhaps best by Thibaut and Kelley (1959) and also by Schutz (1958). As we shall see, there is a commonality in the broad conceptions of Thibaut and Kelley, Schutz, and Helson—at least in their emphasis on the state of the components as influencing the nature of choices. We shall also see that the dyadic, as well as more complex, social relationships are based on a symbiotic exchange not importantly different from that which accounts for the evolution of biologic systems described in Chapters IV and V (cf. Thomas, 1957). The chief difference between social systems and those at lower levels lies in the content or substance of the exchanges, as well as in the nature of the effective and emergent parameters within the system influencing the system's operations. It is our claim that the principles describing the operations are isomorphic throughout the hierarchy of systems.

Thibaut and Kelley (1959, Chap. II) propose that a dyadic relationship will remain viable so long as the cost to each member does not exceed the rewards each receives from their mutual exchanges. They posit on common-sense grounds that each party has a repertory of possible behaviors, but selects from these those which will be acceptable to, and rewarding for his counterpart. By rewards we mean pleasures, satisfactions, and gratifications the person enjoys. The cost of the relationship is any factor that inhibits or deters the behavior. "The cost is high when great physical or mental effort is required, when embarrassment or anxiety accompany the action, or when there are conflicting forces or competing response tendencies of any sort" (1959, pp. 12–13).[4]

[4] This formulation is somewhat different from the model familiar to economists, who think of costs as inputs to the economic system and outputs as rewards. Thibaut

Berrien (1964) has used the term "group need satisfaction" (GNS) to specify what Thibaut and Kelley call the cost-reward difference that may be positive, zero, or negative. GNS has some advantages in that it connotes only those satisfactions which may, but not necessarily, be derived from association (interaction between) with two or more persons. The cost-reward concept, on the other hand, connotes the balancing and comparing of outputs with returning inputs from the other member of the dyad. In the more general terminology of GST, the cost to a person is the energy expenditure necessary to process the inputs to produce the requisite output. The methods of social psychology do not now permit us to measure the ergs per second of each component, but there can be little doubt that the costs, as described in psychological terms by Thibaut and Kelley, may ultimately be expressed in energy terms. Rewards, likewise translated to more general terms, we hypothesize, are maintenance inputs requiring small costs to process. Nonrewarding or punishing inputs are those requiring high energy costs. They provoke nonproductive ruminations, preoccupations, anxieties, tensions, sleep loss, or, in extreme cases, disabling psychotic conditions.

In the early life of a dyad, more than later, each party searches for those behaviors which will provoke reciprocated rewards from the partner. Stated in this way, the relationship is clearly brought under our earlier definition of a coupled system (proposition 4.5). It is not necessary to assume any other mechanism at work than reciprocation of appropriate outputs from one component to the other to account for a pair becoming a dyadic coalition. This does not mean, of course, that reciprocation proceeds smoothly without error. Thibaut and Kelley speak of interference of outputs which raises the costs to the participants of continuing the dyad. Only by gradually minimizing these costs and simultaneously maximizing the rewards can the dyadic bonds gain in strength.

In this description of a dyad, we have ignored for the moment the openness of the system—as do Thibaut and Kelley. It should always be understood that even a symbiotic relationship is not closed. In the extreme case where two persons are completely isolated from other sources of psychological inputs, there are at least the biological inputs from the environment that sustain life on which the psychological exchanges are built. In addition, some dyads may be formed as a consequence of constraining exogenous forces such as threats or economic pressures, as defined in definition 2.4.

and Kelley can be interpreted as looking at a human system in which the economic system intervenes between two or more people. In this view the intervening system delivers products or services (outputs) having utility (satisfactions) for people who, by reason of these reward inputs, put out effort that becomes an input to the economic system. Thus there is no conflict between the economists' and psychologists' conceptions.

Similarities and Differences in Components

Is it possible to look beyond the level of reciprocation to identify any of the characteristics of individuals that may raise the probability of their falling into a symbiotic relationship? Contrariwise, is it possible to describe circumstances under which the formation of a dyad would be inhibited? It may be recalled that in Chapter II we discussed ionic and covalent bonds, pointing out that, in the former, ions are held together by unlike charges, while organic compounds composed of molecules are held together by the weaker covalent bonds. It is one of the properties of a covalent bond that as the atoms approach one another there is first a sharing of their respective electron orbits which accounts for the attractive forces, but, at the same time, the repelling forces from the like charges of the nuclei tend to keep the atoms apart. The result is a balance of both attracting and repelling forces in covalent bonds. These brief atomic considerations suggest that attraction of components may be the consequence of either or both of two different conditions, ionic or covalent.

Folklore as well as serious systematic research has been concerned with whether, at the human level, "opposites attract" or "birds of a feather flock together." Our brief excursion into atomic physics suggests that we look at human attraction to see if there might be something comparable to covalent and ionic bonds. It has been proposed, and empirical evidence is available to support the notion, that people are held in groups (a) because they share the same values, points of view, general aims and objectives; (b) because they have a common idiom and system of communication; (c) because the group, in the eyes of its members, has a valued status in some larger system of groups; or (d) because the members merely like each other. All of this implies that likes attract (cf. Klein, 1956; Cartwright and Zander, 1959). On the other hand, it has been argued that dyads in which the individuals are unlike, but complementary in their differences, are better integrated (Schutz, 1958, Chap. 10). Gross (1956) found, for instance, that those small groups (usually dyads) in a military installation which were most tightly integrated were those in which the members were different, each supplying something the other lacked. (One single, the other married, provided the first with a home away from home, for example.) What Gross called consensual groups were persons of like characteristics and were less tightly integrated. He concluded that "symbiosis seems to be a more powerful tie than consensus" (p. 178). He goes on to argue that on theoretical grounds one should expect some division of labor in groups that are viable and more stable than in groups which merely like each other, since the ties based on liking may be more easily disrupted. If, on the other hand, components develop a mutual dependence for their respective satisfactions, disruptions are less probable. Durkin (1966) has also found that spouses are more co-ordinated in a simple pursuit task which requires their joint efforts than are nonspouses of opposite sex. He interprets his findings as showing that one partner is required to lead and the other to follow, and among married couples this relationship has been worked out. In the stranger-pairs, there is less probability of falling into a complementary and mutually supportive relationship of this sort when confronted with a task requiring co-ordinated behavior.

One cannot, however, conclude that differences among the components of the system are desirable for all kinds of tasks. Lodahl and Porter (1961) found in a study of sixty-four groups at the maintenance base of an airline that the homogeneity of the groups correlated .53 with productivity when the tasks required a high degree of co-operation. Among those tasks needing only a low degree of cooperation, the correlation was essentially zero. Tasks of a creative sort, on the other hand, are likely to be best performed by groups composed of persons having heterogeneous skills and personalities (Maier and Hoffman, 1961). It is clear that what is demanded of the system is one determinant of the kind of system which will meet those demands.

Maintenance vs. Signal Inputs

A possible resolution of the attraction of likes vs. unlikes may be found if we re-emphasize the distinction between maintenance and signal inputs. The distinction is reminiscent of Cattell's *maintenance synergy*, defined as the energy used in operating the "internal machinery" of the group, and *effective synergy* used to carry out the "purposes for which the group explicitly exists" (Cattell, Saunders, and Stice, 1953). In a critique of cybernetic models of perception, Allport (1955) distinguishes between "mainline production" and the feedback controls of the former. At another point (p. 512), he recognizes the need to take into account the "power supplies." Our model equates the stimulus for mainline production with signal inputs, and maintenance inputs with Allport's "power supply." We hypothesize that task-oriented groups require a set of maintenance inputs (satisfiers) which are accepted by the system primarily because of the similarities in values and expectations (states) held by the components. Signal inputs (task instructions) are processed effectively when the components are different in resources, skills, or capabilities.

So far as is known, empirical data bearing directly on such a hypothesis do not now exist. On the other hand, if the distinction between maintenance and signal inputs is valid, one may reinterpret some of the available studies in these terms. Thus, Schutz's theory and supporting data lead him to say, "Compatibility of two or more persons depends on (a) their ability to satisfy *reciprocally* each other's interpersonal needs, (b) their complementarity with respect to originating and receiving behavior in each need area, (c) their *similarity* with respect to the amount of interchange they desire with other people in each need area" (1958, p. 200, italics added). It should, however, be pointed out that Schutz's theory is built around the needs for inclusion, control, and affection, and does not directly relate these with complementary task skills. Schutz and Thibaut and Kelley essentially agree about the requirements for integrated exchanges as the foundations upon which dyads or somewhat larger groups may operate successfully. However, neither explicitly makes the distinction between the conditions that hold the group together and those which are also necessary to permit the coalition to respond effectively to task (signal) inputs.

The situation is illustrated in an example given by Thibaut and Kelley (1959, p. 45) in which one boy has a car, the other a gasoline credit card. Their resources are complementary, and hence they form a satisfactory dyad. The dyad, however, is "put into operation" when they both decide on a common destination. Without knowing where they want to go (signal input), the dyad is merely ready to act. However, as we shall see a bit later, behavior stimulated by signals (progressing toward their destination) augments group need satisfaction as a side effect.

A related question pertains to what has been called status congruence, by which is meant the degree to which the members of a group are assigned roles in a given group task that are congruent with their status in some other organizational hierarchy. Thus, college seniors, if assigned leadership roles over freshmen, would constitute a congruent group. Evidence has accumulated (Adams, 1953; Hughes, 1946; Zaleznik, 1956; Trow and Herschdorfer, 1965) to show that there is a tendency for groups to preserve status congruence among themselves and to reduce status incongruence. Furthermore, Trow and Herschdorfer were able to show that incongruent groups had poorer production, less satisfaction, and greater organizational instability than congruent groups. These findings argue for a complementary organization of people to process task or signal inputs; failing that, they also reveal an adverse effect on maintenance inputs.[5]

After reviewing a number of studies on group composition, Leavitt and Bass (1964) concluded that groups faced with assignments requiring routine, co-ordinated efforts perform best if they are generally alike, but that creative tasks require different group components. Moreover, and

[5] The feedback from signal to maintenance inputs will be discussed in the next chapter.

this comes close to the maintenance-signal distinction, groups composed of members who were similar in Guilford-Zimmerman Temperament scores had less difficulty in regulating their internal relations but more difficulty in creative problem solving than groups of heterogeneous membership (Maier and Hoffman, 1961). These considerations are congruent with proposition 2.17.

This discussion may be summarized by saying that groups appear to be held together by forces comparable to covalent bonds. That is to say, the shared values, goals, and other maintenance requirements held by the members of the group serve to attract one to another; but if the group is to function in any dynamic fashion responding to the varying signal inputs, there must also be some differences (ideally complementary) in skills, capabilities, or resources. It is hypothesized that, taken alone, neither similarity in values nor complementary differences in skills will assure an effectively operating dyad.

Why Any Social Exchanges on Any Basis?

We have so far argued that dyadic relationships are viable when there is a reciprocal coupling of mutually beneficial output-input exchanges between the components. Moreover, we have suggested that the components are more likely to establish such relationships if the individuals are similar in some respects but complementary in their differences. But why should any coalition get started in the first place? Is it necessary to posit a motive for affiliation, a need for social exchanges, some social *élan vital*? At an earlier point (see pp. 55–57), we eschewed such assumptions in discussing biological evolution. Must we recant on that position now? The answer is no.

In Chapter IV, it will be recalled, we developed a model of the self as an adapting system which operated in such a manner as to maintain its stability. Dynamic stability based on a continuing flow of exchanges is, furthermore, one of the fundamental properties of viable systems. If one turns to the theory of interpersonal relations proposed by Heider (1958), the basic posited mechanism is the consistency of cognitions or affections with respect to the multitude of persons, ideas, groups, and the self. Heider argues, with the support of cogent data, that inconsistencies are less viable than consistent cognitions and evaluations. Osgood and Tannenbaum (1953) have presented a somewhat more limited but more rigorous theory of cognitive and attitudinal modifications which also has as its base the assumption of a strain toward consistency. Festinger's cognitive-dissonance theory (1957) likewise rests on the principle that consistency between cognitions from different sources about a common issue or object is more stable, more satisfying, less tension-ridden than the opposite. Newcomb's model (1961) pertaining to interpersonal relations lies in the same category and emphasizes the progression from imbalanced to balanced relationships. For all four models the empirical data are not unequivocal, but to some extent experimental or measurement errors may be responsible for predictive failures. Although these four major approaches have sometimes been placed in competition with each other (and they are different in some important ways),[6] their common feature is at least as striking as their differences. One distills out of these theories and empirical results the following generalization: after the process of transforming physical energies into psychological experience, further transformations are made within the cognitive-affective system which progressively evolve toward a condition of greater, rather than lesser, consistency (cf. Maccoby and Maccoby, 1961). Consistency is the psychological equivalent of stability. This is not merely a verbal ritualistic equivalence. Both consistency and system stability have the same properties, to wit, systems tend to develop toward consistency (or stability) rather than the opposite; the "final" state of a system (see proposition 4.8) is more accurately described by consistency (or stability) than by its opposite; the "final" state of consistency (or stability) is more resistant to change than states which are inconsistent (or unstable).

If we return to the Heider, Osgood, Tannenbaum, Newcomb, and Festinger theories, a second common feature runs through them. They all involve some social relationship or evaluation of a social object (i.e., other people or cultural products) and it is this feature, along with the indigenous consistency forces, that account for coalitions being formed on any basis. Pepitone (1964) has perhaps made this point as explicit as anyone. Given, first, the condition in which individuals are subjected to a never-ending stream of stimuli which, in their primitive state, are formless, colorless, odorless, disorderly, the mere hurrying of physical energies; given, second, the transformation of these inputs first into form, color, tone, and then into significance, meaning, and relationships—there still remains for that individual the necessity to articulate his private experience and his consequent behavior with the behavior of others (Festinger, 1954). There must be at least an approximate correspondence between the cognitions of the dyad components if their behavior is to mesh in any respect. Looked at from the other side of the coin, the only way an individual may confirm his tentative social cognitions of himself and others is via some behavioral act that impinges on the behavior of another (cf. Newcomb, 1950). The unconfirmed cognitions and evaluations are unstable, shifting, unanchored, labile (cf. Asch, 1952; Sherif, 1937; Tuddenham, 1961). Assuming the soundness of proposition 4.8,

[6] The differences pertain to the precise circumstances under which either balance or tension is experienced.

that all systems move toward stability, and assuming second that the only means available for moving the unstable cognitions toward stability is via articulated behavior, it follows that some kind of at least temporary social exchange must occur.

Pepitone's (1964) contribution to this conclusion lies in his model, which proposes that an individual's attraction to another is a function of the extent to which the other supports and confirms the individual's evaluations and cognitions, especially those concerning himself. Contrariwise, hostility characterizes the relationship if the encounter with another tends to threaten, devalue, or undermine the individual's concept of self. Once again, the social exchange becomes the only and necessary means of maintaining the established system of cognitions. The various theories of dissonance, balance, and consistency, with their empirical supports, are attempts to specify the precise conditions that both disturb and reestablish the system's stability. Let it be repeated that we need not assume some unexamined misty need for affiliation or gregariousness residing in the individual, but, instead, the basic assumption underlying social exchanges is found in the tendency of any and all systems to settle their internal states and exchanges with suprasystems in a dynamically stable, rather than unstable, condition.[7]

It is necessary to insert a concluding parenthetical caveat. No value connotations attach to either the more or less stable states. Less stable systems may be more creative, innovating, ingenious; and more "noisy," inefficient, error-ridden. In the value framework of some other system, instability may or may not be a desirable condition.

Extension of Dyad Principles

The principles accounting for the development of a dyad are not unrelated to the relation between an audience and a communicator. Bauer (1964) presents a model of these relationships essentially in the terms just elucidated. If there is to be any genuine transfer of information from one party to the other, they must strike a bargain. He quotes approvingly Davison's statement (1959; italics added) that "the communicator's audience is not a passive recipient—it cannot be regarded as a lump of clay to be molded by the master propagandist. Rather, the audience is made up of individuals who demand something from the communications to

[7] It may be well to recall at this point the distinction between dynamic vs. static stability. By the former, we mean an ongoing process that maintains a near constancy in some respect. A spinning gyroscope has dynamic stability. Stop it, and its static stability is that of a stone. Social systems only exist if exchanges occur between sub- and suprasystems, and hence their stability is dynamic. Obviously, not all dynamic systems are stable, but it is axiomatic that the more stable the system, the longer it will survive.

which they are exposed, and who select those that are likely to be useful to them. In other words, they must get something from the manipulator if he is to get something from them. A bargain is involved. Sometimes, it is true, the manipulator is able to lead his audience into a bad bargain by emphasizing one need at the expense of another, or by representing a change in the significant environment as greater than it actually has been. But audiences, too, can drive a hard bargain. Many communicators who have been widely disregarded or misunderstood know that to their cost."

Bauer speaks about selective exposure, defense mechanisms, and group membership in such a way that they are compatible with the concept of the system boundary, filtering the communicator's inputs to the audience. Although Bauer is not explicit on the point, he is concerned with what Miles (1964) calls a temporary system in which the components by a prior, tacit contract agree to interact for only a relatively short period of time. Certain exogenous forces—announcements of a lecture, attendance requirements of college courses, assignment to an *ad hoc* committee, the receipt of a magazine article, accidentally tuning in a radio speech—bring the communicator and his audience in contact. These exogenous forces are, by and large, weak. Their very weakness, plus the tacit understanding mentioned above, may be sufficient to account for the short life of the system. Even the transitory life of the system, however, depends, as the Davison quotation indicates, upon a transaction of mutually acceptable inputs roughly, but not exactly, balanced.

The communicator—especially the propagandist, advertiser, educator, persuader, even the entertainer—hopes to get from his audience some change in attitude or behavior. What teacher is not gratified by seeing his students advance in knowledge and wisdom? What entertainer is not rewarded and guided by the response of the audience? On the basis of interpreting a wide range of studies, Bauer suggests that the audience accepts those communications which in some way assist them in solving some of their own problems of ego defense, interpersonal relations, or simply economic survival. It is this transaction of "sustenance," or, in the more general terminology of the present theory, maintenance, that keeps the system alive even over the short run. Some may object that such an abstraction leads nowhere; it does nothing to specify the precise circumstances that account for some audiences accepting one communication and rejecting another, while other audiences accept and reject in reverse fashion. Our response is that one may find the same principles operating at lower levels of complexity and in smaller systems. At each of these levels, the specifics are matters for empirical determination, whereas, in this effort, we are providing the model which conceptually organizes the specifics.

Summary

The foregoing analysis of simple dyadic relations and its extension to the audience-communicator setting has shown that the empirical data (not examined in detail) as well as current models pertaining to these relationships are not inconsistent with the logic of general systems theory. In particular, it has been shown that the viable, enduring dyad is a coupled symbiotic system bonded by both attracting and repelling forces comparable to covalent bonds at the molecular level. The initial contact between the components brought about by exogenous circumstances is a necessary, but insufficient, condition to initiate the process of developing stability in the cognitive-evaluation systems of each component. Finally, we have extended these principles to the audience-communicator system and found them to be applicable at this level as well, with the exception that this latter system has only a transitory life, subject as it is to very weak exogenous controls.

THE STRUCTURE OF SOCIAL SYSTEMS—ROLES

Definition 2.6 says that, "A system may exist in various states. A state of the system is a particular pattern of relationships existing among the components and the particular filtering condition of the boundary." Proposition 2.15 says, "The state of the system is one determinant of the output." At the beginning of this chapter we introduced the definition by Parsons and Shils of a role without developing its implications, conceiving of roles as the essential components of a system. In accepting this definition, we make it possible to allow for an individual to move about in several social systems, in each of which he may perform different role functions.

In speaking of roles, we move from considerations of the social system or group taken as a unit to the components of the system and their interrelations within the Black Box. In such an analysis, the individuals become Black Boxes, and we begin to consider the necessary and sufficient internal functions which account for the survival of social systems. As the Parsons and Shils definition reminds us, the social system does not consume the total time or energies of the persons who perform these functions, so we are talking about only those role functions involved in their group life.

Role theorists have generally made the distinction between role behavior and role expectations. The former is the emitted behavior of an individual (output) made in response to the role expectations by others (their outputs serving as inputs to the behaver). These exchanges, although imperfectly articulated one with the other, provide an essential condition for any interpersonal system to operate and survive.

What are the role expectations and behaviors required of a social system? Bales (1950), Thibaut and Kelley (1959), and a host of others have proposed that the role functions may be classified under two major headings, task and maintenance, which in our terms are equivalent to signal and maintenance responses. Parsons and Shils (1951, p. 200) argue for three categories. Although their language is quite fustian, it appears they refer to maintenance ("expressive interaction concern relationships with alters which ego engages in primarily for the immediate direct gratification they provide") and signal ("instrumental interaction concern relationships with alters which ego engages in, not primarily for their own sake, but for the sake of goals other than immediate and direct gratification experienced in contact with the object").[8] In addition to these two kinds of relationships, they propose that there are "integrative problems . . . which arise when one would maintain proper relationships between roles with an eye to the structural integration of the social system." In the paragraph just preceding, we have proposed that the integration of roles is a matter of coupling, as in other collateral systems. Some, if not perfect, coupling is a prerequisite for any system to operate. Only in those special circumstances where someone desires that coupling be improved is it necessary for a third party to perform a mediating role. We thus feel confident that the minimal essential roles performed within a group can be directly related to the two types of inputs previously proposed, namely, maintenance and signal (task). Within each of these categories a number of specific kinds of role functions have been described (cf. Bales, 1950, and Steinzor, 1949).

The number of possible functions an individual may perform in the first instance is limited by his own values, needs, skills, tools, and predisposition to anxiety, which he carries with him as he moves from one system to another (cf. Thibaut and Kelley, 1959). In addition, the role he assumes in a given system is determined by the nature of the signal inputs. That is, in one system an individual may be a receiver and execute directions, but in another he may be the originator of directions. An individual may serve several roles, but not simultaneously, although there may be rapid oscillations or shifts from one to another.

A number of empirical studies have been reported (of which space permits only a sample), giving insights into the conditions that differentiate roles. The often-mentioned "pecking order" in chickens is relevant here. Murchison (1935) found a stable hierarchy after the chicks were about thirty-six weeks of age such that *A* attacked and pecked *B*, *B* attacked and pecked *C*, and so on but never in reverse order. This dominance ladder in infrahumans is an example of role differentiation brought

[8] It would seem that all gratifications have been exhausted by these two statements.

about solely by propinquity and the relative prowess of the chickens. Role differentiation is evidently inevitable where there is some difference in the members and where they are forced to come in contact with each other.

One of the most revealing of role studies at the human level is Guetzkow's (1960). Using seventy-five five-man groups assembled to solve a puzzle by communicating according to certain rules, but without specifying the roles of the individuals, Guetzkow was able to show that roles he labeled end men, relayers, and key men evolved and stabilized after a relatively short period of work. At the outset, so far as the subjects were aware, any one person presumably had the possibility of assuming any one of the roles. Surely the difficulty of the task was not so high that specialized knowledge or skill automatically selected the individuals to perform the available roles. On the other hand, both general intelligence and personal ascendance were related to role differentiation—key men being higher in both respects. This suggests that the role a person may assume in a group is partly determined by certain personal characteristics—a deduction that is hardly surprising.

In an earlier and similar experimental situation Leavitt (1951) found that when roles were established by the experimenter so that four men fed information to a fifth and the latter solved the puzzle, the task was solved quickly. On the other hand, when the group was structured in the form of a circle so that each man could only communicate with those on either side of him, the solution took longer, but the activity was enjoyed more. In the latter case the role of problem solver could be assumed by anyone, as opposed to the former arrangement in which only the designated fifth man could solve the problem. In this case the role of problem solver gradually became identified with one person in each group.

There is no question, either from the systematic studies such as those just mentioned or from common-sense observations, that within a relatively short time a group develops a role structure commonly understood by all or nearly all members of the group. The group comes to expect certain specific behaviors from specific persons. It is far from inevitable that these behaviors will be useful to the group's task, but that is another issue. The Leavitt study along with others further confirms that portion of proposition 2.15 that says the state of the system, as defined by the relationships among its components (i.e., who takes what functional role), is one determinant of its output.

Maintenance and Task Roles

As indicated on page 107, Bales (1950) devised a classification of verbal interactions which made its major distinction between social-emotional responses (shows solidarity, agrees, expresses satisfaction, shows antagonism, disagrees) and task-oriented responses (gives suggestions, asks for information, gives information, summarizes). It was perhaps Heyns (1948) who first devised a somewhat less precise but more flexible classificatory scheme that has continued in use with some modifications. He called his major divisions *problem solving* and *interpersonal patterns*. The first included reality tester, expert, interrogator, idea man, goal reminder, distractor, and passive participant. The interpersonal patterns included rejector, supporter, social oiler, isolate, dictator. Using the former scheme, Bales and others have shown a phase movement in the course of a group discussion in which information giving dropped steadily from early to late stages while positive social-emotional responses and suggestions rose. These data do not mean that each particular person discharged only one role function. Instead, individuals shifted the nature of their roles as the discussion proceeded toward a decision. In therapy groups not required to reach decisions about some imposed problem, the phasing just described did not occur (Talland, 1955). It has also been shown that in initially leaderless groups, the persons who accept the roles, for instance, of leader or follower may change as the discussion develops partly because some people have greater skill at one type of activity, or find the emotional context of one phase more congenial than another (Hare, 1962).

We want to make two points about these data. First, the distinction between maintenance and signal functions agrees precisely with propositions 2.7a, b, and we may therefore confidently conclude that the proposition is relevant to social as well as other systems. Second, the changing pattern of functions in time is in part determined by the kind of signal inputs impressed on the system (tasks assigned). The phase changes reported by Bales are a special case of this second point because in such discussion the definition (as seen by the group) of the problem changes in the course of the discussion.

We could extend the description of various studies of role formation to book length (cf. Sherif, White, and Harvey, 1955; Thrasher, 1927; Ronken and Lawrence, 1952; Newcomb, 1950; Sherif, Harvey, White, Hood, and Sherif, 1961; Simon, 1957). The distillation of these various treatments of the role concept leads to a conclusion not importantly different from propositions 4 and 5a, b. That is to say, as groups form and grow, the members take on specialized functional roles which are only a segment of their behavioral spectrum. They assume these functions because of the capabilities they bring to the group which interact with the pregroup capabilities of other members and the task inputs accepted by the system. If one compares this statement with the description of transplantation studies of embryonic amblystoma or the structural changes in amoebae when formed into slime molds, one may see the operation of a common principle. The coalition and integration of components into a system requires some modification of them in the direction of specialization in structure and function. The "success" of the system—i.e., the degree to which it is maintained and processes inputs—depends, among other things, upon the degree to which these modifications occur, and this in turn is handicapped by the rigidity (memories) of the components (proposition 5.1c). If the components, by reason of established memories, are inflexible, they will not modify their structure to the demands of the system. Given components with the requisite variety of possible functions, they exhibit, initially with some error, the selected functions that permit the system to react in a dynamically stable fashion.

Role Flexibility

We should expect the variability of a social system and its success in dealing with a variety of tasks to depend upon the ease with which the members can assume various roles as they are needed. For instance, the members of a football team all have assigned functions; ordinarily, the tackles and guards do not run the ball. However, if a fumble occurs, a guard, normally a blocker, might run behind the interference of a halfback. The success of the team sometimes depends upon the ability of its members to assume unaccustomed roles quickly.

A study of two work groups, one on the day and the other on the night shift, revealed that the latter had about twice as much work output per man. One, but not the only, distinguishing feature of these two groups, doing identical work, was the ease with which the night shift adjusted its respective roles when one or more men were absent. The day shift was thrown into confusion under the same circumstances (Berrien and Angoff, 1961). Another study of volunteer fire companies revealed that those judged best in all-round performance were those in which the fire-fighting officer hierarchy (chief, captain, driver-engineer) bore the least correspondence to the business organization (president, vice-president, secretary, treasurer) (Berrien, 1963). Those who were in charge of a business meeting were subordinate when fighting a fire. Flexibility in roles and the effect of changing roles have not been widely studied, partly because the mere fact of group development operates in the direction of specializing roles and the concomitant expectations of others that tend to force a member to behave within the group in a specified way.

In the usual situation no counterforces exist to encourage the flexible use of an individual's entire repertory of group-relevant functions. This has been one of the complaints expressed by Argyris (1957) against the typical formal organization. It is his thesis that, because functions are narrowly constrained by typical business organizations, the individual is not able to mature and remain flexible, nor can the organization make maximum use of its available human resources. Although little empirical data are available currently, there are theoretical reasons for believing that some flexibility in role taking (system structure) permits the system to accept and process a wider variety of inputs than if the structure is rigid.

The reverse of role flexibility is role rigidity. The latter condition is revealed by the generation of tension experienced by an individual because of conflicting—sometimes incompatible—requirements placed on him by others. Air force officers, for example, who were temporarily assigned as classroom instructors found themselves in incompatible roles as teachers and commanders. The intensity of this conflict, as perceived by the officers themselves, was found to be related to their ineffectiveness in at least one role (Getzels and Guba, 1955). A report by Wolfe and Snoek (1962) covering fifty-four supervisory and executive positions in six major industries showed that those men whose superiors placed the greatest degree of conflicting demands upon them experienced the greatest tension on their jobs. Likewise, the more the job called for original problem solving as opposed to routinized activities, the greater was the tension. We might view tension as a waste by-product of the individual's performance. Surely the individual's performance in a management position is not valued in these terms. With the system interpretation of tension, one may then deduce that such a waste increases when the requirements for flexibility increase, arising either from the processing of signals (problem solving) or from fluctuations in the kind of signals received from the suprasystem (variety of different tasks expected by superiors). It thus appears that some confirmation in social systems is available for proposition 4.3b (variability of outputs is limited by the finite number of states the system can assume).

BOUNDARY OF SOCIAL SYSTEMS—NORMS

The concept of norm is closely allied with the concept of role in most social psychological theory. They are so closely allied that it is sometimes difficult to distinguish between them. It has been said that the norms of a group define the roles of the members and vice versa. This is an unsatisfactory circular definition, which may be avoided if we conceive of the norms of a group, or the role of an individual, as the filtering boundary that permits certain inputs to flow into the system and certain outputs to flow out. In this sense, norms are the equivalent of the gating or filtering function of the boundary for the social system.

Generally speaking, social psychologists have thought of norms as rules of behavior, proper ways of acting which have been accepted as legitimate for all members of a group. If one accepts the filtering connotation of norms, the term would also apply to the inputs (signal and maintenance) as well as the output behavior. Although this may enlarge the concept of norm, it does it no violence. For example, it is legitimate for a work group to accept certain kinds of work-related directives from their supervisor, but if he were to set up standards for their contribution to a charity drive, they would very probably rebel. It is perfectly acceptable to both parties for a football player to block or tackle an opponent on the playing field during the game, but not in the locker room. A pair of chess players concentrating on a game will look askance at a third person who attempts to engage them in conversation. In this last example, it is evident that what is output for one person (the interloper) is input for the others. However, the norm resides in the chess players and operates to exclude certain kinds of inputs.

Figure 4 is an effort to represent the distinction between the role of an individual and the norms of a group, both of which involve the con-

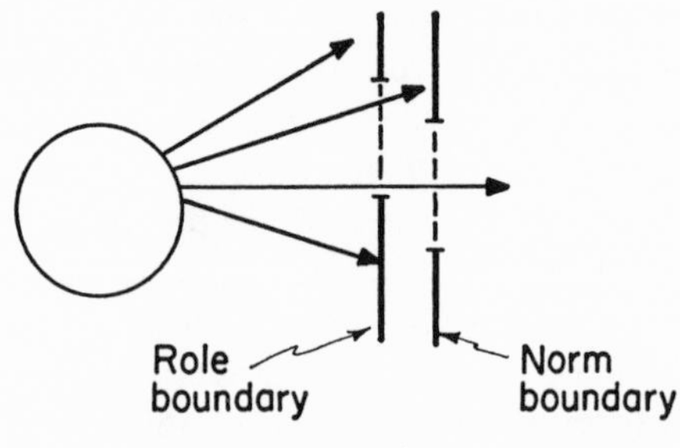

Figure 4

cept of boundary. The arrows extending from the individual represent alternative behaviors of which the individual is capable. Only some of these are permitted by his role and penetrate the "gate" in the boundary. Certain ones match up with the norms of the group. Ideally, the two should match exactly. However, an individual may sometimes behave in ways that he conceives to be appropriate for his role but unacceptable to the group. On the other hand, he may not behave in certain ways that are accepted and excepted by the norms because of the role restriction as he sees it.

We need to recognize that the filtering gate of the boundary in a social system is not as precise in its limits as, for example, an optical or electronic filter which may have sharp cutoffs on either side of its band width. The limits of a social system filter determining what is acceptable (what will pass through the boundary) are more in the nature of gradients than of simple yes-no gates. Some borderline inputs are accepted, but their processing produces tension. This was evidently the situation in the Wolfe and Snoek study (1962) when they found that managers having little original problem solving to do seemed to have about the same level of tension regardless of the variety of demands made upon them by their superiors. The authors interpreted this finding to mean that some role demands by superiors were shrugged off. Stated in systems terms, certain possible inputs were filtered out, while others, although accepted, were processed with difficulty. A work group accepts a message from the supervisor that "we should all give as much to *X* charity as we can"; they might accept, but resent, the message, "*X* charity needs 10 per cent more than you contributed last year"; they would reject the message, "I expect everyone to contribute at least *Y* dollars."

What advantage accrues to what may seem like a mere verbal translation of *norms* to *boundary filtering?* Four considerations are relevant. Norms considered as boundary filters make it unnecessary to introduce a new and specialized concept having relevance only to social systems. The principle of parsimony is served without importantly disturbing the former meaning of the term. Second, it is possible to articulate conceptually social systems with other systems, running the gamut to the very simplest. Third, the notion that norms, like boundary filters, are selective provides an identifiable locus of the selective process, which otherwise is free-floating. Fourth, the filtering concept carries with it the implication that the total range of possible inputs is greater or more varied than the system itself may accept. This last point leads us to the next question.

Why Are Norms (Filters) Necessary?

Newcomb (1950, pp. 267ff.) makes the following observation: "The important thing about a group's norms, you will remember, is that they make possible communication among its members. People can *interact* without any common body of norms, but they cannot *communicate* in the sense of sharing meaning through their interaction. A cat and a canary can interact, and so can a mother and her newborn child, but there is little sharing of meaning in such interaction because there are no common norms. That is, there is no shared 'code' [*sic*] according to which the stalking of the cat or the fluttering of the canary has similar meaning to both of them." Norms, according to Newcomb, are ways of developing meanings about one's private experience of the kaleidoscopic concatenation of multitudinous stimuli that fall on our sensory equipment. The "great buzzing, banging confusion" becomes ordered, organized, related, and meaningful through ordered contacts with other beings subjected to the same or similar "confusions." In Garner's terms (cf. Chap. IV), uncertainty is reduced.

If one compares the Newcomb quotation pertaining to norms with the argument set forth on page 102 accounting for the initiation of social exchanges, one may see a similarity. The physical as well as the social environment is initially a confusion of inputs, resulting in instability of the system. Place a foreigner in a strange culture by himself, devoid of the native language, unacquainted with the written symbols or the meaning of customary gestures (Japanese waving a hand in a manner we would interpret as "go away" or "good-by" instead mean "come" or "follow me"), and he will experience what many travelers have called "culture shock." The bewilderment of strange dress, of odd work habits, of greeting rituals, of traffic regulations, of bargaining protocol—even the currency, and what people find humorous—these and many other items result in a feeling of great uncertainty and instability.

Let us extrapolate this instability from one person in a strange culture to many people in no culture. Let us say several people are cast up on an uninhabited island and say they are a Polynesian, a Congolese, an East Indian, an Arab, an American, and an Italian. Let us also assume that they have readily available housing, food, clothing, and the means to combat disease and physical harm. Let the island be small enough so they must come face to face. While this hypothetical situation has, so far as I know, not occurred and we can speculate on the consequences, what we do know about foreigners in strange cultures leads to the expectation that this collection of people would first feel a marked tension, arising solely from the uncertain social aspects. They have no agreed-upon method of communication, no established "pecking order," no daily routines, no priorities of tasks, no rituals, no certain means of inferring the significance or meaning of any acts of one another. The most "natural" process that would evolve out of such a situation would be a series of exchanges that would bring about some ordering of their relationships, thus reducing the felt uncertainty. Ordering of relationships means that certain kinds of behavior among the total spectrum of each individual's repertory are inhibited within the group. This is what a norm does and why norms are necessary and inevitable.

Some additional indirect evidence for our speculations may be found in the common observation that groups of foreigners, even to the second and third generation, in strange cultures tend to form their own ghettos, compounds, enclaves. In these they find relief and escape from the residual tensions of dealing daily with the different culture in which they are enmeshed. In that showcase of intercultural harmony, Hawaii, there are fraternities, societies, and business associations limited to Chinese, to Japanese, to Caucasians, and so on. Although ethnic discriminations are minimized, one may find neighborhoods that predominate in one or the other of the nationalities represented. For easy[9] social exchange, familiar cultural norms are not just an aid; they are necessary.

In this discussion we see again the operation of a principle transcending the usual compartments of investigation. The system boundary, whether biological, psychological, social, or mechanical, is one that even in its primitive stages selects inputs from a wider range of possibilities. Moreover, such selection is necessary merely because the components of any particular system are structured in a given way, which makes certain kinds of relationships with other components more, rather than less, stable.

SUMMARY

This chapter has been concerned with developing the fundamental concepts of a model within the framework of general systems theory. More specifically, we have attempted to redefine in systems terms concepts which are the fundamental building blocks of social psychology. The emphasis has been upon relatively small face-to-face groups. Perhaps the recurring theme running through the chapter has been the notion that social relationships are those that are selected out of a wider repertory of behavior. Moreover, those that are selected either by means of the filtering function of the group boundary (norms) or by reason of the role functions of the components are those which permit the system to evolve in the direction of greater, rather than less, dynamic stability.

The simple, viable dyadic relationship has been pictured as a symbiotic coupled system, which is enduring so long as the components exchange mutually supporting maintenance inputs. The bonds in a dyad are both attracting and repelling, which places the system in the same category as systems having covalent bonds. Although we shall deal more explicitly with input-output channels in the next chapter, it has been pointed out further that the typical dyad requires not only these reciprocal maintenance exchanges but signal (task) inputs as well. Throughout this chapter we have drawn parallels between the phenomena of social relations and the propositions of general systems. We found that definitions and propositions applicable to nonsocial systems are also applicable to groups.

In the chapter that follows, we shall pursue the exploration of congruities between GST and other social phenomena.

[9] Terms like *easy, tension reduction, congenial* are not to be interpreted as strivings or motives any more than one would attribute to a stone rolling down a rough incline a striving for a resting place. Using familiar psychological terms of this sort avoids the necessity for awkward circumlocutions, but it should be remembered that we are not postulating urges, motives, drives, as they are usually defined in psychological theory.

VII / SOCIAL SYSTEMS: FEEDBACK AND GROWTH

The previous chapter has shown that the problems of group definition, roles, norms, and composition are special cases that fall within the definitions and propositions of general systems theory. Contrary to much conventional theorizing, the terms employed and some of the problems addressed by the social psychologist are not, in their fundamental meanings, significantly different from the meanings of terms used and the crucial problems in the analysis of other systems. The roles members of a group perform are equivalent to the components of any system. The norms of a group are equivalent to the filtering boundary of any system. The way in which member roles are articulated at any point in time is equivalent to the state of any social system. The performance of a group is partly a function of maintaining mutual attraction between members and the performance of an assigned task, just as any system's survival depends partly upon maintenance and signal inputs.

We have not, however, argued that we should therefore replace the term norm in favor of boundary, or role in favor of component function, or make any other translations. Instead, our intention has been to make clear that a core of basic definitions and system phenomena extends through the hierarchy from simple to complex, from nonliving to social. The special terminology of various levels of discourse is too well established to hope for a revolution in terms, even if such a hope existed. The meanings of these are enriched by the discovery that they are the local expressions of much more general phenomena. Furthermore, these conceptual relationships immediately stimulate a search for other similarities among systems, and the discovery of phenomena within classes of systems that would otherwise go unnoticed. It is this latter consequence that gives major significance to general systems theory.

In this chapter we will continue the quest for enriched meanings by examining the phenomena of feedback and growth as they appear in social systems.

FEEDBACK IN SOCIAL SYSTEMS

If one examines the historical development of mechanical or, more generally, engineered systems, it is evident that the feedback principle was not introduced until quite recent times. Watt's steam-engine governor, invented in the early nineteenth century, is often given as an early example. Before that time, machines—aside from some chronometers—operated generally under the direct control of a human operator. We have previously made the point that social systems, like mechanical, electrical, or chemical systems, are the creatures of man's intelligence. It therefore should not be surprising if we may not find clear examples of feedback in social systems, except as they have developed accidentally rather than deliberately and rationally. In our social engineering, we appear to be at about the stage of Watt's steam-engine governor. These considerations suggest that it might be useful to take deliberate steps to invent specific feedback procedures and incorporate them into new organizations.

Chapter II contains the definition of feedback which arose initially out of the design and analysis of mechanical self-correcting systems. Social psychologists and other behavioral scientists have adopted the term and to some extent have corrupted its meaning by using it to refer to a wide range of different communications and different consequences. It will be helpful if we delimit and clarify what feedback refers to in both nonliving and social systems.

Three characteristics of feedback immediately suggest themselves. First, feedback is a mechanism that controls output by sending a message generated by that output to the input regulator. Second, the consequence of feedback is to maintain a relatively steady rate of system operations in spite of external variations that would otherwise cause it to fluctuate. Third, and this is a corollary to the second, systems controlled by feedback have a higher probability of survival. In social systems, what is it that feedback controls, and are these variables controlled in the ways just enumerated?

FORMAL ACHIEVEMENT AND GROUP NEED SATISFACTION

In another place (Berrien, 1964), we have proposed that groups may be evaluated in terms of two kinds of output: the extent to which they achieve the tasks they are expected to perform, and the satisfactions the individuals experience as a consequence of their interactions within the system. The first of these we have labeled formal achievement (FA); it is primarily a function of the signal inputs. The second we have called group need satisfaction (GNS); it is the output side of maintenance inputs. GNS can be thought of in the first instance as a reverberating feedback loop initiated by the proximity and necessary interactions of the components. We have previously shown that the "bonding" of individuals is a consequence of such interactions, the strength of the bonds being a function partly of the predispositions (memories and states) of the individuals and partly a function of the interactions themselves. We shall see later that GNS is augmented or suppressed, as well, by certain other inputs from external sources.

The stability of a group can be evaluated in terms of these two output criteria. It is hypothesized that just as a biological organism foreshadows its eventual disintegration by marked deviations from some "normal" bodily temperature or other steady state, so groups foreshadow their disintegration by marked deviations from some previously established nearly constant level of FA or GNS.[1]

What is it that holds FA and GNS within narrow limits? Why should not these outputs fluctuate solely as a function of their respective inputs? Let us take as a case a work group within an industrial organization. Their upper productivity limit (FA) is a function of their physiological limitations, skills, and methods of work. However, it is well known that such groups rarely approach these limits but, instead, settle upon a rate of production defined more by the norms of the group than by skills, work methods, or physiological limits.[2] The well-known study of the bank wiring room in the Hawthorne Plant of the Western Electric Company (Roethlisberger and Dickson, 1949) was among the first of many that clearly established this fact. On the other hand, the lower limit of productivity is within the control of the suprasystem—the supervision. Various sanctions can be brought to bear on a work group if it produces less than is tolerable for the larger organization. Hence, the permissible limits of fluctuation in FA reside, on the one hand, within the norms of the group and, on the other hand, within the demands of the suprasystem. Figure 5 presents a diagrammatic representation of the situation.

[1] The distinction between FA and GNS is somewhat like the distinction between a psyche group (based solely on personal liking) and a sociogroup (committed to a common task). See Klein, 1956, p. 179. The evidence is weighted in favor of assuming most groups have elements of both bases for existence, which is in accord with our formulation. See Gibb, 1950.

[2] In this statement, we are referring to the FA that can be attributed to the group alone, independent of the machines they operate. The FA of man-machine systems is something else.

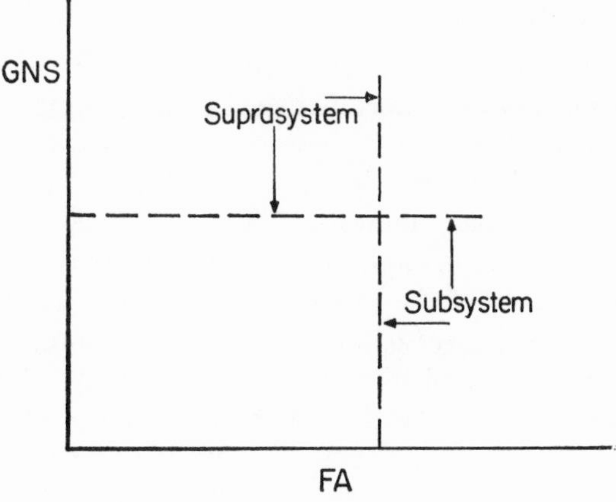

Figure 5

Each limit is controlled by negative feedback signals. If a group member tends to exceed the production norms, his fellow workers resort to a variety of inhibiting measures—the silent treatment, spoiling his tools, withholding materials, or, in extreme instances, minor physical violence. The supervision's method of controlling the lower limit of FA is likewise negative—reprimand, withholding privileges, or, in extreme instances, discharge. As we shall see later, positive feedback from the supervisor is also effective in raising FA.

A comparable situation exists with GNS, except that the sources of negative feedback are reversed. The lower limit of GNS is established by the group itself. If the satisfactions fall below a minimal level, people will leave the group. Bickering, discord, hostility, or merely failure to find one's work associates congenial leads toward the eventual resignation from the group, either physically or psychologically. On the other side, it is the suprasystem that controls the upper limit of GNS. Groups which spend too much time on social activities, take long coffee breaks, and expend energy to excess on purely interpersonal relationships having little direct connection with FA are often reprimanded by the supervision.

To summarize, the suprasystem controls the upper limit of GNS and the lower limit of FA. In this formulation, therefore, we have the possibilities of a balanced system and suprasystem. It can be seen that the model provides for reciprocal and balancing effects from both internal and external sources.

Although we have used a work group as an example in developing the feedback channels controlling FA and GNS, we believe the pattern is applicable to other kinds of groups.

GNS in Various Kinds of Groups

It is necessary to recognize that in conventional social accounting considerable confusion may arise between these two measures. First and foremost, as Gross (1966, p. 216) has argued, it is inconceivable that any social system could long exist if its FA did not contribute to the satisfaction of certain human interests. The identification of these output utilities (or utiles) was a preoccupation of the economists, who early recognized the validity of the proposition. Yet these human satisfactions are most complicated, diverse, and difficult to measure, which probably accounted for the economists' concentration of most of their attention on pure monetary units. On the other hand, the most accessible and accurate information is sometimes grossly misleading.[3] Although pure FA for most systems, at first blush, may appear easier to measure, it too is complex, as the next section will emphasize.

When dealing with relatively small face-to-face groups—the work unit of a firm, the Saturday-evening bridge club, a businessmen's service club, a church or temple—one can without insurmountable difficulties poll the members on their GNS as morale surveys do. When the system reaches the size of a city, state, or nation, the possibilities of capturing more than limited aspects of GNS, even with population-sampling techniques, become remote. In addition, these larger systems presumably have maintenance outputs of a different sort than those of the small face-to-face systems.

In such large systems the satisfaction of certain basic human needs can now be measured, some indirectly, by what Gross (1966, pp. 221ff.) calls surrogate indices. Among these, for example, is the employment ratio. People gainfully employed—in spite of grievances and complaints—are part of some in-group, with a feeling of being needed. Underemployment in any society has long been recognized as a source of discontent, and not alone for economic reasons. The unemployed are the displaced, discarded people who at least initially resent their status and protest against the system which relegates them to society's flotsam and jetsam. Later they may become apathetic, discouraged, submerged in the stream of affairs, giving up a major part of their distinctive humanity. Employment itself is satisfying.

Gross proposes that leisure and recreation are likewise means for satisfying interests not possible in one's employment and a means of renewing those energies expended in gainful work. Paid holidays, reductions in working hours, expenditures on sports, entertainment, and other

[3] Probably the most accurate figure in a financial balance sheet is cash on hand, yet this alone would be a poor measure of the firm's solvency.

leisure-time activities combined in some rational way are possible measures of this segment.

Population survival and general health statistics have possibilities as nonmonetary measures of the extent to which a society produces services directly bearing on another of the fundamental needs of its members. Medicare, free clinics, or the Australian family endowment are examples of such services produced by the system at large which contribute to these health needs. Programs to control or eliminate atmospheric and water pollution, sewage and water plants, roads, bridges, dams, public transport, education, and hosts of other possible services such as police and fire protection may be generated by a functioning society (but are largely impossible for small social systems) and provide the base for surrogate data related to GNS. All such services are possible only by the joint efforts of system components,[4] and are those outputs which contribute to the survival of the system itself.

A confusion, however, may result in using output data such as those suggested when the numbers are taken as conclusive evidence of satisfactions. An increase in expenditures for health may reduce disease and increase longevity, but not necessarily in a linear relationship. It is the data on satisfactions which are more relevant and sometimes less easily or accurately accumulated. Bearing in mind this caveat, our main point is that GNS is, first, a necessary output to be taken into account, and, second, that a basis already exists for believing that with proper attention to its importance it can be measured, although at the moment the technical problems have not been solved.[5]

A second confusion may arise. If the treatment or prevention of disease is the FA of the health organizations, where is the GNS? This question illustrates the necessity of keeping the level of analysis constant. Clearly, GNS for the hospital, the National Institutes of Health, or the Perrineville Mental Health Service comes from the interactions of the people working in these units. The FA of such units, however, interacting with the FA's of the educational institutions, highway departments, etc., become the GNS for the society.

Sources of and Contributors to GNS

One of the complicating conditions in developing a model of a social system lies in the complexity and impurity of the maintenance inputs. Since the individuals performing the roles that compose a social system

[4] Gross deals with other measures of "investments"—security, freedom, consumption—but the above illustrate the point for our purposes.

[5] We are reminded that the Malthusian theory of employment had to wait more than a hundred years until Keynes revived it when the necessary national income statistics became available.

have biological, economic, psychological, and social role requirements extending beyond what any particular group can meet, the inputs in a particular case can be expected to meet only a fraction of the group members' needs. That is to say, Bill Cuthworth's role in the volunteer fire department cannot be expected to satisfy all his psychosocial needs or all his requirements for economic and biological sustenance. Hence, when we model a group and speak of the inputs, we recognize that in no sense are these the sole source of maintenance for the individuals. Contrariwise, a decrement in such maintenance inputs to a social system may have less consequence for the survival of the system than would be the case in systems where the components are exclusively dependent for their entire existence upon the system of which they are a part. Exclusive dependence has been heretofore implicit in the development of both the systems theory and the models within that theory.

This is by way of preamble to the point that maintenance inputs to a social system have at least four roots, some extending beyond the system itself. First, we have already emphasized group need satisfactions, which come from association with other members of the group itself as the primary source. Second, there is (under some circumstances) a GNS contribution from the formal achievement; third, from the immediate agent representing the suprasystem; and fourth, from the more impersonal and more broadly defined social supra-suprasystem. Let us deal with the second, third, and fourth of these in some detail.

If the components of the system fully accept the signal inputs or, in less rigorous terms, are committed to the formal activities of the organization, they will derive some satisfaction from the group's FA. They will relish a sense of accomplishment: a production record established, a job well done, certain obstacles surmounted, a mission carried out with success. Cognitive-dissonance studies (Festinger, 1961) have emphasized that although people tend to work harder for greater rewards, it seems equally true that the harder we work (up to a point) for a reward, the greater it seems. This kind of experience feeds into and augments the satisfactions derived otherwise from mutual association alone. This will only happen, however, if—we repeat—there is a high degree of acceptance of the task inputs. Otherwise, the FA may react against and detract from the net GNS, as is the case of persons exceeding the group-established norm for production ("rate busters"). We shall have more to say about this later.

In work groups, the immediate supervisor is the agent of the suprasystem. Fleishman, Harris, and Burtt (1955) found that the behavior of supervisors could be categorized as "giving consideration" and "providing structure." Their description of this behavior fits our dichotomy of maintenance and signal inputs. That is to say, the supervisor may provide encouragement, promote harmonious interpersonal relations among his subordinates, help to keep open channels of communication, reduce friction, mediate quarrels, all of which contribute to GNS.[6] He may be, and generally is, responsible for giving directions, enforcing standards, providing local rules, administering discipline, conveying information about the larger organization. These are signal inputs. Day and Hamblin (1961) found that punitive and close supervision not only reduced output but also created antipathy toward coworkers. In an experiment by DeCharms and Bridgeman (1961), both productivity and satisfaction increased when supervisors deliberately complied (rather than refused to comply) with requests from their subordinates.

The important consideration for our purposes here is the supplemental source of maintenance, embodied in the behavior of the supervisor. Other autonomous groups—neighborhood associations, recreational clubs, informal cliques—may not have a particular agent linking them with the suprasystem. Hence, for these, this source of maintenance is not available. On the other hand, as one looks at various service clubs, political organizations, local volunteer associations, fraternal societies, and the like, one can usually find a person, comparable to the supervisor although with less power, who represents the larger confederation and provides some maintenance inputs.

The fourth source of GNS lies in the larger context in which the members of a group also have membership, to which reference was made on pages 102–104. This source of maintenance operates indirectly and may take on coloration that is less psychosocial than the others. The group to which an individual is attracted may have a respected status, or membership in it may be a means for achieving some private ends not easily attained otherwise. Membership in a fraternity may be the easiest means of gaining dates with girls in a "companion" sorority. Joining the right club may be a means of making business contacts. In the same way, keeping a job in a given organization may be the most advantageous way of meeting economic obligations. Depending upon the vantage point, these may be looked upon as forces of the suprasystem pushing us into the group, or as attractions of the system pulling us toward it. In either case, it is evident that membership in a group can provide outputs for an individual that contribute to his interpersonal satisfactions elsewhere. Youngberg, Hedberg, and Baxter (1962), for example, found, among more than 1,000 salesmen, great dissatisfaction with their system of com-

[6] The distinction between internally generated GNS and what Fleishman *et al.* call considerations is also made in other terms by Zaleznik, Christensen, and Roethlisberger (1958).

pensation, yet they felt the public prestige of their occupation was the most important factor in their job satisfaction.

It would be well to recall proposition 2.20, which says that the existence of exogenous forces bringing components into a critical proximity is a necessary but insufficient condition for system operations. The private economic needs of individuals satisfied through membership in a particular group may be considered one of these constraining exogenous forces and thus not strictly a maintenance input. One's economic returns from working in a given organization provide a constraint upon his choice behavior. His decisions among alternatives are bounded by what other organizations may offer him compared with what he is already getting (cf. March and Simon, 1958, pp. 100–111). In purely economic terms, these constraints have little to do with group maintenance inputs. Although less constraining than the prison walls surrounding a group, economic factors, especially if directly determining the minimal level of subsistence—food, clothing, and shelter—are more biological than psychosocial and do not require a social system for their satisfaction. Mankind existed prior to even the most primitive enduring social system.

On the other hand, economic returns in our society possess also psychological facets. They symbolize in fairly clear terms the positive or negative attitudes of the work suprasystem, and they also provide the means whereby the individual may gain or display his status in his community suprasystem. In Chapter VI, it will be recalled that we posited a requirement for social interaction as a means—the only means whereby the private experience of one person may be "validated" and his behavior articulated with others. This need has nothing to do with biologic survival but everything to do with social system survival. The level of one's affluence indicates imprecisely to others in the community the favorable regard of one's working associates. Hence the financial returns from one's work group enable the individual to obtain some GNS in the other social systems to which he is attached. Consequently, the economic satisfactions derived from a given social system are a mixture of both constraining exogenous forces and group maintenance inputs.

Although a diagram is a much simplified representation of any social system, Figure 6 may be of some help toward understanding the preceding discussion. The numbers attached to the various channels correspond to the four sources of maintenance inputs discussed in this section.

The agent is placed in parentheses to indicate that he is not always present. Because the preceding discussion has been confined to an elaboration of the maintenance inputs, we have not dealt with the feedback from FA to signal inputs. This, however, is an obvious channel that requires no special treatment.

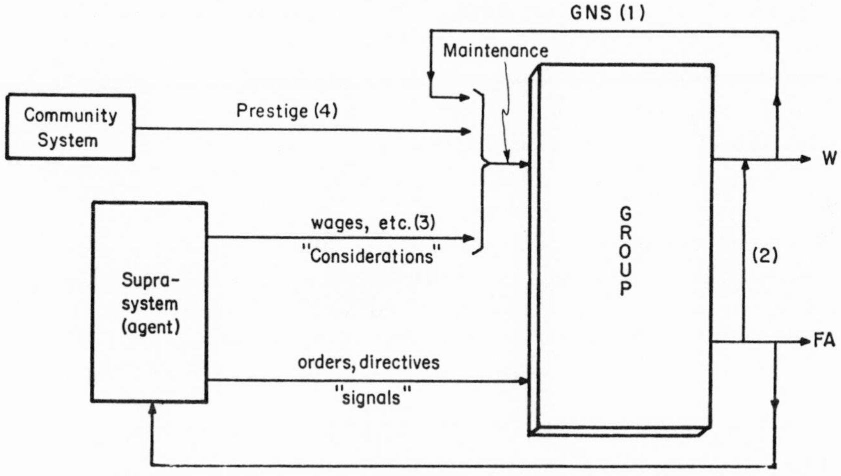

Figure 6

Some Characteristics of FA

It would be a mistake to assume that FA is a single unitary output. Instead we have evidence for postulating that it may be a composite of several "achievements." One or more of these may be sacrificed in the maximization of another. Thus a mental hospital may be evaluated by some measures of its custodial care or its therapeutic successes. Given the limited resources of any such system at a given point in time, it must balance these two aspects of FA. In like fashion, an air force squadron may forgo training flights in bad weather to maintain its good safety record, thus sacrificing the development of flight skills. Although this selective emphasis of one or another of the possible FA components may be under the control of the system, in the long run its survival requires that it be responsive to the demands of the suprasystem (propositions 2.18 and 5.3). Thus Etzioni (1960), in discussing the mental hospital situation, remarks: "When the relative power of the various elements in the environment are carefully examined, it becomes clear that, in general, the sub-publics (professionals, universities, well educated people, some health institutions) which support therapeutic goals are less powerful than those which support the custodial or segregating activities of these organizations. Under such conditions, most mental hospitals and prisons must be more or less custodial."

Seashore and Yuchtman (1968) have provided data from seventy-five insurance agencies, on the basis of which they argue persuasively not so much for a multiple-goal concept as for an optimal mix of FA's of a sort that enables the organization to conserve its sources of inputs and to process these with the least waste consistent with attaining that optimal mix. For example, the costs of adding and training young agents, in the short run, may be greater than relying upon "old reliables." Yet the new agents may aid in a greater penetration of the market, which can be attained only by holding down or reducing the costs of current operations. The Seashore-Yuchtman model is basically an economic one (it says nothing about roles), and lacks the input-output-boundary-feedback features presented herein. Nevertheless, their essential point is that the effectiveness of organizations, like people, flowers, and other living systems, can be conceived as the degree to which they accommodate and adjust in complex ways their inputs and internal resources (capacities) to their environments.

An examination of groups of various sorts reveals both FA and GNS in various degrees of prominence. It is our hypothesis that neither is completely absent in any group surviving over an extended period. However, for groups of a given kind (bridge clubs, factory units, college departments), it is possible that FA and GNS are optimal with respect to each other in some unique way. That is, if it were possible now to measure FA and GNS in the same unit terms, we would hypothesize that an optimal equilibrium would exist when the ratio GNS/FA is some value K_x in groups of type *X;* but GNS/FA would be some other value K_y in groups of type *Y*. Fortunately, it is not necessary to wait for the now nonexistent group taxonomy to test out these hypotheses on groups having similar tasks, although a complete verification of this notion will require the taxonomy and some measures of FA and GNS on a common scale. Since a further development of this proposition leads into the adaptability of social systems, we will delay its presentation temporarily.

The preceding discussion has indicated that groups existing within a well-defined and functioning suprasystem are controlled via "natural" feedback channels. For those in less well-defined suprasystems, the lower level of FA and the upper level of GNS are less rigidly controlled. Our main point is that, in a rudimentary way, feedback channels can be identified for social systems, even in those situations where the concept is unknown to the operators. Such feedback channels appear to have evolved without reference to any deliberate design. They are as natural as feedback found in biological systems.

Feedback in Sensitivity Learning

Some initial steps have been taken to insert feedback deliberately in those teaching laboratories in group dynamics that, in more modern terminology, are sometimes called sensitivity training.[7] One of the practices in these situations is to feed back to participants the way in which their behavior affects others in the group. Considerable emphasis is placed on the prior necessity for developing the norms which make legitimate such frank reflections of behavior. Benne, Bradford, and Lippitt (1964, p. 24) define feedback as signifying "verbal and nonverbal responses from others to a unit of behavior provided as close in time to the behavior as possible, and capable of being perceived and utilized by the individual initiating the behavior. Feedback may serve a validating function with respect to the initial behavior. It may serve to steer and give direction to subsequent behavior. It may also serve to stimulate changes in the behavior, feeling, attitude, perception and knowledge of the initiator." This definition says nothing about maintaining a steady state (unless this is implied in the phrase "serve a validation function"), or counteracting disturbances, or tending to ensure the survival of a system. It does correspond with the feedback definition of nonliving systems insofar as the output (behavior) of an individual generates a signal directed back to the behaver. However, that signal does not necessarily influence the input control. Instead, the signal becomes another input item along with other inputs perceived and processed by the individual. We need to recognize that this use of the term does not carry with it the automatic corrective control which is denoted by feedback in its original meaning.

The discrepancy is not as great as it may seem on first inspection. One may argue that the verbal or nonverbal feedback defined by Benne *et al.* is an example of a loose loop—an imprecise control over subsequent behavior, but otherwise not significantly different in principle from feedback in mechanical systems. The fact that feedback signal "may serve to steer and give direction," or "may serve to stimulate changes in the behavior, etc.," is an indication of the stupendous complexity of the human system, the numerous states that the system may assume, and the initial filtering of each individual's boundary. After all, does not the conventional operation of a feedback "stimulate a change" when an error output occurs such as a deviation from the desired compass bearing of a ship? If we further analyze verbal feedback in these group situations, it becomes evident that the communications tend to bring the individual's role behavior into conformity with group norms that he is expected to adopt within that system. To the extent, therefore, that verbal feedback is effective in achieving these ends, the collection of indi-

[7] This term is derived from the notion that participants become more aware of the effects of their own and others' behavior.

viduals becomes a system with its own boundaries and differentiated component functions.

Because these groups are deliberately temporary—that is, established for a short period of learning—one cannot estimate the extent to which feedback contributes to the survival of the system. It is a common observation that groups which have engaged in this kind of behavior are reluctant to disband and often plan reunions. It may therefore be argued that they have a strong tendency to survive that cannot be achieved because of uncontrollable conditions.

This discussion leads us to conclude that, given components initially unarticulated, the verbal and nonverbal feedback in sensitivity learning groups is a mechanism which assists in the formation of a social system. In the hands of those who have developed the learning laboratories, it has been a deliberately employed mechanism for selecting and channeling behavior into those paths defined by the groups as acceptable. The looseness of the feedback loop may be the consequence of the fact that the group norms are themselves less precise than, say, the temperature setting of a thermostat or the compass bearing of a ship, and, in addition, the verbal communications may also be less precise than the signals in mechanical systems. However, there seems to be no difference in principle between feedback in this kind of social system and in nonliving systems.

This excursion into sensitivity learning is presented as an example of deliberately contriving a procedure that utilizes feedback between components of a social system for the express purpose of "growing a group." Although we have not specified the details of the feedback procedures or the ancillary conditions, it is evident that the method has utility (cf. Stock, 1964, and Bunker, 1965).

GROWTH OF SOCIAL SYSTEMS

Nucleation

From what has just been presented, one might mistakenly conclude that the feedback constraints prohibit the growth of systems. To some extent, this is true; they tend to dampen growth. On the other hand, in Chapter V we presented the proposition that growth may be viewed as structural modifications initiated by some "foreign" input which permits the acceptance of maintenance inputs otherwise rejected. The ongoing established system which has reached some stabilized level of input-output rate is not easily stimulated to increase its size by the addition of new components, except by some out-of-the-ordinary irritant.

Examples of the nucleation principle (Chap. IV) at the social level emphasize the seminal idea or the seminal person, who in more common parlance serves as the founder, or leader, of a social system, drawing about him adherents committed to the promotion and development of an organization. These are the great names: Andrew Carnegie for the steel industry, Clara Barton for the Red Cross, Susan B. Anthony for women's rights, Samuel Gompers and John L. Lewis for labor, and many others, both more and less notable. It is impossible to conceive of a social system developing without assuming some one central person, or, at least, a small coterie of persons taking some initiative to organize and focus the efforts of others around an issue relevant to the concerns they all feel, at least dimly.

Emergent Characteristics

Some emphasis was placed earlier on the square-cube law which says that mass grows by a square. As a consequence of this, it was pointed out that biological systems, as they become larger, must develop specialized emergent structures and functions to maintain communication and articulation among components (proposition 5.1a). Does specialization also occur with growth in social systems and does the square-cube law also hold?

Haire (1959) has provided a number of ingenious analyses of several business concerns which bear out the square-cube law. He assumed that the employees of a firm assigned to purchasing, shipping, selling, reception, and the like were "surface" employees. They met and dealt with systems outside the firm. The remainder were those who made up the internal portion of the system. Each of four rapidly growing firms was followed over a number of years—as many as thirty-five—and the respective numbers of inside vs. surface employees at regular intervals were tabulated. Taking the square root of the second and the cube root of the first and plotting these values gave a scatter plot that was virtually a straight line. If the relationship had been perfectly in accord with the geometric law, the slope of the line would have been 1. The plots for each of the four firms had slopes of .72, .51, .50, and .97, which argues in favor of the view that social organizations appear to grow in accord with a general principle applicable to other systems as well. No measure of the effectiveness of these firms was reported. Had there been such a measure, it would have been possible to determine whether or not those firms most closely approximating a slope of 1 were the most effective.

Proposition 5.1a says that emergent characteristics of systems are the necessary consequences of growth and attendant structural modifications. In addition, we have previously made the point that systems, as they become larger, need to develop specialized communications nets. Haire's analysis throws light on this issue as well. Staff positions within an organization are established when the supervisory or managerial load on an individual becomes greater than he can efficiently handle. Staff, as contrasted to line, supervisors are given responsibility for gathering and sifting information that the line supervisor needs to know but has not the time or capacity to collect or integrate. However, the line supervisor retains responsibility for decision making. Among the four firms studied, Haire found that the number of staff positions increased as the size of the total work force increased—at first more rapidly than the line, and then later at about equivalent rates. That is, in the early growth period, the staff tended to increase geometrically as the line grew arithmetically; but later, the growth curves were essentially parallel. The invention of the staff position in modern organizations is an emergent feature and, according to Haire's findings, appears to be a direct outgrowth of the information overload placed on key individuals. In systems theory terms, the staff assistant is an aspect of the line supervisor's filtering boundary, selecting the significant data for his boss.[8]

It is of interest also that another fairly recent organizational invention—the special personnel officer—was established in these firms when they grew to a size of 177, 152, 138, and 248 employees. The remarkable similarity in the size, except for the last, suggests that the accumulation of special kinds of issues pertaining to the recruitment, hiring, promotion, and morale of people reaches a critical point where the full-time attention of a specialized person is required. Indik (1965) found confirming evidence in three sets of organizations that increased size was associated with increasing task specialization. It is one of the sometimes lamented features of large organizations that too many specialties have evolved. Too few persons are available who possess the global view which holds the specialists in their proper perspective. This is an example of proposition 5.3, which emphasizes the necessary specialization of components when there is an increase in size.

The argument can be pressed a step further. The characteristics of a large social system differ from those of small ones in other ways than size. One of the most obvious of these is the shift from a personalized to a bureaucratic form of control, in which specific regulations, rules, and routines take the place of personal judgment and on-the-spot decisions. The regulations are preprogrammed decisions. When an organization is composed of just a few individuals, the unwritten norms and role expectations of the various components are sufficient to control the transactions within the system and also the interactions the system ex-

[8] Miller (1965) has dealt at length with information overload and mentions filtering as one means of handling the problem.

periences with its surroundings. Issues and problems are dealt with in "humanistic" personal terms. As the organization grows with the addition of new individuals, a point is reached where the "natural" constraints of norms and roles fail to mature fast enough to ensure that all members of the organization either know or are responsive to these controls. It is at this point that the manual of regulations is needed and is frequently produced. Some suggestive evidence of this appears in Indik's (1964) findings that the ratio of supervisors to nonsupervisors declines with the increase in size of the organization. Although he has no evidence of a compensating increase in control by impersonal means, one way of rationalizing the finding is to hypothesize that such controls are a substitute for the personal, direct control embodied in the supervisor. We certainly know from other sources that the written "operations manual" grows as the business corporation grows.

The findings and interpretations we have just presented find a cogent echo in the following quotation from one of the perceptive observers and exceptionally able administrators of our time:

> The development of resistance to new ideas is a familiar process in the individual. The infant is a model of openness to new experience—receptive, curious, eager, unafraid, willing to try anything. As the years pass, these priceless qualities fade. He becomes more cautious, less eager, and accumulates deeply rooted habits and fixed attitudes.
>
> The same process may be observed in organizations. The young organization is willing to experiment with a variety of ways to solve its problems. It is not bowed by the weight of tradition. It rushes in where angels fear to tread. As it matures, it develops settled policies and habitual modes of solving problems. In doing so, it becomes more efficient, but less flexible, less willing to look freshly at each day's experience. Its increasingly fixed routines and practices are congealed in an elaborate body of written rules. In the final stage of organizational senility, there is a rule for everything. Someone has said that the last act of a dying organization is to get out a new and enlarged edition of the rule book (Gardner, 1962).

Indik's data were culled from two types of business organizations (thirty-two parcel delivery stations, thirty-six automobile dealerships), two types of volunteer community organizations (twelve community fire companies, twenty-eight local chapters of an educational "league"), and a union (eight locals of a national union). It appears that the volunteer organizations comparable in size to business concerns or unions have the higher ratio of officers (or supervisors) to the rank and file, suggesting again that those organizations with loose formal controls (volunteers) attempt to make up for these loose controls by having many personalized points of contact with those in the hierarchy. Obviously, the distinguishing characteristic of the volunteer organization is freedom from exogenous economic constraints, with a relative ease in moving in or out of the system and a corresponding freedom from strict impersonalized rules and requirements. It is perhaps significant that Indik's data show a positive correlation between size and frequent complaints of bureaucratic inflexibility in the parcel delivery company, but not in the automobile dealerships or other organizations studied. One may see, in this, evidence of increasing impersonal controls with increasing size, especially in those systems characterized by a wide dispersion of personal and high FA requirements.

The essential point of this discussion has been that as organizations grow and become more tightly integrated, new emergent types of control appear that go beyond the primitive, "natural" controls that reside in norms and role expectations. These data are in harmony with proposition 5.1a.

Dependence-Independence Conflict in Social Systems

One of the features of growth, often experienced but rarely understood, is the resistance of subsystems to stifling control by the suprasystem, sometimes by the reign of rules. Proposition 5.4 stated that some conflict is inescapable between the requirements of the suprasystem and the continued identity of its subsystems. Robert Frost (1938) might have had something of this sort in mind when he wrote:

> Something there is that doesn't love a wall,
> That sends the frozen-ground-swell under it,
> and spills the upper boulders in the sun;
> I let my neighbor know beyond the hill and
> on a day we meet to walk the line
> and set the wall between us once again. . . .
> He only says "Good fences make good neighbors."

Wherever one looks at social systems—neighbors in Frost's New England; the individual working for his employer; a labor union negotiating with a corporation; husband, wife, and children in a family; students within a university; or different ethnic groups living hard by and relating to each other—one can find evidence of opposed forces, one set in the direction of collaborative, conjoint efforts, and the other in the direction of autonomy, independence, and separate identity. This is not to say that the conflict is necessarily hostile or disruptive—only that embedded within the suprasystem are dependency limits beyond which the subsystems will not go except at the cost of destroying themselves. Why should this be so?

The logic of our deductions provides an insight. We start with two defined systems in the simplest case: a social system and an individual. The first we have defined as composed of roles and role behaviors. The second is a complex of several kinds of subsystems, physiological, perceptual, ego, including his various social role possibilities, as an employee, family member, citizen, religious communicant, and so on. One of the special characteristics of a social system is the mobility of an individual in and out of these systems from moment to moment and his movement from one system to another, in which he frequently performs different roles.

If one social system so completely prescribes an individual's role behavior that his other role possibilities are stunted, his output variability is reduced—and this is initially painful. Moreover because social systems are perhaps the most labile, requiring great flexibility to respond to the variability of their supra- and subsystems, the utility of the restricted individual to the suprasystem itself is also reduced. The individual who has so perfectly taken on the role assignments of his employer, for example, that he has become less skillful in other roles (such as those of father, club member, and neighbor), not only limits his own sources of GNS but becomes less useful as his main suprasystem is modified through growth, decay, or reorganization.

It was Alfred North Whitehead who said in less changing times than today: "The rate of progress is such that an individual human being of ordinary length of life will be called upon to face novel situations which find no parallel in the past. The fixed person for the fixed duties who, in older societies was such a Godsend, in the future will be a public danger."

We noted in Chapter IV that the ego can be conceived of as a system. The identity of ego is largely found in the unique pattern of role behaviors which the individual can perform in a manner acceptable to the various social systems in which he circulates. To the extent that he is constricted to a single social system, his identity is blunted. The criticisms of the "gray-flannel-suit syndrome" and complaints of compliant conformity are examples of a pervading resistance against submerging one's identity in any one or a limited number of social systems. It is the preservation of one's uniqueness that operates against the needs of the social system to prescribe the individual's role within it.[9]

We may extend this pattern of analysis to divisions within a firm, the merger of firms, municipalities within a state, on up to colonies within an empire. In all cases, subunits tend to maintain some independence

[9] See Trow (1965) for an experiment that partially confirmed this.

in the face of their dependency on the suprasystem. If either "wins" completely, both fail.

The Form of Social System Growth

Proposition 5.1d states that growth follows a "plan" embedded in substructures of the initial system modified by localized specialization. It will be recalled that this proposition was exemplified in biochemical data. How does it apply to social systems?

If we look about at various types of social organizations—universities, business corporations, religious organizations, community associations, professional bodies, political bodies, military units, philanthropic foundations, governmental agencies or bureaus—one is immediately struck by the almost universal adherence to the pyramidal shape of the hierarchy. It matters little whether the organization is small or large; as one moves from the lower level to higher echelons, the number of persons becomes smaller and smaller. This has been true at least from the days of Moses, when his father-in-law advised him to "provide out of all the people able men, such as fear God, men of truth, hating covetousness; and place such over them to be rulers of thousands, and rulers of hundreds, rulers of fifties, and rulers of tens" (Exodus 18:21). If there is a "natural" plan of development in social systems associated with survival, the pyramidal shape seems to be it.

But is this form of organizational growth "embedded in the substructures of the initial system"? Obviously, one cannot have a pyramid with less than three components. Research conducted by Vinacke and Arkoff (1957), using triads in a competitive game situation, has repeatedly shown that two of the players often and quickly pair off to form a coalition against the third. Sometimes the coalition is between the weakest and strongest member against the third or, as Caplow (1956) and Vinacke and Gullickson (1963) have shown, the most powerful may prevail over the other two. Although the evidence is slim, one may suggest that in triads there is a strong tendency to establish a hierarchy with the power triangle either inverted or in its more usual position. The most primitive condition in which the pyramidal form of organization can display itself does in fact occur. Vinacke and Gullickson's data further indicate that such forms are less likely among young preadolescents, which further suggests that the general cultural influences have been somewhat responsible for the patterning of the triads.

Going beyond these experimental data, we are repeatedly impressed with the fact that all organizations of any extended permanence establish for themselves some sort of charter, constitution, or set of by-laws. Even in primitive societies the unwritten codes and customs prescribing the form and structural pattern of their relationships can be viewed as the societal counterpart of the DNA template. The structural form assumed by such systems as they grow is partly determined by these charters—written or unwritten. In the so-called established societies, these are transmitted from generation to generation in written form. Of course, such charters may be altered in time, perhaps more easily than DNA molecules. A rough parallel has been suggested (Gerard, Kluckhohn, and Rapoport, 1956, p. 6) between the mutations in genes which alter hereditary characteristics and data about innovations, such as woman suffrage, representative government, or high-speed transport, that may alter the fundamental structure of a society. However, there has not been a rigorous test of this hypothesis.

SUMMARY

This discussion of growth phenomena in social systems has been handicapped by a regrettable poverty of both relevant empirical data and earlier theoretical formulations (McNulty, 1962; Guetzkow and Bowes, 1957). Obviously, it is more difficult to observe or manipulate organizational growth than the growth of fruit flies or corn. Apart from the time requirements, the absence of more than a rudimentary conceptual framework has resulted in little empirical effort. We therefore cannot claim that the growth phenomena of social systems do, or do not, fit in major respects into the general systems theory, yet some data are understandable within such a framework. Much is yet to be learned about the expansion of organizations and the concomitant changes associated with growth.

In this chapter we have continued the development of our systems model of groups, defining group needs satisfactions as the maintenance inputs and formal achievements as the outputs linking one group with another. We have identified the mechanisms whereby both the inputs and outputs are controlled by feedback loops. The sources of GNS have been shown to be (a) the interactions of the individuals themselves, (b) a by-product of FA, (c) the agent of the suprasystem, (d) the larger suprasystem or the exogenous forces over which the group has minimal control.

The growth of social systems appears to be initiated by some benign irritant which serves to trigger the process, just as growth in other living systems appears to be initiated by the nucleation principle. Although the empirical data are meager, it is evident that specialization within social systems emerges as size increases. As in other systems, the preservation of subsystem identities in opposition to the growing control exerted by the suprasystem is an unavoidable built-in conflict. There is some possibility that the form of growth in social systems is in part determined by certain nascent conditions embedded within the "charter" members of a new group.

VIII / SOCIAL SYSTEMS: ADAPTATION

It is somewhat paradoxical that adaptation as a process has been of concern to biologists for a century or more, yet the social scientists have given it scant attention—surely less than it deserves. Instead, the latter have cast the issues largely in terms of the strategies for bringing about social change through modifications in the structure, function, or goals of an organization. This chapter will address itself, not to the ways in which social systems may be changed, but to the conditions which must be stabilized when changes occur. We will be talking about the homeostatic conditions that permit changes to occur without sacrificing the ongoing life of the system. Toward the end of the chapter we shall offer some methodological suggestions for researching the adaptation process as it works out in social systems.

Proposition 4.7 says that adaptation is a survival-extending process and occurs when a potentially harmful maintenance input (an error) from the suprasystem is blocked or dissipated at the boundary or neutralized within the system. How does this apply to social systems?

We propose that two kinds of adaptation may be identified for social systems: internal and external.[1] External adaptation pertains to those adjustments the system makes in response to potentially destructive conditions in the milieu surrounding the system. The system's capacity to deal

[1] Miller (1965, p. 224) implies the same distinction, but lumps the two kinds together under the label of *values*. That is, strains resulting from some incompatibility between the system's template program of growth and stressing inputs from the environment, he calls values. The relative urgency of reducing specific strains represents the system's hierarchy of values. These latter priorities are, in our model, internal adaptations. See also Bennis (1966).

with such disturbances may be traced to a set of conditions different from those that affect its capacity to cope with internally arising disturbances. These latter pertain to the relations between the system and its subsystems. In the previous discussion of adaptation (Chap. III), we dealt with only the former of these—disturbances arising from some external source.[2] Accordingly, we shall deal with this kind of adaptation first.

ADAPTATION TO EXTERNAL STRESS

We have previously defined the mutual satisfactions of role performers as the reverberating maintenance inputs-outputs of a social system. The processing activities of the system itself contribute to the generation of GNS, which then feeds back as an input. In another place (Berrien, 1964), the proposition was also advanced that the degree of adaptability is a function of both FA and GNS. That is to say, the extent to which these outputs remain stable in the face of external disturbances that would depress them is some function of both. Figure 7 illustrates the proposition.

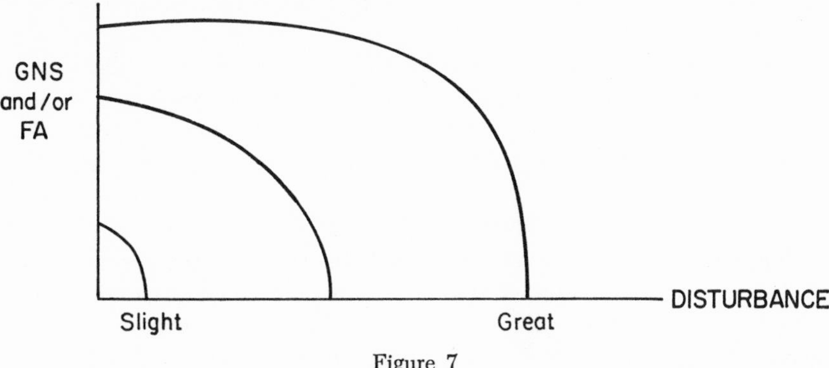

Figure 7

The figure is meant to show that if GNS and/or FA are initially at some high value, no matter how severe the disturbance is, little if any change will occur in the two output values until the system collapses. At moderate levels of GNS and FA, the greater the disturbance, the greater will be the decrement in the output. For very low initial levels

[2] It will be well to recognize at the outset that this distinction between internal and external is a difficult one to maintain because it depends upon one's vantage point in any particular instance. What may be viewed as an external disturbance for system *a* could equally well be seen as an internal disturbance for the suprasystem *A* of which *a* is a component. For purposes of explication, the distinction, we believe, has merit since it will help to resolve the apparent contradiction that adaptation is a process whereby stability, viewed from some external viewpoint, is maintained by internal change.

of the outputs, a slight disturbance will cause a precipitous decline in output. (The accelerating slope of the curves is purely hypothetical.)

Some corroborating evidence supporting this proposition was provided by Indik (1962) in a study of six remedial reading classes observed over seven periods. In the middle of the seventh period, the teacher was called, without prior knowledge, from the room. Those classes having high GNS and FA (measured during each of the previous sessions) continued to work more effectively than did those with low output scores.

Two other studies (Berrien and Angoff, 1958; Berrien and Indik, 1961) —one based on thirty-two work groups and the other involving twelve volunteer fire companies—produced the correlations shown below.

Adaptability of	*GNS*	*FA*
12 fire companies	.47	.75
32 work groups	.41	.57

Another study in the same series (Indik and Tyler, 1963), this one dealing with college students in a semilaboratory situation, revealed that combined measures of FA and GNS taken before disturbance correlated .70 with adaptability.

It is evident from these quite different sets of groups that the general hypothesized relation between the outputs and adaptability is at least supported, even though we have no information yet concerning the course of any changes in the output variables as a function of the disturbance magnitude.

On purely logical grounds, why should the output, especially in GNS, decline with increasing severity of the disturbance? If the members of a group are receiving a high degree of satisfaction from their mutual association, it is reasonable to assume that a temporary decrement in this respect will not push them past a critical point where the group would disintegrate. But if the group is operating at a low marginal level of GNS, a comparable decrement—even for a short period—may be just enough to cause at least some members to dissociate themselves. Such decrements in GNS may be triggered by a variety of circumstances, both internal and external. March and Simon (1958, Chap. 5) have suggested that where a felt need exists for joint decision making, interpersonal conflict and probably lowered GNS will develop if there is a difference in goals or a difference in perceptions of reality, or both. Moreover, they also argue that if the total resources of the organization are plentiful and the suprasystem is benign, interpersonal conflict is less likely. Some evidence on this latter point is found in the study of community volunteer fire departments, the most effective of which were in communities that supplied some support without creating a paternalistic control or dependency

(Berrien and Indik, 1961). Likert (1961), distilling the results of some fifteen years' work on large-scale organizations, also came to the conclusion that those managers and groups were best which existed in a context of supportive relationships with higher echelons. It is reasonable to interpret this conclusion to mean that the suprasystem, as represented by the supervisor, assisted the subsystem to maintain itself via the generation of GNS (cf. p. 123).

What about the FA component in adaptability? Work groups, as specific examples of subsystems, provide considerable evidence of FA's contribution to adaptability. In many incentive-paced situations, the groups often "hide" some of their output so that, in periods when demands are increased or they are indisposed to keep up the normal pace, the groups' output will remain essentially stable. The warehousing of output within a firm is a comparable phenomenon clearly designed to be adaptable to fluctuations on both the input and output side of FA. The profit of an enterprise is likewise a surplus of FA, which enables it to ride out periods of depression. The previously mentioned classroom groups making good grades are better equipped to continue their work in the absence of the teacher. In all instances, either the actual or potential FA of a system—if high—aids the system to hold a steady level of output.

Some additional supporting evidence for the general proposition was found in a study (Berrien and Angoff, 1960) of two working shifts in a warehouse. The night shift was known to pack about twice as many orders per man as the day shift. It was also known that the night shift had a higher level of GNS. The day shift was less adaptable to emergency situations that called for rush orders or required changes in work assignments. Moreover, directives from the supervisor were often evaded by the day-shift workers. Although the study was largely qualitative in nature, the thrust of the findings in no way contradicts the proposition that the higher the FA and GNS, the higher is adaptability and disturbances in routine activities will adversely affect the outputs least.

INTERNAL ADAPTABILITY

Internal adaptability refers to those adjustments stimulated by some disturbance arising within the system, rather than from an external source. On page 126 it was proposed that for each class of groups, the ratio GNS/FA has some optimal value, *K*. It has also been argued that the upper limit of GNS and the lower limit of FA are normally under the control of the suprasystem.[3] Contrariwise, the lower limit of GNS and the upper limit of FA are normally controlled by the subsystem. It follows

[3] Here we are assuming that the system under study consists of just two levels and the internal disturbances arise between these levels.

that if one or the other system loses control of either variable, the ratio will depart from its "normal" level.

The first of the above propositions—namely, that for each class of groups the GNS/FA ratio is relatively stable—has pervaded organizational theory in various forms for some time. Barnard (1938) spoke of the *efficiency* and the *effectiveness* of an organization in terms that approximate our GNS and FA, and argued that they need to be balanced. The firm cannot long exist if it has the major features of a country club or a sweatshop. Roethlisberger (1944) raised as a central question, "How can a plant be organized so as to fulfill its technical objective of manufacturing a product at a minimum cost, and at the same time fulfill a social function of providing for its employees a socially significant way of life?" (p. 112).

Simon (1947) and later March and Simon (1958, Chap. 4) advanced an organizational equilibrium theory which held that a surviving organization is one in which a certain balance is struck between inducements and contributions. This was framed mostly in individual terms, the central proposition being that "each participant and each group of participants receives *from* the organization *inducements* in return for which he makes *to* the organization *contributions*" (March and Simon, 1958, p. 84). The meaning of this statement would not be significantly altered if we substituted GNS for inducements and FA for contributions. We seem, therefore, to be in good company in proposing a variant on a basic concept of balance between production and satisfaction that has been around for some time (cf. Parsons, 1949). The hypothesis can be diagrammed as in Figure 8.

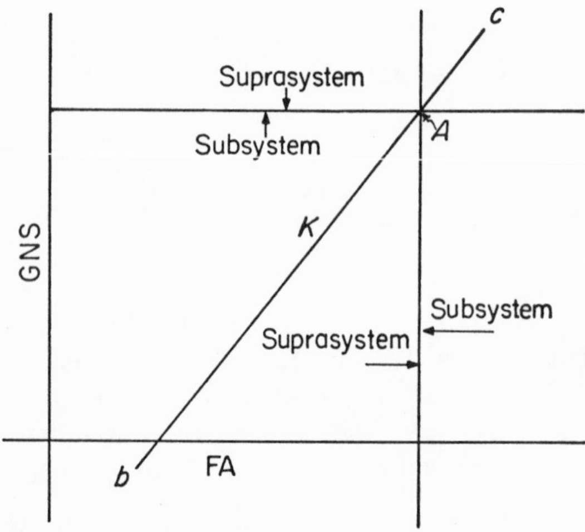

Figure 8

In the previous chapter we argued that the suprasystem generally operates so as to depress the GNS level and to increase FA. Each of these forces, we assume, is opposed by the subsystem, which tends to increase the GNS and to depress the FA. This is merely a restatement of the views explained on page 119. The resolution of these forces and counterforces is represented by the intersection of the two variables at point *A*. Moreover, the hypothesis says that point *A* should fall on or near some line *b*, $c = K$, if the total system is to remain adaptive or balanced. If, for some reason, one or the other of the sets of forces manages to depress its variable without a corresponding decrement in the other, the point of intersection will depart from the adaptation zone. It is hypothesized that so long as there is a tendency for correction to take place such that the intersection point is forced back toward the adaptation line, the system will readjust. On the other hand, should the countercorrecting forces be sufficiently weak, the intersection point will depart farther and farther from line *K*.

Two things should be noted about this model. First, it borrows unashamedly from the concept of a quasi-stable equilibrium proposed many years ago by Lewin (1947) in which he argued that any ongoing, relatively stable pattern of behavior could be conceptualized as the resultant of "driving" and "restraining" forces. In our model, these forces originate in the sub- and suprasystems. Lewin conceived of a single variable held in balance by opposing forces; our model has two such variables. Second, the model also incorporates the notion advanced by Cannon (1945) to the effect that "if a state remains steady, it does so because any tendency toward change is automatically met by increased effectiveness of the factor or factors which resist the change." What has been presented seems, therefore, to be congruent with the general concept of adaptation.[4]

Some Further Deductions

The model has heuristic utility. Suppose that the subsystem fails to limit the eastward movement of FA or a decrement in GNS. In either case, point *A* will fall to the east of line *K*. Similarly, should the subsystem relax its normal control functions, point *A* will fall to the west of line *K*. Thus the model provides an automatic indicator of the source of imbalance and is a diagnostic aid in determining where corrective measures might be taken. Major departures from *K* become symptoms

[4] The model is also strikingly similar to Boulding's model (1965) describing the bargaining relationships between two parties (firms). Boulding uses the model as a basis for defining three kinds of moves within the area which he calls benign, malign, and conflict. Successful bargaining or benign moves are very close to what we call adaptation here.

of some maladaptation in the internal relations of the total system when one or the other or both sets of constraints are defective.

Figure 8 shows *K* with a slope of 1. This is purely hypothetical and is not meant to be fixed. Any other positive slope may be characteristic of a set of groups. The specific slope for a given case is a function (linear or log) of the scaling of the two measures which has not been specified. However, it is likely that the intercept of *K*, when GNS is zero, will be some positive value of FA. Exogenous conditions (e.g., economic pressures) sometimes compel individuals to be productive even when GNS is at low or zero levels. Prison camp groups working under the pain of punishment or death would be examples.

The resolution of forces at point *A* cannot be considered a sudden or immediate consequence which comes about quickly. For those groups which have existed for some time, point *A* is "norm-determined." That is, the norms of both the sub- and suprasystems play an important part in bringing about the resolution of their respective needs. It should be clear from our earlier discussion of norms that these, in turn, may vary from one group or organization to another. Within one firm having a given reputation, kind of work, and personnel policy, the resolution at point *A* may be quite different from that in another kind of firm. The Michigan studies, for example, of a large insurance company revealed that work groups having "employee-centered" supervisors were more productive than groups with "production-centered" supervisors. The norms were such as to lead employees to expect a moderately high degree of personal consideration. This finding was not confirmed by the same team of investigators when studying railroad section gangs (Katz, Maccoby, Gurin, and Floor, 1951). The railroad workers, whether in high- or low-productivity gangs, evidently were operating within norms that did not require supervisors to give them as much consideration as was true of the office workers. Both studies, however, are silent on the question of adaptability.

The model further leads one to expect that if some exogenous or other suprasystem conditions operate in such a manner as to force FA westward to a low value without simultaneously reducing GNS, the subsystem will tend to counteract the FA movement. Such a condition would be a reversal of the usual direction in which the forces operate and would constitute a case in which an out-of-the-ordinary adjustment is required. This is essentially what has happened in those organizations whose FA becomes irrelevant or no longer useful to the suprasystem. Consider the National Foundation for Infantile Paralysis. After the vaccines were discovered and distributed to large masses of the population, the original mission of the foundation was largely accomplished. The suprasystem thereafter had no use for the FA of the foundation. But it did not disband. It modified its name and found a new target for its FA. This has been the history of several other similar organizations. Garden clubs often evolve out of organizations originally formed to protest a real-estate developer's failure to complete his portion of a contract. If an organization accomplishes its mission (suprasystem no longer requires its FA), the organization will disintegrate unless it finds another FA that is acceptable. In terms of the model, if the suprasystem forces augment—rather than counteract—the subsystem forces, the subsystem is in grave danger of collapsing.

How far may the point of resolution, *A*, deviate from line *K* before the system may be considered in danger of disintegration? A small piece of empirical information gives a hint. The night and day shifts in a shipping room were studied over a period of months (Berrien and Angoff, 1960). The day shift was ill-adaptive to changes in work loads, assignments, or methods of work. There was a continual undercurrent of antagonism toward one another as well as toward the supervision, frequently punctuated by open hostility. Work output averaged about one-half that of the night shift. In the latter group the reverse was true; they easily adapted to the same kinds of changes, were much more congenial, and packed by actual count twice as much as their daytime counterparts.

Each of the men in both groups was asked how much of a cut in wages he would accept before looking for another job. For the night shift this averaged 10 per cent of current wages and for the day shift 14 per cent. Assuming as we did in Figure 8 that GNS has several sources including wages, "considerations" from supervisors, and the satisfactions from interpersonal interactions (in unknown proportions), these decrements in wages alone represent a small portion of the total GNS. Hence the results suggest that for these groups a slight drop in GNS, and therefore a small departure from line *K*, would at least initiate the disintegration process.

Another way of getting some idea of the tolerable deviation limits of line *K* in more general terms comes from Ashby's "law" of requisite variety (Ashby, 1956). This declares that any controlling system must possess a greater degree of complexity and variability than the system which is controlled. Before applying this "law" to our model, we must be more specific than we have been about the system whose GNS and FA are under examination. It must be the subsystem, for the suprasystem is presumably composed of other subsystems and is, therefore, more complex. With this specification, we may hazard the guess that Ashby's law of requisite variety leads to the deduction that when the subsystem develops a complexity greater than its suprasystem, it will tend to break away, assert its independence, or fail to return the point of resolution to the vicinity of *K*. This will happen whenever either or both of the "normal" subsystem forces reverse direction. We shall discuss on pages 150–151 a situation in which this happened.

Consider the case of the subsystem attempting to increase its FA, the direction of GNS forces remaining "normal." (Note that these initial conditions are the opposite of those given in the case of the National Foundation for Infantile Paralysis.) Presumably, in the early stages of such a developing situation, the suprasystem's resistance would be minimal. Point *A* will move in the northeasterly direction partly because the subsystem will derive some GNS feedback from its FA (Figure 6, p. 125). This is the direction in which *K* increases, representing the subsystem's increasing adaptability to external disturbances—that is, external to itself.

In more concrete terms, such a condition may occur in an academic department which expands its staff and attracts more students, engaging in more research with the initial blessing and encouragement of the university's administration. Subsequently, it receives, from outside the university's resources, grants and awards which support additional students, additional facilities, more staff. Its internal organization and sources of financial support come to match or exceed that which the university can allocate to that department. It therefore becomes less dependent upon the university and can, with greater impunity, ignore the policy controls of its "parent" system. This is precisely one of the organizational problems facing university administrations in the last half of the present century, and, unless appropriate suprasystem controls are exercised, the various segments of the "multiversity" are united only in name. The "law" of requisite variety provides a useful addendum to the model which helps to specify the upper limit of *K* that will be tolerable to the suprasystem.

Suppose a second case in which the suprasystem operates in conjunction with the subsystem to increase GNS with "normal" balanced pressures on FA. Such an organization might be described as paternalistic. Point *A* would then move northward. The model would then predict that such an organization might shortly become unstable. If the subsystem became dependent upon the suprasystem for generating the major source of GNS, its own cohesion would suffer and its unique identity would disappear. The punch line of a recent advertisement, "I would rather do it myself!" echoes this need for identity. Paternalism in its extreme forms in American industry has, in fact, proven to be only a temporary defense against the organizing efforts of unionism. Once a group becomes articulated, its principal maintenance, we postulate, must be self-generated. If the suprasystem takes over *all* that function, it does so at the risk of fatal disorganization.[5] We are forced to conclude that

[5] It is also possible to interpret the effects of extended welfare programs on family disorganization in these terms.

such a pattern of forces on the FA and GNS variables does not lead to an adaptive organization.

Let us suppose a third case in which the subsystem is so organized that it is capable of producing greater FA than the suprasystem finds acceptable. (Suprasystem is opposing FA.) In addition, the suprasystem, as in the second case above, is contributing a major part of GNS. Under these conditions, point *A* moves in the northwesterly direction. These general circumstances fit the example of a dedicated military establishment during a period of nonwar demobilization or gradual disarmament. It would also apply to an organization like the Red Cross during periods between major disasters. The difficulties of maintaining such organizations under these circumstances are well known. Not only is there a tendency to generate some substitute forms of FA (war-game exercises, blood-bank campaigns, life-saving and first-aid classes), but the substitute GNS inputs (financial subsidies, "morale-building" activities) are sometimes less effective than when the organization is working at the tasks for which it was designed. One can hardly imagine the continued existence of a baseball team which did not compete, or a drama group which did not produce a play for an audience, or a first-class concert orchestra which did not give concerts, no matter how well they were subsidized.

It is possible to construct other cases in which the net effect on point *A* is away from line *K* and show that in these the organization is, in some fashion, moving toward disintegration. Some further examples are given in the final chapter. Rather than continue with this line of argument from hypothetical situations which find some tentative support in general experience, let us turn to more concrete empirical findings.

Relevant Empirical Studies

Some indirect supporting evidence of the *K* hypothesis comes from a study by Adams (1954), which indicates that a moderate level of authoritarian control by officers of bomber crews was associated with the best crew performance. Officers who were extremely authoritarian or extremely "equalitarian" commanded crews who performed less well. Superior performance, in this case, is assumed to mean highly adaptive performance in which the GNS/FA ratio is "on line." For those crews with highly equalitarian or highly authoritarian officers, GNS is assumed to have been high and low respectively, resulting in departures from the on-line ratio. We have no way of exactly specifying yet when an "off-line" ratio becomes such a severe departure that the systems are unable to make effective corrections. Nevertheless, Adams' study lends some, albeit tentative, support for the validity of the model.

A report by Guetzkow and Gyr (1954) points in the same direction. Decisions were eventually reached with a high degree of consensus in small committee conferences (even though, in the decision-making process, disagreement flared) when (a) self-oriented needs of the members were expressed and tended to be satisfied, (b) there was a recognized need for unified action, and (c) the chairman maintained order, focusing attention on one issue at a time. Condition (a) appears to be related to GNS, while (b) and (c) may, with some charity, be translated into signal inputs that promote FA. In contrast, those groups in which the "affective needs" of many members remained in conflict reached decisions only as the conflicting members withdrew from the problem and each other. Translated into our model, these latter group members suffered some deficiency in GNS, leaving the decision to others.

Bales and his colleagues (1955) have examined what they call the phase movement in small discussion groups, making content analyses in a manner that has now become well known. They found productive groups to be ones in which there was a certain "orbit of activity" such that a disturbance created by one remark was corrected or adjusted by a later counterbalancing statement. Bales says (p. 433), "Theoretically we tend to assume that a preponderance of positive reactions over negative is a *condition* of equilibrium or maintenance of the steady state of the system. The reasoning goes something like this: We assume that the instrumental-adaptive goals of the system involve the maintenance of a certain level of accomplishment output, and that this level *tends to fall* without the constant application of effort, energy, and activity applied successfully to the realities of the external situation. But the level of accomplishment cannot be maintained for long without also maintaining the level of diffuse *satisfaction*, which depends upon the achievement of expressive-integrative goals." This, from our standpoint, is another statement of the GNS/FA ratio proposition. It is of some interest that Psathas (1960) confirmed Bales's hypothesis in psychotherapy groups when several sessions were analyzed as a unit.

It might be helpful if additional quantitative studies already published, starting from other assumptions and using different models, were reinterpreted within the model presented here. This is a somewhat hazardous procedure, as already exemplified above, because the operational definitions of GNS especially would obviously differ from one to another in subtle and perhaps significant ways. Moreover, our model of GNS sources is sufficiently complex that previously published quantitative data can be reanalyzed only by making a number of gratuitous assumptions. We are, therefore, discouraged from following that course.

It would be foolhardy to insist that the studies cited above and others like them (Bales, 1953; Whyte *et al.*, 1955; March and Simon, 1958; Hare, 1962) provide more than tentative support for the model. On the other hand, none of the reports which have come to our attention frankly and directly address the question: By what means or mechanism within a system is a balance of psychic and tangible outputs achieved? It is often assumed that the output of a group is primarily under the control of some leader, supervisor, or other person in a power position. On the other hand, the norms of a group and the expectations of its members have also been recognized as influencing the outcomes. The model presented attempts to bring these two sources of influence into a co-ordinated picture. It is our contention that reciprocal relationships between the components and their suprasystem account for the relative stability of the GNS/FA ratio, which, in turn, is the indicator of internal adaptability. Marked departures from some narrow range of fluctuations foreshadow, or at least accompany, conditions recognized as maladaptive or conflictive.

ADAPTATION, INTERNAL AND EXTERNAL

Are the two kinds of adaptation, internal and external, related? We are not sure. Certainly on the basis of our initial assumptions, external and internal adaptation are not the same. Adaptation cannot be both the sum of GNS and FA and also some unique and stable value of the GNS/FA ratio. On the other hand, it would seem reasonable that if a system were internally adaptive (variations in GNS and FA were co-ordinated so that they approximated K at all times), it would thereby be better equipped to deal with external disturbances. In Figure 8, it is possible by the Pythagorean theorem to write the equation:

$$K = \sqrt{(\text{GNS})^2 + (\text{FA} - e)^2}$$

In this case, K is not the slope of the line but its length (between GNS $=$ O and A). The length *may* represent the degree to which a system is capable of adapting to external disturbances. No empirical evidence is available to support such a deduction, but a further examination of the model suggests the possibility.

In order to explain the main features of Figure 8, it was assumed that the opposing forces were essentially equal in all respects. We may relax this assumption now. It is evident from Figure 6 that a high degree of FA in a group that takes satisfaction in its FA will generate a somewhat higher level of GNS. Transposed to Figure 8, this condition would indicate a stronger driving pressure on GNS than the resisting force against FA. If the suprasystem in such a circumstance relaxed its resisting force against GNS by an appropriate degree, point A would move upward along K. From an intuitive standpoint, a system of this sort looks like one of increasing adaptability. That is to say, it functions in a positive feedback manner so that increases in FA tend to contribute to increases in GNS, and the total system develops surplus outputs well beyond a critical survival level.

On the other hand, as we indicated earlier, Ashby's "law" of requisite variety, when applied to this model, suggests that a point may be reached at a high level of *K* where the subsystem may become so adaptive (see Figure 7) that it may not be responsive to its "parent" suprasystem. When such a point is reached, the subsystem may break out of its earlier controls and instead become a component of a suprasystem collateral with its former "parent." Examples of this development are found in spinning off segments of a firm as independent units, in the breakup of colonial empires, in research institutes and consulting organizations begotten by universities.

Under the condition that the subsystem does not find satisfaction in its FA, this source of GNS would be cut off and the level would be lower than in the previous case. This condition is represented in Figure 9 by

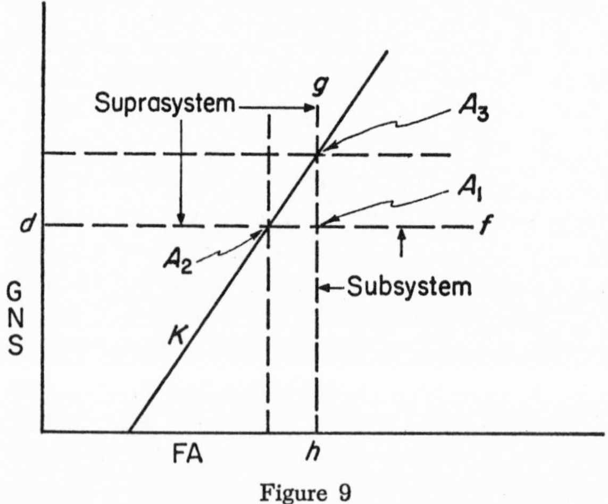

Figure 9

the intersection at A_1 of lines *d-f* and *g-h*. In order for *A* to approximate line *K*, either of two options are available to the suprasystem. First, it could relax its driving forces on FA, allowing line *g-h* to move to the west and re-establishing adaptation at A_2. Alternatively, the suprasystem could provide additional "considerations," rewards, or other maintenance inputs, relaxing its restraining forces of GNS, thus moving the point of resolution toward A_3 at a higher level of *K*. Again from the intuitive standpoint, the latter option seems to carry a higher probability of resulting in a better adaptation than the first option. The model agrees with that intuitive expectation.

It should be emphasized that these are deductions from the geometry of the model for which we have only the most general observation of the manner in which organizations function. On the other hand, these observations projected against the model immediately suggest a program of empirical studies to test the hypotheses generated. Rather than present other model deductions of this kind, it would seem wiser to forgo these in favor of seeing whether the model is useful in interpreting organizational problems as they arise "in the field."

Zaleznik-Christensen-Roethlisberger Study

The work of Zaleznik, Christensen, and Roethlisberger (1958) is particularly useful for this purpose because they not only gathered data from an ongoing organization but in addition brought to their observations a theoretical framework bearing some correspondence to the one presented herein.

Zaleznik *et al.* propose essentially that FA (productivity) and GNS (satisfactions) are a complicated function of the individual's acceptance by the work group and the rewards offered by the suprasystem (supervision). Their statement of hypotheses (p. 327) follows:

1. When an individual is rewarded both by management (external reward) and by the group (internal reward), he will be satisfied and produce close to the norms of the group.
2. When an individual is rewarded by the group but not by management, he will be moderately satisfied and produce close to or slightly lower than the norms of the group.
3. When an individual is rewarded by management but not by the group, he will be moderately dissatisfied and produce above the norms of the group.
4. When an individual is rewarded neither by management nor by the group, he will be the most dissatisfied and produce below the norms of the group.

This set of hypotheses grew out of a more basic proposition that the individual in the group has needs which are satisfied on the one hand by the rewards of the group (acceptance, belonging, sharing sentiments of loyalty, friendliness, and affection) and on the other by the external rewards from management that give status, job security, and pay. We proposed earlier that the lower limits of FA and the upper limits of GNS are controlled by the suprasystem, while the upper limits of FA and lower limits of GNS are controlled by the system or group itself. The above-quoted hypotheses, especially the second and the third, strongly imply this sort of mechanism. Unfortunately, some aspects of these hypotheses were not confirmed in their data. We can perhaps do no better than quote from the original report (p. 328). The findings were based on systematic observation of a manufacturing group over a period of months.

> The findings of this research showed that those individuals who were rewarded by the group (i.e., regular group members) tended to produce "on-the-line" or in conformity with the output norms. [In terms of our model, the system of forces was like that presented in Figure 8.] They were also relatively satisfied. Those individuals who were not rewarded by the group (i.e., nonregular group members) tended to deviate in output (by producing high and low) and were relatively dissatisfied. The degree to which an individual was rewarded by management showed no relationship to his level of satisfaction. Reward by management did however show some relationship to productivity among those individuals not rewarded by the group but in a direction opposite to expectations. Those individuals who were not rewarded by the group (nonregulars) tended to produce high under conditions of nonreward by management, and to produce low under conditions of reward by management.

Diagrammed for those (nonregular high-producing) members not rewarded by management, the situation looks as in Figure 10. It can be

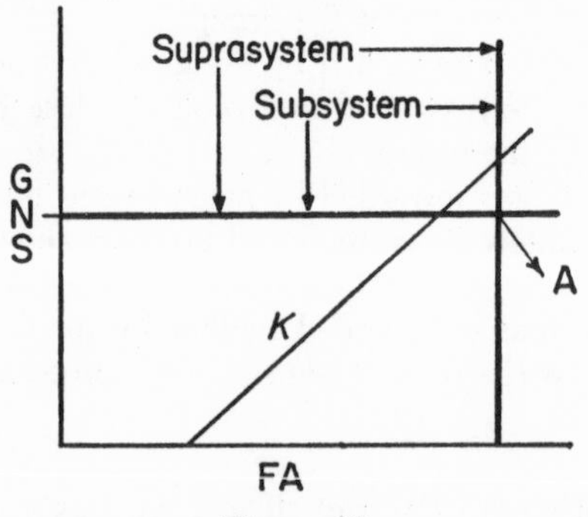

Figure 10

seen that the forces in the situation are out of balance, and one would expect such persons to provide problems primarily for other members of their work group and eventually for the management as well. The point of intersection will be driven toward the southeast corner and away from the *K* line.

In the case of the nonregular members rewarded by management but not by the group, an imbalance is found, but of a "nonnormal" sort (Figure 11). If we refer to Figure 8, we will see that the forces on the

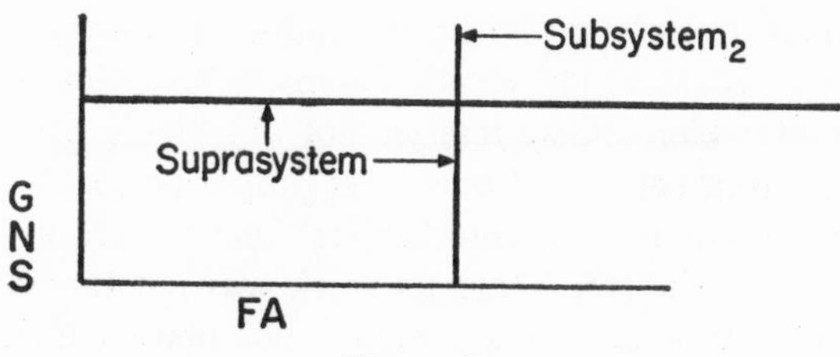

Figure 11

GNS level have been reversed; the subsystem here tends to lower GNS and the suprasystem to increase GNS. If we then overlay Figure 11 with Figure 12, thus combining the forces for all nonregular members, we get

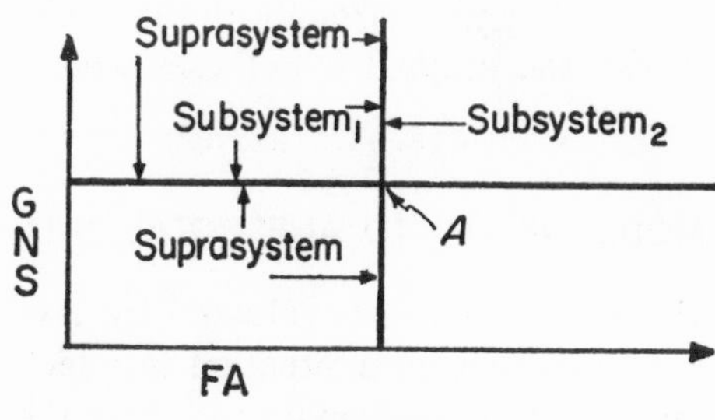

Figure 12

a picture that is clearly out of balance. It can be seen that the effects of the suprasystem on the GNS are contradictory with respect to different members of the nonregulars. The subsystem's effect on the FA level is also contradictory, with the result that the suprasystem is nearly unopposed in its pressure for greater FA, and both subsystems' "unnatural" suppression of GNS is likewise countered by uncertain forces from the suprasystem.

The original report indicates that the nonregulars (those with low GNS) came from social backgrounds that tended to predispose them to be "loners"—persons who valued individual accomplishment over group identification. Many were, indeed, hostile toward the "regulars," and to some extent toward each other. Consequently we are faced, not with a homogenous subsystem, but instead one which is composed of a "regular" subgroup and two sets of nonregulars. The fact that the nature of the tasks performed by the total set of workers was not such that one man's work depended heavily upon the accomplishments of others made it possible for the total output (i.e., the sum of individual outputs) to be acceptable to management. Had this not been the case, we would have expected the subsystem to have come into major conflict within itself and with its suprasystem.

These interpretations lend plausibility to the proposition that the maintenance inputs to a system (in social systems, GNS) provide a fundamental basis without which the system cannot effectively process the signal inputs. The apparent contradiction to this proposition in the above example of the nonregulars results from the fact that the work group was not a true subsystem in the sense that its work was not interdependent, nor did the members have in fact a common boundary which filtered both maintenance and signal inputs by the same criteria.

This exercise in translating the Zaleznik *et al.* data into our model illustrates a way in which the forces may be displayed so as to reveal their contradictory and net effects. It should be pointed out that we are making no assumptions about the relative strength of the forces, yet the direction of forces alone suggests strongly the unbalanced nature of the system and shows why the original hypotheses were not confirmed for the nonregulars.

MODEL APPLIED TO ANECDOTAL DATA

The utility of the model may be evaluated by laying it figuratively beside or beneath a case study of a situation in which an internal conflict arose. Such an exercise may demonstrate that the model possesses utility in helping to organize social phenomena as they come to us in "raw" descriptive form. This is our immediate objective. A second benefit of such an exercise is that it may give flesh and blood to some of our abstractions.

We have selected a case whose description required a book-length account (Ronken and Lawrence, 1952). We quote from the abstract with italics added and interpretations inserted in brackets.

> This is the case history of an industrial project, the story of how an entire organization felt the impact of a technological change in its factory. The technological change was the introduction of a new product (the Amicon tube); the impact of that change was on the social system in the organization—on the men who originated the design idea, on the *engineers* who had to perfect it, on the *production people* who had to absorb it into their daily routines, and on the *top management,* whose job was the administration of the change.
>
> [In what follows, we shall define the suprasystem as the management of the plant which had the responsibility of maintaining co-ordinated relations between the development engineers, industrial engineers, and production workers led by a foreman. These latter three groups we define as subsystems.]
>
> The idea for the new product originated in the "wrong" functional group, the *industrial engineers.* When management gave them the go-

ahead to experiment with their idea, no one realized that that step involved a basic change in the customary relations among the functional groups in the organization. In working out a major modification of product design, the industrial engineers were doing work which the *development engineers* customarily performed. Their activity did violence to a fundamental assumption (role) of the development engineers: that they and they alone were the technical experts on matters of design, within that company.

[The behavior of management in assigning the development task to the industrial engineers depressed the GNS level of the development group. Assuming that the latter had other work to do, the GNS/FA ratio for their subsystem therefore departed from the *K* line (Figure 8) and point *A* was to the "east."]

The ideas of each group about itself were reinforced in interaction with the other group. When the development engineers made a design suggestion which the industrial engineers rejected, the latter were confirmed in their belief that they were properly the design experts on the Amicon tube project—and that only they fully understood the new tube. The development engineers, on the other hand, saw in the rejection of their suggestion a confirmation of their belief that the industrial engineers were not qualified to handle a design problem. Gradually each group came to regard their test results more as an evaluation of the other group than as an evaluation of the product. *For the first six months of the project the two groups of engineers disliked and distrusted one another, contacted one another only rarely, and succeeded in producing no fundamental technical advancement on the product.*

[A breakdown in mutual support, possibly traceable, in the first instance, to the fact that the development group was "off line" and unable to raise its GNS to the customary level for two reasons: (a) management withheld some "considerations" input by assigning a development task to the industrial engineers, and (b) the rejection by the industrial engineers of their proffered FA, from which they might have derived some GNS. See Figure 8.]

In the meantime, with an eye to the competitive situation, top management had decided to put the new product, the Amicon tube, into production "while the remaining bugs are being ironed out," as they thought. [The plant's FA level was threatened; hence, management pushed for more FA, unbalancing the ratio for the industrial engineers.] The remaining "bugs" proved to be both more numerous and more stubborn than had at first been anticipated. But before that became clear, the foreman had been given responsibility for producing this item and for living up to some optimistic production schedules. Some of the basic assumptions of the foreman and his group can be stated as follows:

1. Our job is to produce.
2. The development engineers are to supply us with operating specifications.

3. The industrial engineers are to give us help on methods, processes, layout, etc.
4. But in the last analysis the project is our responsibility; we are the ones who get the product out.

It is obvious that these assumptions were incompatible, at certain points [(2) and (3)], with certain assumptions held by the development and industrial engineers. One of the significant aspects of these relationships was the persistence with which people maintained their assumptions about themselves in relation to others, even in the face of behavior which denied their validity [an example of the persistence of a self-image or, more generally, of the autonomy of components.]

An additional complication for the foreman was the necessity of learning how to work with new supervisors and a new group of subordinates. When the foreman experienced difficulty in communicating with his superior, he was not able to understand his subordinates' problems or to gain their spontaneous cooperation, and the work suffered. When he felt more confident of his relations upward, he administered his own group with greater skill.

[An instance of the benign or supportive suprasystem influencing the subsystem in a beneficial way, as discussed on page 150. In addition, it may not be too farfetched to imply that the positive inputs through the "considerations" channel to the industrial engineers and foreman compensated partly for deficiencies in GNS from a lack of FA.]

During such periods his operators showed considerable initiative in their work, contributed more useful suggestions, and raced with themselves and each other to increase output.

The Amicon tube, with which all these people were concerned, involved mechanical, chemical, metallurgical, and production know-how. As the unit itself had to combine these various aspects into a functioning whole, so the specialists in the plant who had expert knowledge of these aspects had to coordinate their efforts to get results on the project. Cooperation was not automatic, however; coordination was not easily achieved; the work was not effective. Six months after the project had been "put into production," not a single salable unit had been produced.

[Failure of maintenance inputs to generate sufficient GNS between and within collateral systems results in zero FA that feeds back negatively on GNS while the pressure for FA is high. Result: further deviation from *K*.]

On July 1, 1949, top management formally recognized that the Amicon tube was "in production" in name only. Responsibility for the design was turned over to the development engineers with the industrial engineers limited to help on production methods. When some of the *emotional pressures were relieved or handled* [a rise in GNS?], the people began to learn how to work together. After some months, the Amicon tube was again considered ready for production. Once again, technical matters went badly; once again the coordination of several functional groups was needed. This time their joint work was effective, and by the spring of 1950 the product had begun to return a profit to the company.

The failure of several subsystems—industrial engineers, development engineers, foreman, and workers—to have their FA accepted by other collateral systems deprived all of one customary source of GNS—their own production. In this instance we see a decrement in both FA and GNS, but in proportions that cannot be accurately assessed from the description. The model would lead us to expect that the GNS/FA ratio for each of these subunits would be "off line," but we have no way of determining whether this was true. When the management reassigned work to the development engineers, they released the downward pressure on the latter's GNS level, thereby restoring the GNS/FA ratio for that subunit to its former level. There was also a simultaneous decrement in the GNS level of the industrial engineers by reason of the reassignment and its clear message from management that they had failed. Shortly after, however, they returned to their regular work, in which they could achieve, and once again established their customary levels in both FA and GNS.

The following concluding statement of the case writers clearly indicates that the primary source of difficulty did not lie in unsolvable technical problems, nor in the skills available within the total system, but rather in the integration of these skills. The skills resided in subsystems and had to be "exchanged" across subsystem boundaries. Such exchanges could take place smoothly if the several systems maintained their appropriate ratios. Disturb one of these systems in that respect, as was done to the development engineers, and it becomes less capable of integrating with other systems.

Out of all this detail about a single new product come some uniformities which the authors believe to have implications for administering changes in other kinds of situations. The generalizations may be stated in abbreviated form as follows:

1. The technological change concerned in this study involved changes in *interpersonal relationships* in the organization.
2. It was largely around those modifications of relationship, rather than around technical change per se, that resistance arose.
3. Until the problems of relationship were at least partially resolved, progress on the technical aspects of the project was seriously impeded.
4. A critical element in the acceptance of changes was the skill of the administrator in understanding the various points of view represented and facilitating the development of *satisfying new relationships.*

This exercise in translating a descriptive account into model terms is clearly open to a number of objections, not the least of which is the charge that another model might be equally or more appropriate. On the other hand, it is offered as a demonstration that the model, as presented, can be used as a means of interpreting raw empirical observations. Were this not possible, it might be thought that a model is irrelevant as an abstract representation of groups. The generalization of the case as given by Ronken and Lawrence, especially those numbered 1, 2, and 3 directly above, are fully in accord with proposition 4.7, which says that adaptation occurs when a potentially harmful maintenance (error) (in social systems, GNS) input from the suprasystem is blocked or dissipated at the boundary or neutralized within the system. The major part of this case was an account of the failure to adapt because, in our terms, GNS was deficient.

ADAPTATION AND GROWTH

We are now in a position to deal with the relation between growth and adaptation. It is self-evident that if maintenance inputs are restricted, growth will be restricted. We have also argued that growth brings with it necessary modifications in structure which require new mechanisms for delivering maintenance inputs to the various components of the system. These new mechanisms we have called adaptations. The study by Haire (1959), previously referred to, indicated that as the business firms increased in size, the number of staff personnel grew rapidly in the early phases and then reached a stable level. He interpreted this to mean that such staff personnel were required to maintain the necessary communication links within the organization. Of course, no one could claim that all communications contribute to GNS, yet, on the other hand, communications are the vehicles whereby GNS is generated. Consequently, it appears at least plausible that the growth of the staff in Haire's studies can be interpreted as an adaptive mechanism.

The description and interpretations of the Amicon tube case further point to the importance of appropriate maintenance as a precondition for growth. It is true that the case does not deal with growth directly except as the development and introduction of a new product contributes to the growth of the organization. In this instance the GNS variable was unwittingly depressed by the actions of the suprasystem at the same time as the pressures for greater FA increased. Under these conditions, growth was inhibited.

IMPLICATIONS FOR RESEARCH ON SYSTEM ADAPTATIONS

We are still not in a position to claim that adaptation in social systems has been shown to be primarily confined to disturbances in the maintenance feedback channels. There are, moreover, important theoretical reasons why most, if not all, extant data pertaining to the question cannot provide a proof.

One needs to be reminded of the fact that, on what appear to be reasonable grounds, four sources of GNS have been postulated: (1) mutual interactions, (2) FA concomitants, (3) considerations from the suprasystem agent, (4) suprasystem constraints and inputs. In addition, (2) depends upon the degree to which the group norms accept the signal inputs as appropriate, which makes possible a fifth indirect control over GNS as a take-off from FA. (FA may be low because the task is difficult, regardless of the acceptance of the signals by the subsystem.)

If we make the further assumption that each of these sources may vary in value so that ten discriminable steps are possible for each, we then have 10^5, or 100,000, possible combinations of these inputs. Not all of these combinations will, of course, ensure the system's survival. A zero reading on all five would mean no maintenance input, and by proposition 2.16 and definition 2.7 we would have a dead or dying system. It is an empirical problem to decide what combinations above this limiting case do permit the system to function over an extended time period. However, even this work would probably require the lifetimes of several investigators.

What, then, is the implication of such a model for research strategy? Does it lead us to a blind and frustrating conclusion that social systems are so inherently complex that they defy analysis? Does the logic of the propositions based on plausible assumptions merely confirm what behavioral scientists have always claimed, namely, that our problems are far less simple than is true of the physical sciences? The situation is not quite that pointless.

The model shows why much of our past research strategy has been unfruitful and suggests an alternative. Past and current research pertaining to group effectiveness, while recognizing the multivariable nature of the problems, has been characterized by a search for a single criterion of effectiveness (output) and a pattern of contingent variables that might be predictors. In the first category, one may find various measures of production, absenteeism, scrap, sales, accidents, morale, job satisfaction, and so on. The second, or predictor variables have included quality of supervision, leadership, ambition of group members, satisfaction with the organization, wages, job security, avoidance of risk, strictness of regulations, technical competence of supervisors, and so on. These have been thrown into various kinds of statistical hoppers and analyzed to discover which ones or combinations paid off as predictors. Moreover, the vast bulk of the research has been on a "one-shot," cross-sectional design in which variability across groups provided the basis for correlational or other analyses of data. From these analyses, it has been customary to infer that if the least effective groups were changed so that they had the "predictor" characteristics of the more effective groups, the former would approximate the latter in criterion measures. It goes almost without saying that where checks have been made on these inferences, they have not been verified, nor have the predictors generally stood up in replications or cross validations. (See Pfiffner, Comrey, Beem, High, Wilson, and others, 1952; Katz, Maccoby, Gurin, and Floor, 1951; Indik, Georgopoulos, and Seashore, 1961.)

The model of a social system that we have drawn permits us to see two fallacies in the past approaches and the inferences drawn from the data. First, the conventional research designs make no provision for distinguishing between the feedback effects and the inputs themselves. True, the feedback gets intertwined with the pure inputs, but in the case of the FA output the feedback may feed into both the signal and maintenance channels and these need to be separated. The more serious fallacy in the bulk of the research lies in its cross-sectional nature, which essentially ignores the dynamic interrelationships over time among the variables that are measured.

The general systems propositions presuppose a continuing flow of information, or energy, into and out of the system. A social system survives by a continuing interaction with its sub- and suprasystems. The state of the system or the state of the inputs at any one moment has almost no meaning unless it is related to what has gone before and what comes after. To take a set of cross-sectional readings on several groups and then plot levels of "considerations" vs. output is somewhat like taking the first word from one sentence, the second word from a second sentence, and so on to form a notion of how sentences are constructed. Doing this for the last ten sentences would give: "Moreover, these almost a make with the flow with several." Clearly, what is required as a research strategy is a longitudinal design, as exemplified in case studies, but supplemented by quantitative measures taken as often as feasible. Under these conditions, one may then plot changes in parameter values and more legitimately infer the interrelationships among them. At the present time this is a possible, but not an easy, task, partly because the interruption of continuing activities for the purpose of probing satisfactions, feelings, attitudes, or whatever is disruptive in itself. In this, we run against the problem of disturbing what we wish to measure.

These considerations suggest two possibilities, both of which are in their struggling infancy. The first is the development of games that simulate organization, and the second is the more ambitious pure computer simulation. The first of these has been more often used for management training (Stewart, 1961), although Guetzkow and his colleagues have simulated international systems primarily for research purposes (Guetzkow, 1962, and Noel, 1963). In the business games, players are provided with a rich array of information pertaining to cost of plant, equipment, labor, and distribution. Decisions are required as to how they should price the product, divert resources to advertising or research, borrow capital, or reduce costs by various means. The game may be played against some preprogrammed market or against other "companies" operated competitively by other players. Although the nature of the "givens" and objectives are different in international simulations, in general principle they are similar. One instance is reported in which an airline discovered an efficient means of routing and maintaining its aircraft by means of simulating a maintenance service (Meier, 1961).

Pure computer simulations of organizations have generally been designed for research purposes to check the validity of various system models. This has already been accomplished for various models of manufacturing and distribution systems, in which easily identified unit products can be followed through various stages from their input into a manufacturing process, then are transferred to warehouses at the distributor and retailing levels, and finally to the customer. The flow from one point to another is influenced by the time delays in ordering and delivery, the capacity of the respective storage points, and anticipations of future requirements based on the rate at which the goods are flowing during given periods (cf. Forrester, 1961). Models of this system which make mathematical assumptions about the interrelationships of these variables provide the basis for a computer program that is "disturbed" by introducing a percentage increase or decrease in orders from any portion of the system. The computer is programmed to trace out the consequences of such a disturbance over an extended period and at each level of the distribution system. If the consequences are adverse, it then becomes possible to consider what corrections in assumptions or delays are needed at what point to prevent these adverse results from occurring. Thus the model and its simulated behavior may be progressively refined to bring it in accord either with what is known about the gross input-output variables or with what would be desirable in order to achieve certain specified results.

An effort in this direction, using Homans' (1961) model as a basis, has been reported by Gullahorn and Gullahorn (1963). They describe a computer flow diagram which allows not only for the cognitive evaluation of interactions between two people but also for affective responses that may contribute to or modify subsequent cognitive evaluations.

A more elaborate computer program has been developed for the IBM 7090 that simulates the interactions of several individuals, taking into account their interest in a specified issue, their attitude toward each potential conversational partner, a "given" or initial evaluation of known assertions about the issue, and a predisposition to accept or reject certain new assertions about the issue (Abelson, 1964). In addition, the "individuals" may, under specified conditions, forget certain assertions. Abelson reports that, although the program makes certain well-founded assumptions about the relations between the separate variables and the degree of correspondence of assertions with predispositions, he has not developed a model which will stand or fall in any empirical run of the computer. "When data is inconsistent with the model, there are many possible ways to make readjustments; when data is consistent with the model, it could be right for the wrong reasons" (p. 159).

Perhaps the most ambitious computer programming relevant to social organization is the Leviathan project in the Systems Development Corporation. This aspires to simulate a large-scale "productive organization," including the transformation of "raw materials" into finished products, but is governed by an associated system which operates in a fluid manner through an enormously complex set of nested and hierarchically related feedback loops. When completed, it is expected that it will provide information on the consequences of fitting together the components of a social system in one way versus another. However, the underlying model of the organization assumed for this program is not compatible with the model proposed in the foregoing pages (Rome and Rome, 1962).

Rather than start with the distinction between signal and maintenance inputs, Rome and Rome make their major distinction between the technological (manufacturing?) and governing (managerial?) systems. In the latter they include something called "social energy," which is as close to GNS as they come. The fact that a start has been made on programming social interactions that takes into account both probability functions and subroutines which simulate emotional responses is strong support for the feasibility of such computer experiments.

So far, we have been limited for a number of reasons in applying this strategy to group behavior. First, we have had few group models that even in qualitative terms approximated the requisite conditions for computer simulation. There must be at least clear stipulations of input, output, and feedback features. These have been provided in the model presented herein. Second, assumptions as plausible as possible must be made concerning the relationships among the variables. And third, the variables and their relationships must be reduced to quantitative terms that the computer may process. The second and third conditions have not, so far, been detailed to the point where generalized group behavior may be simulated. On the other hand, there appears to be no reason to believe that efforts in this direction would not be fruitful, if it is recognized that the initial runs would represent only approximations of real groups.[6]

Let us summarize the implications of the social system model. First, it reveals why previous research strategy based on cross-sectional data has failed to provide conclusions on the basis of which we can safely generalize. Second, it suggests that we must move in the direction of longitudinal studies of real groups. This line, while ultimately providing the final validation of a model, may be both costly in time and subject to the uncertainty principle. Third, it leads to the possibility of computer simulation of groups if the inputs, outputs, feedback, and their interrelations can be reduced to quantitative terms.

Finally we have called attention to some of the research implications of the model, emphasizing that it will be necessary to develop strategies which permit continuous, rather than periodic, cross-sectional measurements.

SUMMARY

The adaptation of a social system may be considered from two aspects: internal and external. The latter, we hypothesize, is a function of the levels of GNS and FA, and internal adaptability is possibly related to the ratio of these two variables. Adaptation and growth have been shown to be related to each other in that growth is limited by the adaptability of the system to maintenance inputs as well as the established roles and norms (memories) of the group.

[6] Developments in computer technology and programming are proceeding at such a rapid pace that these statements may be outdated before publication.

IX / CONFLICT BETWEEN SYSTEMS

In this development of a general systems theory, little mention has so far been made of conflict phenomena. We have instead been concerned with developing a theory of surviving systems that directs attention to the conditions which promote and account for the evolution of coalitions and symbiotic relations. In systems containing more than two components, we have emphasized feedback as it relates to growth, learning, and adaptation. The main thrust of our propositions has been to account for integration, articulation, the reduction of randomness to order and organization.

It hardly needs to be mentioned that the line of development toward order and organization is not a smooth one, no matter whether, in the long sweep of evolution, increasing order amidst complexity is the dominant characteristic. Although it might be possible within the framework of general systems theory to develop a model of "systems in conflict" that would apply to both living and nonliving systems, we shall not cast the net that far. The common-sense view of conflict is confined to living systems and is focused on individual human and group interactions. In what follows, we shall accordingly take a similar focus with references to infrahuman systems where these are appropriate. Furthermore, we shall be concerned only with an effort to specify the *conditions which precipitate conflict* rather than the strategy and management of conflict once the conflicting forces are joined. The latter area has attracted a great deal of attention—particularly from those interested in conflict resolution, simulation of international negotiations, and war-and-peace gaming (Guetzkow, 1962, and Noel, 1963). As the term *conflict resolution* suggests, these efforts—exciting and insightful as they are—start from a condition of at least incipient conflict. Our purpose in this chapter is to probe into those conditions which predate the conflict but lead, perhaps inexorably, to its exacerbation.

CONFLICT DEFINED

Why does conflict occur? This is not as simple a question as it may at first appear, particularly within the context of the systems model so far developed. We have proposed that systems are adaptable—blocking, dissipating, or neutralizing inappropriate inputs (proposition 4.7)—and further, that such systems develop co-ordinated outputs that move them in the direction of greater, rather than lesser, stability (proposition 4.8). Given these propositions, under what circumstances could conflict arise?

We have previously proposed that the variability of a system's output is limited by the structure of components and the finite number of states the system can assume (proposition 4.3). For many systems, the last of these imposes the first line of defense against inputs that would otherwise destroy the system. The skin of an organism, for instance, serves to block the invasion of antigens. Other neutralizing defenses came later. However, circumstances may be such that the boundary may be pierced. The skin may be lacerated; the national frontier may be overwhelmed; the group norms of appropriate behavior may be violated; the management of a company may disband a division; the cell wall may disintegrate under excessive pressure. In short, exogenous forces can, and sometimes do, outweigh the counterforces of a system.

The disruption of the boundary is the prelude to a destruction of the entire system, and this represents not the beginning, but the penultimate end, of conflict. For human and some infrahuman systems, the beginning of conflict occurs when there is a perception [1] of the possible disruption of the boundary. A wealth of data indicates that humans and many animals begin to take aggressive or defensive postures (both overtly and attitudinally) under conditions of threatening harm that precede the actual experience of harm.

We shall attempt to show in what follows that one class of conflicts arises out of a threatening breakdown in the internal adaptive mecha-

[1] We have deliberately avoided a treatment of perception in system terms, believing that it would require nearly a full chapter. At this point, it may be sufficient to call attention to the fact that all adaptive feedback systems, living and nonliving, must be equipped with sensors. Some of these are so designed that they respond only to proximate stimuli; others, to distant sources of energy, e.g., pressure vs. radar or light reflections. Moreover, radar–like human systems—may be so designed as to anticipate future events, such as the course of an object moving in space. Although human perception connotes more than the prediction over a short range of future events, for purposes of the present discussion this aspect of perception is assumed and will probably suffice (cf. Campbell, 1956a, 1956b).

nisms (proposition 3.6). This type of conflict is always potentially possible within growing systems which incorporate previously "autonomous"[2] subsystems. A second class of conflicts includes those in which two or more systems reach out to "capture" an additional, relatively passive but always limited, source of maintenance resources. These are conflicts involving external adaptation, as discussed in Chapter VI. The prototypes of these two classes at the national level are insurrections for the first and foreign aggression for the second.

INTERNAL CONFLICT AND GROWTH

In Chapter V the proposition was also developed that suprasystems evolving out of their subsystems may gradually gain control over the latter (proposition 5.3). Many subsystems operate relatively autonomously, as do the amoebae before they join up to form slime molds, or before the craftsman who joins a union, or before an auto-parts supplier is merged with a giant automotive manufacturer, or before a consultant joins a consulting firm. As the suprasystem requirements for specialization increase, the components become more dependent and less autonomous. In opposition to these searching, tentaclelike bonds tying the components to the suprasystem are the inherent adaptation mechanisms of the components themselves, whose net effect is to prolong the survival of the components as relatively autonomous, self-regulating, identifiable units.[3] The processes required for the expansion and integration of the suprasystem are thus potentially destructive of the subsystems' adaptive mechanisms. It is from these opposing trends that internal conflict arises.[4]

Let us carry the analysis somewhat deeper, still making use of the propositions already developed. It has been said earlier that social systems possess two outputs: formal achievement (FA) and group need satisfactions (GNS). It was hypothesized on page 119 that the stability of these two outputs was controlled in such a way that the upper limit of FA and the lower limit of GNS were under the control of the sub-

[2] No open system is, of course, completely autonomous. The term emphasizes only the system's relative autonomy.

[3] Note that previously, and on other grounds, we have argued that systems are composed of components with both attracting and repelling forces. Although we have not attempted to develop a systems model for personality in this book, a number of parallels may be found between the group-conflict model and the theories of personality proposed by Rank (1936), Murray (1938), and Harvey, Hunt, and Schroder (1961). Common to all of these and several others is a conflict between dependence on some other persons and a need for independence.

[4] It is of more than passing interest that international alliances have tended to fall apart, for instance, when France developed her own atomic "independence" and placed strains on NATO; the same thing happened also in the case of mainland China vis-à-vis its alliance with the U.S.S.R.

system, while the opposite limits were under the control of the suprasystem. It was further proposed (p. 126) that for each class of systems a certain balance between GNS and FA was necessary to ensure an optimal level of functioning. Stated in slightly different words, each type of system (work group, fraternal club, nation, political party) is characterized, among other things, by a given GNS/FA ratio, departures from which represent disturbances requiring correction to re-establish the appropriate ratio.

ORGANIZED VS. UNORGANIZED INTERNAL CONFLICT

We may now apply these propositions to the conflict situation. The "appropriate ratio" means that condition most advantageous for symbiotic relationships of a subsystem with its suprasystem. This is the condition under which both sub- and suprasystems provide mutual maintenance, not excluding maintenance from sources external to both. We display the situation in Figure 13.

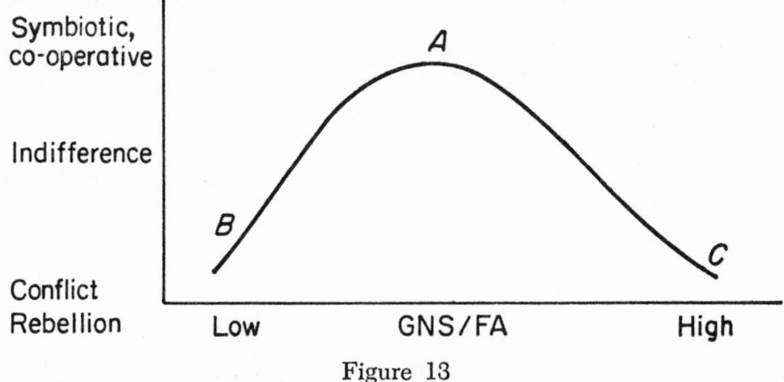

Figure 13

The shape of the curve is obviously only hypothetical. It indicates that as the GNS/FA ratio departs in either direction from some optimal value, *A*, the subsystem moves in the direction of indifference and then conflict or rebellion. When the ratio is some low value, *B*, we propose that the nature of the rebellious conflict is characterized by a fragmented opposition in which the members of the subsystem are poorly organized among themselves and are mainly galvanized into action by the source of their discomfort. This is mob action.

The right side of the curve, where GNS is high relative to FA, represents those situations in which the initial discontents stimulate the subsystem members to coalesce more tightly than under the optimal conditions. The early stages of such a conflict in an industrial setting might be an organized slowdown. GNS may remain nearly constant, but the

FA denominator decreases. At the extreme high values the conflict is characterized by a high degree of group solidarity with little or no FA delivered to the suprasystem. The right tail of the curve represents the organized rebellions.

One should not assume that the curve in Figure 13 in any way represents the course of conflict over a time span. Neither is it meant to suggest that a system in conflict, represented at point *B*, needs to pass through the peak of the curve before it can take on the characteristics of a conflict, represented at point *C*. Instead, the early stages of a violent conflict are often poorly organized, but, as time goes on, the dissonant components come together to offer an organized opposition. If there is an intermediate stage, it is one of relative quiescence in which indifference with respect to the domination of the suprasystem more properly describes the situation rather than co-operation.

The fluctuations of the GNS/FA ratio over a time span are shown in Figure 14. The ratio is shown to oscillate between arbitrary limits deter-

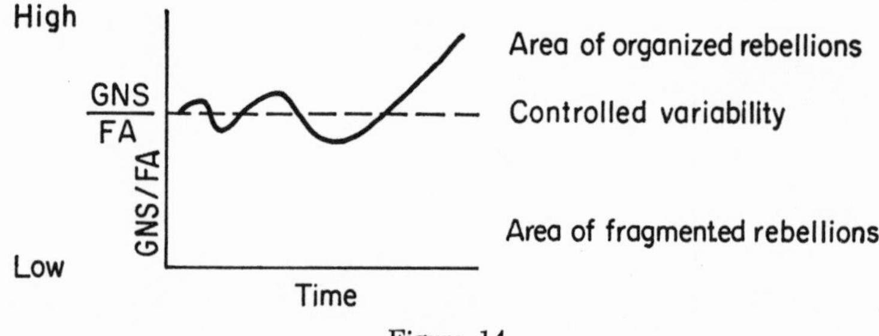

Figure 14

mined by the respective controls residing in the sub- and suprasystems, as indicated on page 119. It is obvious that we will have a high and increasing ratio of GNS to FA if GNS increases or FA decreases. Now, in an adaptive system, the upper limit of GNS and the lower limit of FA are both within the control of the suprasystem. Contrariwise, the ratio will be prevented from falling below a given level if the subsystem discharges its stabilizing function by controlling both the upper limit of FA and the lower limit of GNS. We can therefore deduce that if either system loses control of its respective outputs, the system will move outside its tolerable adaptive limits.

It can be seen that if the suprasystem loses control of the upper limit of GNS or the lower limit of FA, the subsystem will move toward an organized rebellion. On the other hand, if the subsystem loses control of the upper limit of FA or the lower limit of GNS, the ratio drops, with the result that the conflict moves toward a fragmented, moblike insurrection. In the first instance, it is the subsystem which gains organized revolutionary dimensions; in the second, the suprasystem itself may be destroyed by the fragmentation of its necessary components, or at least must deal simultaneously with a large number of separate and unrelated dissonant elements.

Supporting Data

It is not our purpose within this book to carry the analysis through the alternations between organized and disorganized conflicts. The earlier chapters have been devoted to the mechanisms whereby disorder may gradually be brought to a stage of order. However, the following quotation from Stanley Loomis' exciting and informative *Paris in the Terror: June 1793–July 1794*[5] (p. 12) provides an interesting historical backdrop for further discussion:

> Pre-Revolutionary France had presented the curious spectacle of a people technically at the mercy of medieval monarchic law enjoying freedom in a way that would not for an instant be tolerated by many of today's republican societies, where conformity of idea as well as manner is often considered the ideal. An ill-administered, ineffectual tyranny induces a climate hospitable to ideas in which are planted and nourished the seeds that grow into revolution.
>
> It is ironic that of all countries in Europe, France was the only one that could have had a revolution—not because she groaned under the lash of tyranny, but on the contrary because she tolerated and even invited every conceivable dissension and heresy. Restlessness, a passion for novelty and the pursuit of excitement were everywhere in the air. They were the fruits of idleness and leisure, not of poverty.[6]

In the barren language of our model, Loomis' synoptic description fits the case of a suprasystem losing control of both GNS and FA limits—resulting in an organized revolution that culminated in a year of terror and near national suicide. Although lacking precise empirical data, Davies (1962) argues that revolutions are likely when a period of objective economic and social development is followed by a sudden, sharp reversal. The expectations of the general population, based on a period of relatively steady growth, are then unfulfilled; or again, in the terms of our model, the FA output drops, bringing about deviation in the GNS/FA ratio. Davies says, "There appears to be no sure way to avoid revolution short of an effective, affirmative, and continuous response on

[5] From *Paris in the Terror, June 1793–July 1794,* by Stanley Loomis. Copyright © 1964 by Stanley Loomis. Published by J. B. Lippincott Company.

[6] These conditions bear a striking resemblance to those which accompanied the "long, hot summer" riots of 1967–1968.

the part of the established governments to the almost continuously emerging needs of the governed."

Davies' reference to the "almost continuously emerging needs of the governed" is reminiscent of Katona's (1964) principle of habituation, which he derived from more than two decades of surveying the buying plans and proclivities of the American public. In effect, Katona believes that people react to news about the state of the economy against a background of expectations. Increasing prices for given commodities and rising standards of living become accepted as normal during some periods. Under these circumstances, plateaus in the economic indexes are often interpreted as danger signals. We have here something very like Helson's adaptation level.

For those less impressed by the interpretations of a single case by a single historian or the speculations of a sociologist and an opinion-taking psychologist, we are fortunate in having a systems analysis of disintegrating "empires" that begins with a set of definitions somewhat in the same manner as we have adopted herein. Merritt (1963) draws a major distinction between the direction of (a) policy decisions (downward from supra- to subsystem) and the direction of (b) loyalties, (c) communication, and trade balances (upward from sub- to suprasystem). The policy decisions he defines as the "distribution of power and income, the establishment of the principles of legitimacy, the use of force, the allocation of scarce resources, the distribution of honors and other symbols of social status." This appears to be analogous to the inputs from the suprasystem in Figure 6 and is a mixture of exogenous constraints (force, power, income), signal inputs (allocation of scarce resources, principles of legitimacy), and considerations (honors and social status). Loyalties are defined by Merritt as the "sense of community"—an awareness that the members are interdependent. Again, this is at least comparable to our maintenance inputs that, for the social level, we have labeled group need satisfactions. Trade and communication for Merritt pertain to the flow of goods, mail, and other interpersonal exchanges and habits of communication. This definition contains elements that look like our FA variable (trade) and others that look like the "pick-off" from FA of GNS feedback. (See Figure 6 and Merritt, 1963, p. 92.)

Merritt's model of the functioning empire assumes that the balance of exchanges in the third area (FA) is in favor of the empire rather than its colonies, and this, along with other conditions such as the absence of reciprocally balanced exchanges of policy decisions and loyalties, makes for an unstable system. The instability is further compounded by the minimal exchanges of any sort between the subsystems.

The model suggests that disintegration is promoted by the failure of the empire to supply the colonies with adequate status, rewards, and scarce resources while simultaneously requiring unilaterally an overbalance of goods and services. ("No taxation without representation.") In the framework of Figure 6, it appears that inputs through channels 3 and 4 were deficient, with the consequence that the GNS output and feedback were likewise reduced. Furthermore, in terms of our GNS/FA ratio hypothesis, that ratio suffers a decrement leading to the expectation of a disorganized rebellion. Notice that in this translation of Merritt's model the emphasis is first on the reduction of the maintenance inputs and their repercussions. Essentially the same phenomena occurred in the industrial case study in Chapter VIII of the Amicon tube, although the specific "messages" in the two cases sent from the suprasystem were obviously different and the real-life circumstances were far from similar in both time and extent. For both instances, the initial disturbances are found in the maintenance channels, and from these flow adverse consequences that impede the production of FA. The "less than expected" output of FA feeds back to the signal inputs that call for increased FA, which further imbalances the system.

The Merritt model helps us to understand the parasitic growth and later disintegration of several empires, particularly the Anglo-American relations during the eighteenth century, and to some extent the more recent disintegration of the French and Dutch empires. Although Merritt does not emphasize the applicability of his model to the reverse development of subsystems joining to form a "more perfect union," it has this possibility.

The Feierabends (1966), a husband-and-wife team, have provided additional support for the main theme of our analysis. Making use of national statistics, extensive descriptions of national polities, and historical records, they developed, among others, indexes of internal instability and the permissiveness-coerciveness of the polities. On the basis of such data for eighty-four nations, they found a product-moment correlation of .41 between the coerciveness of the polities and internal instability for the period 1955–1961. However, they had hypothesized that a strongly repressive coercion from the suprasystem would prevent dissonant elements from expressing their displeasures, while permissiveness would not generate protests and overt instabilities. Medium levels of coercion, on the other hand, would arouse frustrations and yet not be sufficiently strong to prevent instabilities. This curvilinear hypothesis was supported in the Feierabend data, as represented by an eta of .72. Moreover, if one examines the criteria employed in rating nations on the permissive-coercive dimension, they pertain, as was true of the Merritt study, largely to communications from sub- to suprasystem (civil rights, effective public opinion, frequency of elections, functioning of legislative bodies, respect for constitutional procedures, and so on).

Thus the Merritt and Feierabend studies converge in finding the excessive dominance of supra- over subsystems at the expense of the latter is the central issue in internal conflicts. It is worth emphasizing also that this issue is inextricably tied up with the growth phenomena of systems. For systems to grow and remain viable, it is essential that the suprasystem gain such an ascendancy. Building on our proposition 2.14 and the discussion on pages 133–134, it is clear that such growth may occur only if the components maintain their identities (i.e., boundaries) and enjoy reciprocal exchanges with the suprasystem and with each other. Internal conflict develops when this proposition is violated.

CONFLICT BETWEEN COLLATERAL SYSTEMS

We have emphasized that internal conflict is a growth-related phenomenon and represents a breakdown in the adaptive mechanisms. We propose that external conflict is also growth-related, but in a different sense. It is axiomatic that as systems increase in size, their maintenance must also increase. If one assumes that the internal adaptations to growth are adequately made, there remains the problem of gaining access to further sources of maintenance to sustain the growth process. When growing collateral systems find themselves in competition for a common maintenance source, we have a condition on the brink of conflict.

Let us begin the analysis of these conflicts by looking briefly at the static model proposed by Boulding (1962) and the dynamic models of conflict developed by Richardson (1960). Both start from a basic assumption that two parties seek an advantage over their respective opponents. This is less evident in the Richardson models, which start with a degree of hostility attributed to each contestant, provoked no matter how. Behind this hostility lies Boulding's explicit assumption that each is attempting to occupy a behavior "space" [7] that cannot be occupied by both simultaneously. Following Boulding, we diagram the situation in Figure 15. The behavior spaces *A* and *B* represent not the present posi-

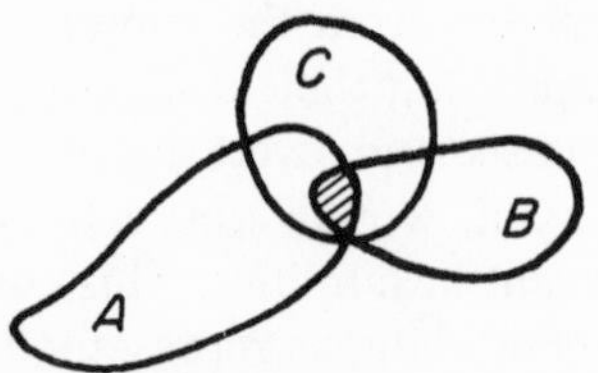

Figure 15

tion of each party but the behavior possibilities open to the respective parties. The shaded area within the dotted boundary represents the por-

[7] This term is used in the same sense in which Kurt Lewin (1951) defined it.

tion of the field in which the interests of the two parties may come into direct conflict. Although Boulding carries the analysis of this model further to define a bargaining area, making certain assumptions about the order of preference each party may have for each of the points in the space, our main point is that the conflict is not between *C* and *A* or between *C* and *B*, but rather between *A* and *B* concerning *C*.

What might *C* be in any real situation? For competing firms, the shaded portion of *C* is customers; for political parties, voters; for warring nations, strategic positions; for family members, the use of their only automobile; for hungry pelicans circling over the surf, the fish; for members of the executive suite, the presidency; for the contesting blocks of nations, the loyalties of nations "uncommitted."

This class of conflicts has different characteristics from those of the first class, which include protests, riots, insurrections, rebellions against the controls of a suprasystem that is extending what, for it, is its integrative power over subsystems already somewhat dependent. Conflicts between collateral systems pertain to limited resources, markets, prestige that each covets. The differences between these two classes are diagrammed in Figure 16. In Figure 16(a), subsystems *C* and *D* are

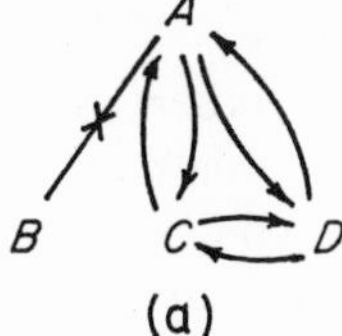

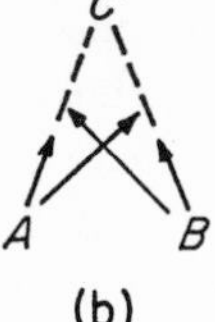

Figure 16

linked with suprasystem *A* and with each other by mutually supportive exchanges. Subsystem *B*, however, is at loggerheads with *A* to the extent that *A* is attempting to generate a bond, but is being resisted by *B*. In Figure 16(b), the contending parties are attempting to block each other from attaining a third resource.

Suppose that we amplify the details of Figure 16(b) to see how the model of two systems such as *A* and *B* would look when placed in a conflict situation. The essential features of each system will be the same as those presented in Figure 6, simplifying the details on the input side but detailing the connections with the community, *C*, which we left vaguely defined in the earlier diagram.

The meaning of Figure 17 can perhaps be understood better if we assume that it represents two firms, *A* and *B*, in a competitive relationship. The dotted area, *C*, represents the community (not the neighborhood) in which they compete. From the upper portion of *C*, they draw

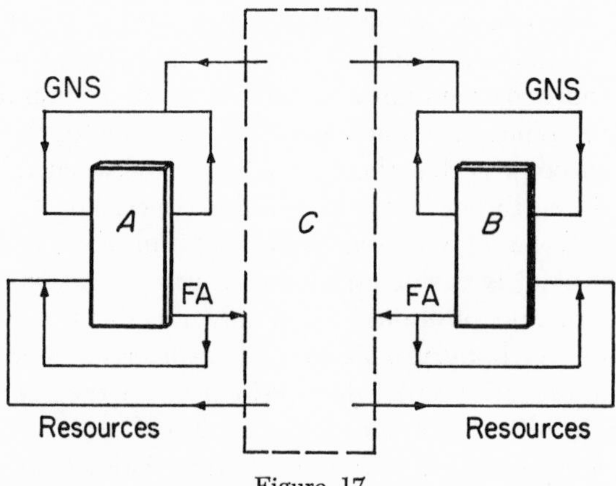

Figure 17

status, reputation, and good will. It is an uncontestable fact that a firm's reputation for financial responsibility, reliable service to consumers, considerate personnel policies, and other intangibles have important bearing on its access to the resources of the community. Furthermore, these matters are a source of group pride in and of themselves. This is no less true at the international level, as witnessed by the space race, which is sometimes justified on the grounds that the winner will thereby gain an advantage in the competition for the loyalties of other nations.

The FA inputs to *C* represent the competition for markets, the sales of each firm's goods or services. These likewise contribute to the firm's ability to draw from the community those tangible supplies essential for its continued operations. As indicated above, this FA input to *C* also feeds back through the community to the GNS channel.

As pictured, there are two kinds of "returns" each system may "drain" from *C* and one channel in which the outputs of the two systems may be in direct opposition.[8] Such an initial orientation toward *C* precludes the possibility of any mutual supporting exchanges between *A* and *B*, and the stage is set for a struggle. With this more detailed picture of the situation as shown in Figure 16(b), let us examine the precipitating circumstances, given two more assumptions: (1) that the systems are composed of persons capable of perceiving and anticipating events at

[8] This distinction bears a resemblance to that proposed by Mack and Snyder (1957), who argued that conflict may be provoked by two kinds of scarcity—position and resource. The first arises when the two systems attempt to occupy a single location, perform identical roles, or serve the same function where only one role function is possible, e.g., president. Resource scarcity is a condition in which supplies of desired objects are limited, so that neither of the parties may have all they want or need.

least over a short time span; (2) that *C* is the only, or major, source of inputs for *A* and *B* beyond those needed to maintain the status quo.[9]

Given the anticipatory capability of the system, when *B* perceives—correctly or incorrectly—that *A* is moving toward *C*, *B* will anticipate that its own future welfare may be in jeopardy and will take such steps to protect that future by moving toward *C*, or by directly blocking *A*'s movement. This movement will be perceived by *A* in the same manner as *B* originally perceived *A*, and the conflict is joined in an escalating fashion. This may occur before either is, in fact, denied access to *C*.

Without the anticipatory perceptions, the conflict would commence with experience of harm and would probably be resolved quickly. This is by no means a profound deduction. The Cold War is a current example of just such a conflict, stimulated and maintained by anticipatory perceptions. The significance of the deduction lies in the fallibility of the perceptions and their implied predictions, which may lead to unwarranted anticipatory defensive or aggressive actions. A mistaken perception on either side may lead to an unnecessary escalation of conflict; or, if one side fails to anticipate early enough the moves of the other, *C* will be "captured" to the eventual disadvantage of the misperceiver.[10]

Some evidence of this phenomenon and also the postulated competition for position or limited resources is found in an analysis of Soviet and American views of each other's major foreign policy goals. Singer (1964) analyzed the contents of three authoritative "elite" publications reflecting the policies in each of these countries during the period extending from May, 1957, through April, 1960. Each attributed to the

[9] It is of some relevance that Ash (1951) postulated a "constant power curve" of maximum security which rises ever more steeply as reserves are depleted. His thesis is that a country's desperation increases as its reserves approach a vanishing point.

[10] This model bears a number of similarities to the "World Politics Game" developed by McClelland (1959; quoted in Brody, 1963, pp. 675–676) for the purpose of simulating the international behavior of states. Decision makers representing two or more opposing states compete for "target regions" in a series of diplomatic-military moves. The states are free to pursue several different kinds of strategies—aggressive, passive —or they may back a "United World movement." It is, furthermore, of interest that McClelland found it necessary to provide for two classes of capabilities in each state, basic and military. In the Northwestern University "Internation Simulation Game," each nation is provided with prototype variables of capacity, including public opinion, consumer demands, military level, economic level, and decision latitude. From the published account, it is not possible to classify these with great confidence, but one might hazard the guess that the "economic and military levels" are roughly equivalent to what we have called FA, while "public opinion and consumer demands" are at least aspects of GNS viewed as bonds within any nation. "Decision latitude" seems to be the freedom of the central decision maker to manipulate the other two given capacities in dealing competitively with other nations. This appears to be analogous to the adaptive capacity that, in our model as well as in this simulation, is a function of the levels of both GNS and FA (see Brody, 1963, pp. 699–712).

other, with about the same frequency (24 per cent and 31 per cent), the aim of world domination. Alternatively, each saw the other's policies as designed to retain and expand its spheres of influence also with about the same frequency (73 per cent and 68 per cent). However, when considering its own motivations and the criteria influencing its own foreign policy decisions, each believed it was guided by certain moral principles (73 per cent and 79 per cent). Secondarily, they considered the gain or loss in vital national interests, or how the nonaligned countries would view the act. Thus each saw the other but not themselves as threatening. The value of this analysis is heightened by the fact that the publications from which the data were drawn (*The New York Times; Pravda;* U.S. State Department *Bulletin; Kommunist; Foreign Affairs,* the U.S. publication; and *International Affairs,* a comparable journal published in the U.S.S.R.) were sources largely uncontaminated by outright propaganda. Furthermore the data were "unobtrusive" in the sense that they were abstracted from the sources rather than just produced by respondents for purposes of study.

Figure 17 permits us to deduce further that external conflict may be in terms of a struggle to feed FA into *C* or to "drain" *C* of resources and maintenance, or both. Among competing firms, both are probably involved, although the initial struggle often pertains to the FA channel with subsequent feedback drains on both the resources and maintenance sides. At the international level, during the present era, the situation is similar, although this has not been the case formerly. The relatively affluent nations since World War II have been competing in the export of foreign aid to the less developed nations, with the anticipation that the new independent nations will reciprocate by channeling their resources and loyalties (maintenance) to that country which wins in the export of aid. Thus competition in the FA channel feeds back via the maintenance route.

It has been pointed out by others that this kind of international competition represents a major turning point in the nature of international conflict. Prior to World War II, the struggles were largely confined to draining resources from colonial areas for the enhancement of the dominant powers. For several hundred years, the growth of nations had required material resources from beyond their immediate national boundaries. Hitler's cry for *Lebensraum* was one such example of justifying foreign expansion—a justification that had previously carried a species of historical approval. So long as such expansions did not encroach upon the boundaries of other colonial holdings, there was small likelihood of a serious confrontation. Africa, Southeast Asia, the subcontinent of India, the Near East, South America, and even North America were colonized with relatively little conflict compared with the wars that rent Europe prior to the fifteenth century.

Some historians have argued that tacit agreements among the dominant powers on "spheres of influence" during the century between the battle of Waterloo and World War I may go a long way toward accounting for the relative absence of major international conflict in that period. The Monroe Doctrine, a unilateral declaration of the United States' sphere of influence, is a concrete and familiar example.

In this broad-brush, oversimplified historical reference, we are emphasizing that intersystem conflicts may arise out of the competition for resources when the expanding system boundaries begin to approach those of other expanding boundaries. When these "touch" and remain relatively resistant to change, further areas from which resources may be drained are unavailable.

Subsequently, intersystem conflicts under these circumstances shift from the struggle merely to drain or exploit *C* in ever greater amounts to feeding into *C* greater amounts of FA. We are not implying that the export of FA is wholly altruistic. It is evident that with foreign aid goes an envelope of political philosophy and an expectation that the receiving country will eventually develop closer dependence on the donor. The fact that many recipients of FA have discarded the envelope from both the U.S.A. and the U.S.S.R. while retaining their contents does not deter the donors from continuing the competition, partly because the system provides no other ready channel for competition. The manufacturer who gives out free samples of his product in the hope that he will thus gain the recipients as steady customers operates on the same principle, although in the latter case other specific means are available through competition in quality, service, or price.

It would, of course, be a mistake to leave this model with the implication that *C* is completely passive in the conflict between *A* and *B*. The customers for which the firms compete, the uncommitted nations for whose allegiance the major nations compete, the students for whom academic departments compete, the funding agencies for which universities compete, are not indifferent victims. So long as *C* in any particular instance is composed of people who are to some extent integrated into a system, they—like other systems—tend to resist maneuvers which would destroy their autonomy. The American Indians resisted the French, English, and Spanish invaders, yet the major confrontations were among the invaders. The potential customers of competing firms are not indifferent; through the mechanisms of public regulatory agencies, they protect themselves from some forms of exploitation by any of the competitors. Private and public funding agencies contributing to universities require detailed information on the merits of appeals for grants and support. These relationships, upon examination, turn out to be governed by the principles pertaining to the development or inhibition of symbiosis (Chapters IV and V). It is only when a second (third, fourth, and so on) system begins to maneuver to gain a portion of *C*'s resources that competition enters the picture, and it is then that the *A* and *B* systems must be open to input signals emanating from each other as well as from *C*. The conflict begins when either *A* or *B* perceives the other as potentially threatening its own unstable relation with *C*.

In these and other examples of competition which may lead to intense conflict, the major struggle occurs at the point of contact between the systems within the area labeled *C*.

One final point of explication with respect to the model. In the previous chapter, we proposed that a system's adaptation to external disturbances is a function of both its FA and its GNS, perhaps in the form:

$$A = \sqrt{(\text{GNS})^2 + (\text{FA} - e)^2}$$

If this hypothesis is temporarily assumed to hold, it follows that if system *A* has a greater GNS and FA than *B*, the "defeat" of *A* in a struggle for *C* will be less disastrous than if *B* were defeated. That is to say, if one system has a greater margin of surplus outputs beyond that required for survival, the failure to gain additional sources of maintenance and resources or to find additional outlets for its FA will be less disturbing than for a system operating closer to its survival level. This is to some extent a circular inference, which rests on the validity of the first hypothesis of a relation between the combination of FA and GNS, for which we have little empirical evidence.

It is not our purpose in this chapter to go beyond the distinction between internal and external conflict. From what has already been presented, it is clear that the system-to-system relations in the latter are far different from those involving internal conflict, where the issues do not revolve around the capturing of limited resources but rather the autonomy of the subsystems vs. their integration into, and control by, a suprasystem.

Supporting Arguments

Some empirical support for this distinction may be found in Rummel's (1963) analysis of conflict within, and between, nations. After reviewing some twenty-four earlier studies, he concluded that they failed to converge on any common dimension characteristic of conflict in and by itself. That is to say, the sources of conflict could not be attributed to any common concept, such as aggressiveness, economic deprivation, political ambition, clash of ideologies, or similar common-sense "causes."

He proceeded to define nine measures of domestic conflict (number of assassinations, general strikes, presence of guerrilla warfare, major governmental crises, purges, riots, revolutions, antigovernment demonstrations, all forms of domestic violence that resulted in death) and thirteen measures of foreign conflict (number of antiforeign demonstrations, negative sanctions, diplomatic protests, severed diplomatic relations, expulsion of ambassadors, of lesser diplomatic officials, threats, military action short of war, troop movements, wars, mobilizations, accusations, and all forms of foreign conflict that resulted in killing). The frequencies of each of these measures were factor-analyzed for seventy-seven countries, and "showed a clear separation of domestic and foreign conflict into distinct dimensions" (p. 17). The first factor Rummel labeled *aggressiveness;* it had high (>.60) factor loadings on seven measures of foreign conflict, while none of the domestic measures exceeded .24. The second factor he labeled *instability,* and the high (>.54) loadings were confined to those among the domestic conflict measures, with none of the foreign measures exceeding .21. Although labels for factors are at best arbitrary, it is nevertheless an interesting coincidence that Rummel's labels serve remarkably well to describe the two forms of conflict diagrammed in Figure 16. Rummel found further that the measures of domestic conflict, when inserted in regression equations, were not predictive of measures of foreign conflict, or vice versa. Moreover, the nations that ranked high in domestic turmoil, revolution, and subversion were (with the exception of France) not among those involved to a major degree in foreign conflicts.[11] (The *r*'s were in the .26 to .31 range.)

These data are entirely consistent with the model proposed. The two classes of conflict occur in different systems and their expressions take different forms. Rummel found that the correlation of threats and wars was .55, and protests correlated .51 with wars, whereas neither of these correlated to any significant degree with incidence of domestic conflict. The data suggest that at least the threats and protests rather regularly precede the outbreak of wars, but obviously are not the essential causes. His intercorrelation for domestic conflict, although high, provides no clear suggestions of the precipitating or contributing causes. This is merely because the possible causal variables were not included in the analysis.

Although Rummel does not carry his analysis backward to the instigat-

[11] The Feierabends (1966), using data similar to Rummel's, drawn from fifty-three nations for the period 1955–1961, found a moderately strong correlation (.49) between internal instability and external aggression. Although this finding tempers Rummel's conclusions, some differences in statistical treatment and in the basic data defining the parameters may account for the discrepancy. In any event, the Feierabend findings are not contradictory to Rummel's.

ing conditions for both types of conflict, our model provides a heuristic device which may be of assistance in speculating about such conditions. In the first class of conflicts, the instigations are hypothesized to be an imbalance in the GNS/FA ratio among one or more subsystems for whatever reason; while in the second class, the trigger is the threat of losing sources of either or both maintenance and signal input.

FRUSTRATION AND CONFLICT

It has often been observed that things which are different are also alike. The two classes of conflict so carefully discriminated in the preceding pages have some similarities. In neither class were we able, purely on the basis of deductions from system propositions, to account fully for the turning point in the relations between sub- and suprasystems or for development of hostility and destructive aggression in the competition of collateral systems. It is, after all, true that not all growing and expanding systems suffer an internal rebellion, nor do all competitive contests run an inevitable course that culminates in violence. We will attempt to show in what follows that, in both forms of conflict involving people, the feature which converts the adjustive processes into a fight is the emergence of frustration and its accumulation within at least one system to a critical level. Conflict cannot be accounted for solely in terms of the relations between systems, but must, according to this notion, include some account of the systems' states.

We should first of all note that frustration is not a necessary concomitant of anticipatory responses. Airborne radar systems designed to track a moving target do so by "locking on" and computing (anticipating) the future position of the target. They may be so designed that if the airborne pursuing radar system and the target are on a collision course, the lock will automatically break and another control system will take over, thus diverting the pursuer in a "safe" direction. Such a nonliving system exhibits anticipatory behavior, yet it would be ridiculous to ascribe frustration to it.

On the other hand, the famous studies by Maier, his colleagues, and others (Maier, 1942, 1949; Maier, Glaser, and Klee, 1940) demonstrated that frustration is a necessary concept to account for certain kinds of nonadaptive behavior in rats and presumably other infrahumans. How far down the hierarchy of biological systems one still finds frustration is perhaps a matter of definition. The determination of the limiting level may be an interesting, but not an important, problem for our purposes. It is sufficient merely to assume as a definition that *when the anticipatory outputs (responses) of a living system are blocked and negative feed-*

back signals are delivered to the system, the state of the system is disturbed in a certain way.[12]

When human beings (either individually or in groups) are the systems under study and the blocking circumstances are such as to inhibit many other attempted anticipatory responses, the disturbed state is reported as frustration. Implied in this definition is the proposition that the greater the number of blocked alternative responses, the greater will be the frustration.

The above definition agrees in substance with one proposed by Berkowitz (1962), with one omission. Berkowitz, following Brown and Farber (1951), posits not merely outputs (responses) but also drives which may be frustrated, leading to anger. There seems to be no need to make the assumption of a number of differently categorized states within a system with their attendant difficulties of definition. The state concept is both general and specific enough to account for the alternative outputs under either the same or different input patterns. As we have indicated before, the superior capacities for communication between humans make it possible for us to report on our own internal states, though with imperfect accuracy. To confound these imperfections with discreet definitions of anger, pleasure, rage, disgust, etc., may be reaching for a misleading level of descriptive accuracy, as well as discriminations which are unnecessary (cf. Rogers, 1963). We take the position that when outputs are repeatedly rejected by a suprasystem with attendant negative feedback signals, the system is disturbed; and when humans are the system under study in this situation, they frequently report this disturbance as frustration.

What is the connection between frustration and aggressive behavior? We propose, along with Dollard and his colleagues (1939), Stagner (1956), and a long list of others, that whatever the nature of this disturbed state is in hormonal, neural, or other physiological terms, it is a necessary prelude to aggressive behavior. Moreover, again following Berkowitz, such aggressions may occur as thoughts, fantasies, or symbolic behavior as well as overt actions. These are the specifics of the general principle that the component relations are not in their accustomed pattern. When the blocks to behavior are attributed to some other system (physical barriers, other social or living systems), the situation is such as to increase the probability of aggressive, destructive outputs against the blocks.

[12] It will be recalled that Campbell (1956a) conceptualized perceptions as anticipatory responses that, in the higher order of animals, including man, may be substituted for overt trial-and-error responses. Moreover, in computers, an instruction that is inappropriate for a given component will either be rejected, and the processing will cease, or the program may continue with an output that is entirely irrational.

The last paragraph implies correctly that not all frustrations necessarily result in aggressions. We need not here review the literature, which shows that frustrations may result in other alternative responses such as apathy, retreats, denials, compensation, or constructive problem solving. On the other hand, it does assume that, without the development of frustrations to some as yet unspecified level of intensity in one of the systems, relations between systems will remain adaptive. This means that in the competition for scarce sources of maintenance, or in the jockeying for mutually supportive relations, the otherwise adaptive process is converted to aggression as frustrations mount in intensity.

We have emphasized in the previous paragraph that frustration may occur in only one of the competing systems. Buss (1961) pointed out that aggressions may occur in response to attacks or to noxious conditions, but even these two classes of inputs will not inevitably be followed by aggressions. An attack may provoke passive resistance, retreat, resignation, or a stoic acceptance of the attack, much as Hitler's army was accepted in the Sudetenland in 1938. Although Buss declares (pp. 38–39) that frustrations are not necessarily involved in aggressive responses to attacks, he does not suggest any mechanisms whereby an aggressive response is selected from among the other possibilities. We see therefore no reason for abandoning Miller's position (1941) that "the occurrence of aggression always presupposes frustration [at least as] a useful first approximation of a working hypothesis."[13] An attack may be initiated by one party out of his frustrations, and the counteraggression, rather than retreat or stoic acceptance, is mounted because the initial attack generates frustrations that in the view of the victim can be dissipated by such actions. Singer's data, referred to on page 174, are consistent with this view.

With the recent popularization of territoriality (Ardrey, 1966) as a contributing factor in animal conflicts, one might consider whether frustration is involved in such situations. (See also McNeil, 1965.) The essence of the territorial doctrine developed by Ardrey with delightful but not always persuasive literary skill affirms that virtually all species, including man, protect their "turf" against all strangers and will attack when that territory is invaded. Ardrey refers approvingly to the Dollard, Doob, *et al.*, frustration-aggression hypothesis, but does not make much of it. The view advanced here is that while the defender may not be frustrated prior to his defensive aggressions, the invader is. Otherwise, the latter would have no reason to move out of his territory. This, of

[13] A closely allied hypothesis has been proposed by Brehm (1966), which affirms that "if a specific behavioral freedom of a person is eliminated by impersonal events, he will experience reactance and subsequently will see increased attractiveness in the eliminated behavior."

course, does not rule out the possibility that once a defensive counter-aggression is mounted, it may not convert into an expansionist aggression by reason of the immediate arousal of frustrations generated by the initial attack.

It was Maier (1942) who extended the frustration concept as a helpful tool in accounting for the development of social movements. He pointed out that those which are militantly aggressive focus on the frustrations of their members, while other social movements appear to be positively and rationally oriented toward achieving certain identifiable goals.

Berkowitz (1962, pp. 167ff.) offers the following further conditions as necessary ancillary circumstances which encourage conflict at the group level: (1) The opposing group must be "visible," easily identifiable. (2) There must be some contact. This is not limited to physical contact (e.g., U.S.A. and U.S.S.R.), but may include "perceptual" or cognitive contact, where the behavior of one is known to the other. (3) Some differences between the customary behavior patterns of the two groups help to promote conflict. The first two of these are circumstances, in addition to frustrating competition, that appear to be necessary and sufficient to set the stage for aggression.

Pruitt's Version of Richardson's Model

A theoretical contribution to a generalized understanding of conflict has been offered by Pruitt (1967), who used Richardson's mathematical model of the causes and origins of wars (1960a, b) as his point of departure. The central idea of both models is that each of the contending parties reacts similarly to the actions of the other in a spiraling fashion. Figure 18 displays one such pattern of interactions.

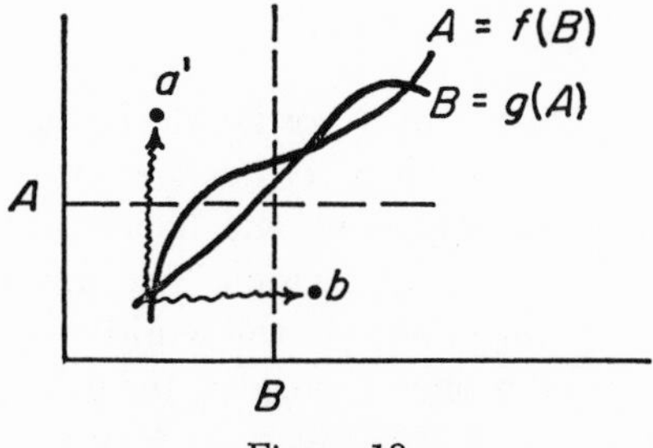

Figure 18

The co-ordinates of the figure may represent *A*'s and *B*'s actions to (1) improve their export of FA, (2) drain maintenance from some third system (Figure 17), or, as Richardson proposed, (3) increase their military resources or power. Other similar variables could be used as well. Both Richardson and Pruitt draw a number of deductions from this model, some of which do, and some do not, fit with our own. On the other hand, if the curves are seen as representing the usual response paths of each party as a function of the other's action, it is reasonable to assume that the area between the shaped curves is the area of adaptive responses. The crossover points represent conditions of maximum stability in the relations of the two systems.[14] Pruitt points out that a major move by *B* (represented by the wavy line) to a position greatly to its advantage beyond some critical level (represented by the dotted line) will stimulate *A* to do likewise if the action persists and the position is maintained. Areas beyond the dotted lines Pruitt calls "points of no return." In more psychological terms, the dotted line west of *b′* is *A*'s frustration-tolerance level; the line south of *a′* is *B*'s frustration-tolerance level. When either of these levels is exceeded, the conflict may be joined.

In view of the deductions which have been developed earlier in this chapter, it would seem that Pruitt's "points of no return," rather than being defined by orthogonal lines, might be better represented by the dotted lines as shown in Figure 19. This is meant to suggest that as each

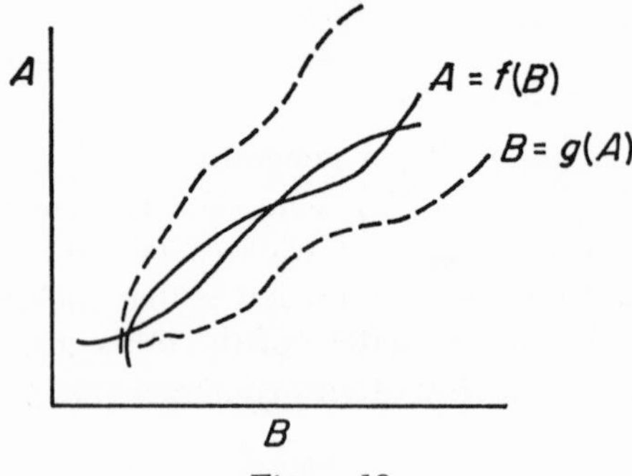

Figure 19

adjusts at levels which move in a northeasterly direction, the tolerance levels are widened because each party has greater resources and greater potential for destroying its opponent, and hence, as Pruitt also deduces, is less likely to be provoked to aggression. This appears to be consonant with the fact that the great powers in the world are less likely to engage each other than the smaller ones (consider, for example, the U.S.S.R. vs. the U.S.A. as compared with tribal wars in Africa or the conflicts in the Middle East).

[14] The figure could just as easily represent the relation between GNS and FA in which the subsystem functions to raise GNS while the suprasystem attempts to increase FA and a balance is struck close to some curve very like the mean of the two curves in Figure 18.

Pruitt has argued that the S-shaped curves of Figure 18 are not the only shapes possible. Straight lines, positive or negative accelerating curves, or any combination can be assumed, but the basic principle is that conflict is generated out of an initial stabilized state when the actions of one party give it a marked advantage over the other and exceed some critical level which we interpret to be frustration.

Maladaptive Stereotypy

Maier, Glaser, and Klee (1940) have emphasized that frustration-instigated behavior, once established, is highly resistant to change. Hamilton (1933) and Patrick (1934) were among the early experimentalists who showed that stereotypy characterizes the behavior of individuals subjected to emotional stress. One of the chief features of behavior under conditions of frustration is its fixated, maladaptive nature. In the famous studies of Maier and his colleagues (1940), the frustrated rats persisted in jumping toward a nonrewarding, punishing stimulus. The angry child kicking a closed door and the alcoholic drinking his way into head-splitting hangovers are common examples of maladaptive human behavior instigated by frustration. Such behavior patterns seem not to obey the principles of extinction and nonreinforcement which are the foundations of much learned behavior. It is this intransigence and lack of variability in behavior which often, but not always, accompanies frustration that contributes to the failure to find those system outputs (behaviors) which are rewarding and adaptive.

Although the strategy and tactics of military operations reveal elements of variability, these are employed in the service of an unwavering objective to destroy the opposition. In this sense the conflict relationship is stereotypic. Furthermore, the cliché has it that each war is fought initially with the strategies of its predecessor. The Maginot Line of World War II, and the massive, heavily armored attacks against small, lightly armed guerrilla bands in the unhappy Vietnam conflict, are examples of such stereotypy.

Moreover, at the conclusion of a successful military aggression, the victor's frustrations have been largely dissipated and it therefore becomes possible for him to negotiate an armistice with the vanquished, who has little or no power of resistance. The experience of negotiating an armistice with the North Koreans while hostilities continued for more than two years suggests that the failure to reach a clear win-lose condition at the end of a conflict, and thus to dissipate frustrations on at least one side, creates a condition unfavorable for finding those alternative system outputs which promote adaptive rather than conflictive relationships. That is to say, the problem of accounting for the transformation of a conflict relationship to a noncombative or collaborative one also requires that frustrations be minimized, if not eliminated.

World War I Study

Up to this point we have depended heavily upon studies of animals and individuals to support the hypothesis that the emergence of frustration is a necessary condition that transforms adaptive relations between systems to conflicting and aggressive relations. Holsti and North (1965) have made a valuable contribution by analyzing documents and authenticated statements made by the principal decision makers in the Triple Entente (Russia, Great Britain, and France) and the Dual Alliance (Austria-Hungary and Germany) in the five weeks just prior to the outbreak of World War I. Their data showed an initial plateau of perceived hostility directed at each of the antagonists by the other, lasting about three weeks. It was during this period that the Archduke Francis Ferdinand of Austria-Hungary was assassinated by a young Serbian. A week later, Germany promised a "blank check" support for the Vienna government in its dispute with Serbia. On July 23, Austria-Hungary, now confident, and in part forced by the sense of national injury, presented Serbia with an ultimatum. Five days later, war was declared on Serbia. In the subsequent two weeks, the curve of perceived hostilities rose markedly with mobilization by Russia in support of Serbia and the later involvement in quick order of France and Great Britain.

It is of interest that Holsti and North took the position that the *perception* of hostile *threats*, regardless of their veracity, was a major determinant of action. Moreover, their quotations, primarily from Dual Alliance sources, suggest that the decision makers felt helpless to stem the course of events. They all perceived themselves as offering more friendship than they received, and as a total system each was more often the target than the agent of hostility.

Although Holsti and North do not speak of frustration, but instead code the statements in terms of perceived hostility and friendship, there is a clear implication that an underlying base of frustration existed. They derived indexes of rejection, persecution, and sense of injury based on various ratios of self-perception as agents or targets of hostility or friendship. Frustration is the common denominator or generic term which includes as specifics a sense of injury, persecution, or rejection. Moreover the stereotypy and fixedness of the military responses is suggested by the reported beliefs on the part of all decision makers that the stream of events could not be stopped or diverted.

A similar analysis, with some refinements in methodology, has been made of the documents and official statements in the Egyptian-Israeli confrontation just prior to the Suez crisis of 1956. The general results were comparable, although the basic data issuing from Israel were meager, and the presence of the United Nations as a mediator provided an additional target for Nasser's hostility, which mounted as the events unfolded (Holsti, 1965).

The Feierabends' study (1966), previously referred to, represents a more generalized approach to the relation between national frustration and aggression. In addition to developing indexes of coercion and internal stability, they were able to arrive at indexes of "systemic frustration" and external aggression. The first of the latter pair was the ratio of social satisfactions to "social want formation" (expectations). The correlation between these indexes was .23 over fifty-three nations. On the other hand, the correlation between frustration and internal political instability was .50. The frustration index developed by the Feierabends, it should be noted, was based on data that refer to intranational rather than international issues and, as indicated, is more closely associated with internal stability. Although these results provide some general support for the frustration-aggression hypothesis at the level of large social systems, the very modest correlation between frustration and external aggression suggests that it will be necessary to find an index which more clearly pertains to externally rooted frustrations. In the meantime we are forced to suspend judgment, although the case studies of Holsti and North, as well as the statistical analysis by Rummel (1963) provide a reasonable basis for further exploration of the hypothesis.

System Differences in Frustration Tolerance

In the previous chapter we proposed that the state of a social system is one of the parameters influencing both the acceptance of inputs and the pattern of its possible outputs. It is a plausible extension of that proposition that some social systems may be more or less tolerant of frustrations and that the social norms may permit greater or less destructive aggression. A wealth of anthropological observations testify to the brutalities of some cultures in circumstances that would not be countenanced in others. Primitiveness does not necessarily account for the differences, since some tribal cultures (such as the American Hopi Indians) are notably unaggressive and others equally primitive are not. Moreover, even among the more advanced cultures, considerable differences may be observed. For example, the Filipinos compared with Spaniards seem to have less compunction about assassination, murder, or rape. It is therefore necessary to recognize that any generalized index or measure of frustration as an instigator of aggression must be related in some fashion to the system's frustration tolerance. In the studies referred to above, this has not been done, but it might provide additional insights.

Simulation Studies

Coe (1963) has developed a computer program that simulates the development of aggression out of an initial condition in which two parties with different expectations or intentions confront each other. This is of some interest as an example of the use of computers in social organization research, to which reference was made in the previous chapter. The program was based upon an analysis of laboratory studies (Thibaut and Riecken, 1955; Day and Hamblin, 1961; Wilkins and DeCharms, 1961) which found that about 80 per cent of the time subjects responded aggressively in order to coerce the agent of frustration to comply with the aggressor's wishes. In the remaining situations the aggressions were of a revengeful, retaliatory nature. The simulation takes into account differences between the two parties in expectations, intentions (goals), power, frustration tolerance, relative reward-cost payoffs, and level of aggression. Coe was able to show that by changing the difference point (i.e., from power to frustration tolerance) the simulation closely approximated empirical results obtained with humans.

Of course, the advantage of the simulation, once some validity can be shown for the program, lies in the ease with which the various parameters can be shifted and new outputs obtained. Of interest here is the finding that tolerance for frustration appears in the simulation to be at least as important, if not more important, than the relative degree of power. Even though this comes from a simulation, it is nevertheless suggestive of the international conflicts between those powers which have great military resources but are unable to subdue weaker countries inured to privation and low standards of living. The simulation results also lend additional, although indirect, support for the basic features of our model.

Some results from international simulation studies (see p. 173) fit in with the conclusion that frustration tolerance, conceived as an internal state of the contending systems, is a significant variable as a precondition for aggression. Driver (1965), on the basis of sixteen "runs" each of which used seven simulated nations, found that some aggression developed in every run, but to differing degrees of seriousness (from provoked arms increase to war). By means of a careful analysis of the progress of each run, the personality features of the national decision makers, and the situational factors, he concluded that the power differences were a necessary but not sufficient explanation for aggression.[15] In addition, there must be threat from some external source and a "low

[15] In at least one run a weak nation militarily attacked a stronger nation. An analysis of the circumstances leading to World War II (Holsti and North, 1965) revealed that it was the weaker nations which, in the grip of frustrations, took the initial aggressive actions.

aggression threshold" (which is merely the reverse of high frustration tolerance).

In this discussion of nonadaptive aggressive behavior, we have been compelled to introduce one new emergent condition that characterizes living systems—frustration. Without positing a disturbed state of a system that cannot be corrected by the usual adaptive mechanisms, there is no logical way of accounting for behavior that is destructive of other systems rather than that which eventuates in symbiotic, integrated behavior. Some turning point must be established or some new characteristic of systems must be assumed to emerge to account for the turning point. Frustration is that new characteristic.[16] We have not, however, departed from a fundamental proposition (4.1) that open system outputs are probabilistic. A "frustrated" system is one in which the most probable, and many of the less probable, outputs are not accepted as useful to its collateral or suprasystem. So long as the system is able to vary its outputs, it may eventually find one or more acceptable to the constraining system(s). Below a certain level of system disturbance, the system searches for outputs that bring supporting returns; above that level, the search is for outputs that will break and destroy the sources of frustration.

SUMMARY

We have attempted in this chapter to confine the discussion to those conditions which lead to conflict rather than to deal with the management of conflict once it is joined. Simply defined, conflict is the failure of adaptation. Growth requires adaptation, and internal conflict may arise when the adaptation processes related to growth are overtaxed. Two kinds of internal conflict may occur. If the suprasystem loses control, the subsystem will move toward an organized rebellion. If the subsystem loses its normal controls, there follows a moblike insurrection of fragmented unco-ordinated elements. Conflict between collateral systems arises indirectly out of growth and the consequent search and competition for scarce resources or GNS. We have proposed that the emergence of frustrations in the otherwise adaptive process is a necessary precondition for both internal and external conflict. Disturbances arising from the rejection or the anticipated blocking of outputs from one system by another generate frustrations which may, but do not necessarily, result in aggressions against the blocking system. On the other hand, frustration, we hypothesize, is always a forerunner of aggression.

[16] Dollard and his colleagues (1939) of course emphasized the significance of frustration as a precondition for aggression. Our point here is that from a systems standpoint frustration is a necessary condition.

X / A LOOK BACKWARD

In this concluding chapter we shall take a look backward over the ground we have covered in an effort to draw together some of the loose ends, point to some issues we have not covered, deal with some objections to this approach, and suggest some implications. In one sense this may be a summary; in another sense no summary is possible, partly because the theory itself is a summarized abstraction of phenomena running the gamut from cosmology and molecular physics to some references to international conflict. The spectrum over which we have ranged gives one pause—more than that, it raises profound doubts whether anything of genuine significance can be abstracted from such diverse materials. Mankind, however, has been infected with an incurable disease to make sense out of experience, to raise to higher and higher levels of abstraction the heterogeneous phenomena that surround and impinge upon us. This book is one symptom of that disease.

All theory builders repeat with tiresome regularity that their structures are oversimplifications of the empirical facts, the latter rich in variety but incoherent in the "raw." The current effort is obviously of this sort. We have not dealt with all particulars; but like other theories, this one, we believe, may claim to have provided a framework and strategy for an enlightened examination of many particular cases. Again, as in all other theories, we are confident that when enough particulars are compared with the theoretical framework, this too will be modified or displaced by another framework that makes more sense. This continual process of construction, revision, and perhaps demolition of theories is the nature of the "theory disease," which at times takes on the aspect of addiction; we search for a better, bigger "kick."

SCIENTIFIC AND ADMINISTRATIVE COMMUNICATIONS

These deliberations have been based on the conviction that nature, including that "nature" which man has constructed in his interpersonal and intergroup arrangements, has some identifiable unifying threads. By examining the concepts developed within several fields, we have attemped to find these common conceptual threads. We have also been persuaded that it is high time such a search was begun, for scientists may become so engrossed in the pursuit of the empirical facts each within his own domain as to lose sight of what may be useful and provocative from fields apart from his own. One of the early proponents of general systems theory (Boulding, 1956) had this to say:

> The more science breaks up into subgroups . . . the less communication is possible among the disciplines; however, the greater chance there is that the total growth of knowledge is being slowed down by the loss of relevant communications. The spread of specialized deafness means that someone who ought to know something that someone else knows isn't able to find out for lack of generalized ears.
>
> It is one of the main objectives of General Systems Theory to develop these generalized ears, and by developing a framework of general theory to enable one specialist to catch relevant communications for others.

There is in addition a very practical difficulty of maintaining significant communication among specialists in the institutions of learning and research. For several years I sat on an executive committee of a graduate school. One of the functions of this committee was to approve all proposed new courses. It shortly became evident that as a committee we were totally incompetent to discharge this function. The course descriptions and justifications from microbiology were incomprehensible even to the chemists, those in sociology were so much gibberish to the physicists, a course in musicology made no sense to the psychologist, and so on. The committee's activities dropped to the level of criticizing the grammar of the descriptions and inspecting the forms to make sure the proper signatures were on the proper dotted lines! I do not recall that we rejected any proposals. No doubt the situation is not very different in many other graduate schools.

Some may ask, is this bad? We cannot say it is good or bad in any absolute sense; it depends upon our criteria of an effectively operating system. We are reminded, however, of Ashby's dictum that intelligent systems are selective. Presumably, positive value was placed on some degree of control over the proliferation or quality of courses within the suprasystem (in this case the graduate school); otherwise, the rituals would not have been established in the first place. If, on the other hand, we accept the view that the development of a graduate school can best proceed by permitting each department to evolve as it sees fit without regard to some general plan, without intermeshing between specialties, then the absence of an effective control by the approving committee is highly desirable. If the deductions from our systems theory have any validity, one would expect that the latter path would lead to fragmented disorganization and internecine conflict over the "capturing" of limited sources of maintenance (budget, space, additional personnel). These, I gather, are characteristics found in many universities. It has been emphasized in the earlier chapters that self-regulating systems are those which possess effective negative feedback channels. In the situation just described such feedback is slight and largely ineffective.

One could hardly justify the development of a general systems theory as a means of dealing with the administrative problems of a graduate school, nor do we hold out much hope that, if the propositions of this book were embraced by a significant body of academic people, the administrative problems would disappear. In presenting this vignette we are only illustrating the consequences of nonvalid communications between subsystems coupled with weak control exercised by the suprasystem.

EARLIER BIOSOCIAL SYSTEMS

The general proposition with which we have been dealing is by no means new, although our particular formulation that cuts across levels of analysis is perhaps unique. Durkheim (1912) argued more than fifty years ago that society placed an indispensable restraint on the desires of men which would otherwise expand without limit. He conceived of society as "represented" in the shared norms (although he did not use that term) which both prescribed and proscribed certain forms of behavior; and because they were shared, they provided a base for the essential "spirituality" and rationality of men. That is to say, the restraints of society compel men to think rather than merely act. Society and its representations were for Durkheim abstract, normative, and emotional, operating to maintain order and consensus, neither of which is possible in the absence of societal forces. Thus the restraints of society, far from having negative effects alone, were the very source of enrichment, development, and innovation (cf. Pitts, 1961).

In its main outline Durkheim's account is a special case of the more general theory pertaining to the interrelations of sub- and suprasystems. His language may be French, but the meanings are not inconsistent with GST.

This is not the place to review the historically significant theories of society proposed by Max Weber, Karl Marx, Herbert Spencer, Thorstein Veblen, Thomas Hobbes, Auguste Comte, and a score of others. They have all in one manner or other addressed themselves, as we have herein, to the interconnections between the behavior of man taken in its theoretical pristine form and the requirements of the social organizations, formal or informal, which surround men. How do people manage to cope with the institutions of their own making? What accounts for their construction, development, long life, or eventual death?

In the search for answers to these and related questions, biological analogies have often been proposed, particularly by Hobbes, Plato, and Spencer. Walter Cannon reversed the analogies; he extrapolated his principles of biological homeostasis to the social level. The present effort is somewhat more ambitious—perhaps overly ambitious. It has attempted to deal with the age-old issues within *a framework of generalized concepts and propositions in which the various levels of analysis represent not analogies but special cases.*

In one respect this effort to find the overarching principles that apply to suborganic, organic, and social systems has suffered from a deficiency that earlier efforts of the same general sort have displayed. It will be recalled that Cannon jumped from homeostasis in men and animals to some speculations about homeostasis in social systems. More recently Gerard, Kluckhohn, and Rapoport (1956) drew parallels between a number of interesting features of biological and cultural evolution, pointing out that biological mutation, selection, migration, and the random drift of gene (now DNA) patterns had their counterparts in cultural changes. This effort, like Cannon's, although considerably more sophisticated than Spencer's or Hobbes's, jumps over those systems which are of an individual psychological sort. In this book we have also made a similar jump except for a brief excursion in Chapter IV, where we presented a discussion of ego adaptation.

The failure to deal with individual psychological phenomena in general systems terms has been deliberate, although perhaps indefensible. Stagner (1961) has employed homeostasis as a central theme in his personality model and within this has incorporated systems-like principles pertaining to perception and affective responses. Although Stagner's model has much to commend it, the assumptions and propositions are less explicit than those provided herein. It would require a treatment of nearly book length to build upon Stagner's beginnings and to bring individual psychological systems within our framework. It is possible that someone in the future will fill in the gaps that now exist. Sanford's plea (1965) for a holistic approach to these and other psychological issues expresses the need eloquently and vigorously.

In presenting our general model of social systems we have rejected—not merely omitted—the concept of drive and its companion, motivation. Perhaps we should explain why.

IS MOTIVATION NECESSARY?

It is a mark of the shifting emphasis in psychology that the *Nebraska Symposium on Motivation,* which began in 1952 as an annual collection of relevant papers, contains an article in both the 1962 and 1963 volumes which questions the concept directly (Kelly, 1962, and Rogers, 1963). Rogers did not eschew the concept entirely, but did question the usefulness of its subcategories. "Given the motivational sub-stratum of the actualizing tendency,[1] is anything added to our theories by postulating more specific motivational constructs? How helpful has it been in the past and how helpful is it likely to be in the future to specify and try to give meaning to a variety of special motives? I am not arguing that these differing types of seeking do not take place. Men do seek food, and they do tend toward increasing their competence in dealing with the environment and most people wish to increase their self-esteem, but I am not at all sure that there is any profit to thinking of a hunger motive, a competence motive, or a self-esteem motive. Are these heuristic concepts? Do they lead to significant discovery? Are they provocative research? Obviously I am dubious" (pp. 6–7).

Kelly was more direct. He declared in the first sentence, "I have no use for the concept of motivation." He went on to argue that the concept arose from the early Greek philosophers, particularly Democritus, who conceived of primary particles being pushed this way and that by "secondary forces." Apply this idea to psychology "and you come up with the notion of a person either being propelled by 'motives' in spite of himself, or stuck tight in his own fundament." Kelly's alternative explanation for the directedness of behavior was a concept he called a "construct." If I understand him correctly, a construct is a relatively persistent (memory?) state of an individual's psychological system which permits him to "construe" his environment into "similarities and contrasts." It is "an abstraction of the linkage and differentiation which inside each man's own tight little world constitutes a generalized pair of alternatives. . . . A system of constructs constitutes a ready-made format for future thinking, and for lower order processes as well. To have constructed such a system means that a person has somewhat prepared himself to cope with all sorts of strange things that have not happened yet." And somewhat earlier he declared, ". . . the fundamental thing about life is that it goes

[1] We questioned even the usefulness of this on pages 71–72.

on. It isn't that something *makes* it go on; the going on is *the thing itself*" (pp. 85–86).

Our own formulation is wholly consistent with this view. The behavior of a system is the consequence of the state of the components and the nature of the inputs. A system does what it does because it is constructed in a certain way and because the inputs are of a certain character. No further assumptions have to be made about the components. Motives considered as "activators" are not distinguishable from signal or stimulus input. Motives, considered as "energizers," are equivalent to life itself, or, as Kelly says, the thing itself. On the other hand, if one wishes to label a certain state of a system as "hungry" or another state as "angry" and still another state as "prejudiced," no one can object, provided each state can be described and discriminated from each other.

Aside from being able to describe some states resulting from physiological deprivation, our knowledge of most other states (i.e., "status-seeking," "ego-defensive," "explorative," "prejudiced") is vague and indistinct. About all that we can say with confidence is that a system is ready to accept and process certain kinds of inputs while resisting others. Furthermore, we know the system is ready only after it produces some output.

This critique of the motivation concept should not be interpreted as a complete rejection of efforts to describe the states of a system. Instead, if one defines motivation as a system state, the task of differentiating between motives takes on a different aspect. It requires that the states, indeed, be different and that some correspondence can be found between the verbal report of a person's state and the physiological, neural, hormonal conditions. Until this information becomes available, our only recourse is to view the system as a Black Box. To do otherwise is to imply greater knowledge than we in fact possess, making distinctions of doubtful certainty.

O'Kelly, writing in the *Annual Review of Psychology* (1963, p. 59), made this observation: "A sustained reading of the Nebraska series leads to the reflection that a major difficulty with attempts to erect physiological theories of motivation is that they all have the aim of describing the physiological and anatomical basis of some group of psychological constructs, with little regard to the suitability of the constructs for either the empirical facts of behavior or the biological 'facts of life. . . .' Much of our present attempt to look for anatomical structures on the map of current motivational concepts is probably as doomed as was the search for the Seven Cities of Cibola." Perhaps we have already reached the point anticipated by Cofer, when he said in the same series (1959) "that if the present trends continue, motivation as a distinct concept coordinate to other psychological concepts may well disappear." General systems theory does not require the concept.

POWER AND INFLUENCE

Gaining currency in social system theory is the concept of influence and power, which we have also not mentioned in the model here presented. Is this an emergent feature of social systems, or is it a concept like motivation that is unnecessary? Is it possible that the power to influence another is embedded, unrecognized within the model as it stands, or is it a concept which must wait to be integrated in some extension or refinement of what has already been presented?

French and Raven (1959) and later Raven (1965) distinguish between six forms of power. First is *coercive* power, which results from a person's belief that another has the capability to inflict punishment and harm. Second is *reward* power, based on the perception that another person may mediate rewards, benefits, or desirable returns. Obviously, these two forms of power may be exercised by a single agent. Third is *legitimate* power, based on "broad, general norms about the beliefs, opinions and attitudes" of what influences are appropriate and proper. The policeman, the foreman, the priest may exercise legitimate power in various segments of behavior. Fourth, *informational* power is based on the cognitive elements in a communication which to a greater or lesser degree influence the subsequent behavior of the recipient of the information. Fifth is *expert* power, which in some instances may be additive to informational power for the reason that the source of the information is perceived as a person of special knowledge. Sixth, and finally, is *reference* power, which stems from the reference group with which the individual identifies himself. This power has been demonstrated by numerous experiments, of which the Asch studies (1955) are the prototypes. With these six definitions before us, let us see how the various forms and sources of power may be interpreted within the propositions already presented.

Coercive power may be conceived as an input from a collateral or suprasystem that at least threatens or actually destroys the existing boundary or the internal processes of the system on which the inputs are impressed. A sudden explosive increase in atmospheric pressure may destroy the microphone's mechanism, and thus the pressure may be said to be coercive. The thief's threat of harm to the houseowner may not actually result in harm, but the threat would be without effect unless it carried some credibility. (We have previously dealt with the issue of systems being capable of anticipating future events.) Hence coercive power can be seen as a special case of possible harmful inputs that may be resisted up to the point where destruction of the system is perceived as imminent. It is an attribute of the input.

Informational power is likewise a special case of signal inputs which influence what the system will process and, to some extent, the manner in which the processing will occur. Information read into a computer is of this kind.

Expert power clearly depends upon the perception of the receiving system that the "communicator" or input agent is especially acceptable, to the extent that the input from such a source is readily passed by the boundary. A computer cannot respond to expert power. Unlike coercive power, the receiving system does not anticipate harm in the event that the input is rejected, but, on the contrary, anticipates greater congruence with other systems.

There appears to be a close correspondence between expert power and reference power as Raven has defined them. The latter appears to refer to the special acceptance of signal input by reason of the fact that the source also supplies a high degree of GNS. That is to say, I accept information and subsequently engage in certain appropriate behaviors because by so doing I will gain, or at least not lose, sources of GNS. Expert power is much the same sort of thing, except in the latter case the input comes not from a group but an individual whom I regard highly and with whom I wish to align myself.

Legitimate power again is a characteristic of the input that makes it more acceptable than if the input lacked this characteristic. Legitimate power depends upon the broad norms of the social system in which the recipient of power is embedded. A priest of a given religious order exercises legitimate power over those within that order, but is legitimately powerless over those outside the sect. It is the acceptance of the group norms that forms the basis for legitimate power and in this sense is no different in principle from the influence of norms generally on behavior. The sanctions which enforce legitimate power are those also determined by the norms, unless they reach the point of coercion, and then legitimate power becomes coercive power.

These translations of the various kinds of power into systems terms indicate that the concept most often is descriptive of the inputs, or the relationship between a system and its suprasystem. Although it may be useful to invoke the concept as a shorthand way of describing certain conditions obtaining in social systems, it does not appear to be a necessary cornerstone for social system theory. The effects which one could reasonably expect to flow from the various definitions of power may also be deduced from the propositions pertaining to boundary filtering, norms, symbiosis, and exogenous forces.

ANOTHER SOCIAL SYSTEM MODEL

In the development of our basic social systems model presented in Chapter VI, we passed over some comparisons with other models in an effort to get on with the main argument. Now that the picture has been developed, it may be appropriate to consider in greater detail the way in which this model is similar to the proposals presented by March and Simon (1958).

March and Simon (p. 84) present the essence of their model in five propositions:

1. An organization is a system of interrelated social behaviors of a number of persons whom we shall call *participants* in the organization.
2. Each participant and each group of participants receives *from* the organization *inducements* in return for which he makes *to* the organization *contributions.*
3. Each participant will continue his participation in an organization only so long as the inducements offered him are as great or greater (measured in terms of *his* values and in terms of the alternatives open to him) than the contributions he is asked to make.
4. The contributions provided by the various groups of participants are the source from which the organization manufactures the inducements offered to the participants.
5. Hence the organization is "solvent"—and will continue in existence—only so long as the contributions are sufficient to provide inducements in large enough measure to draw forth these contributions.

The similarity between these statements and our own model hardly needs emphasis. Inducements are defined by March and Simon in such a way as to include what we mean by GNS, the rewards of wages or other tangible returns, and what we called exogenous forces. The March-Simon model declares that if the inducements-contribution ratio falls below a given level, the participants will engage in search behavior for alternative arrangements. In this respect the model is similar to our proposal that the GNS/FA ratio must be kept within a narrow range of values for the system to survive. March and Simon consider absences, turnover, and production output as primary evidences of the stability of the organization, and their model is well suited to dealing with these matters. On the other hand, they do not consider the possibility of applying the model to the problems of conflict, either internal or external, which is a possibility within the framework provided herein.

The March-Simon model is different from our own in several respects, but one is important. We have placed considerable emphasis on GNS as a reverberating feedback loop, fundamentally accounting for the cohesion of the system with contributing inputs from FA, the immediate control "operator" (supervisor), and the larger suprasystem. March and Simon have not differentiated these. Furthermore, as the paragraph above has already suggested, the appropriateness of the outputs of the system for its suprasystem has not been explicitly considered. They take into account only the matters of absences, turnover, and productive level as evidences of the system's stability. The concept of FA and the proposition that this must be acceptable to some larger organization provide a more general basis for determining stability. A growing body of empirical studies shows that the criteria for group effectiveness and survival depend upon what the suprasystem requires and that this is different from system to system.

Seashore, Indik, and Georgopoulos (1960), for instance, analyzed measures of productivity, chargeable accidents, unexcused absences, errors, and rated effectiveness in a collection of twenty-seven groups within a given company and found virtually no stability in the intercorrelations from group to group. Comparable evidence has been reported by others (Morse, 1953; Brayfield and Crockett, 1955). This means that instead of these measures being homogeneous and useful to indicate stability, *any* measure of FA established by the suprasystem may be the feature that bears heavily on determining the system's survival. The March-Simon model as well as our own emphasizes that the inducements must be measured in terms of the participants' values. Our model emphasizes, in addition, that the contributions must be measured in terms of the suprasystem's values, which in some instances may be absences; in others, productivity; in still others safety, or something else. Our main point is that the model based on general systems propositions is one that encompasses a wider variety of specific instances.

One more point of comparison is of interest. March and Simon emphasize the alternative groups or paths of activity available to a participant as a factor contributing to search behavior, on the one hand, and stability, on the other. If his skills are only useful to organization *A*, or if the available inducements from *B* are less than *A*'s, or if geographic factors limit his mobility to *B*, the participant will remain with *A*. Matters of this sort we have grouped under the heading of exogenous forces that reside in the broader supra-suprasystem. Conceived in this way, the March-Simon "alternatives" are included within the systems model rather than being somewhat extraneous and dangling opportunities that float around the central model.

The March-Simon model is essentially based on a theory of rewards that has been carried to an extreme by Homans, who attempted to account not for just group behavior but for the basic two-person social interactions as an exchange of rewards (1961, p. 378). Newcomb (1961) criticized this extreme form of the theory on the ground that although based on Skinnerian reinforcement, which is relevant as a partial explanation of much social behavior, instrumental conditioning is incomplete as an explanation.

FUNCTIONS OF COMPONENTS RECONSIDERED

Early in our definition of components we assigned them the functions of combining, separating, or comparing inputs to produce outputs (definition 2.2). It may appear that we have not specifically dealt with these functions. They have not been mentioned since they were introduced. On the other hand, we have gone to considerable length in developing the concepts of growth, adaptation, and conflict. We hold that the component functions are exemplified in these latter phenomena. Growth is a process of combining subsystems or dividing and subdividing. Viewed in this way, growth includes both the combining and the separating functions. It is true that we have talked about growth in terms of "foreign" inputs, and the requirement for increasing specialization as the system expands, but lying behind these changes are dynamic relations that may be reduced to the mathematical relations which include adding or multiplying and subtracting or dividing. Thus growth includes both the combining and separating functions.

Internal and external adaptations involve comparisons. Mathematically this refers to *equal, not equal, greater, lesser.* We have said that a system must produce outputs acceptable to its suprasystem. This requires that a comparison be made between what is produced and some criterion of what is acceptable. The seat of the comparison process we located in the boundary. Furthermore, the feedback concept has embedded within it an implicit comparison. That is to say, a negative feedback message is one which says, "The output is too great, too fast, too something." It can only be *too* anything if it is compared with something. Since we have postulated that systems are "nested," one inside the other, basic functions true of a system are true of its components; for a system at one level of analysis becomes a component at a higher, more complex level.

For anyone interested in mathematizing these concepts, there is a model that comes close to the descriptive model given herein, which was developed by Rosenblatt for neurological systems (1962). The similarity between our own general systems definitions and Rosenblatt's "perceptron" may be gleaned from the following quotation: "A perceptron consists of a set of signal-generating units (or neurons) connected together to form a network. Each of these units upon receiving a *suitable* input signal (either from other units in the network or from the environment) responds by generating an output signal, which may be transmitted, through connections, to a *selected* set of receiving units. Each perceptron includes a sensory input (i.e., a set of units capable of responding to signals emanating from the environment) and one or more output units, which generate signals which can be directly observed by the experimenter, or by an automatic control mechanism" (p. 4; italics added). The italicized words emphasize the comparison processes which we have been discussing. The inputs cannot be *suitable* or *selective* unless we posit that some other inputs are not suitable.

For purposes of exposition we have found it more meaningful and significant to consider the phenomena of growth, conflict, and adaptation as general system features rather than constrain language to the basic functions of the components, since it is in these former ways that the functions reveal themselves. On the other hand, as we already implied, the functional relationships are immediately translatable into mathematical operations. If someone sophisticated in mathematical modeling wishes to develop such models from these propositions, we believe they are amenable to treatment and may well be sharpened thereby.

IS GENERAL SYSTEMS THEORY MECHANISTIC?

Raising such a question is tantamount to drawing a line between two sets of entrenched philosophies: those who hold the view that mankind possesses control over its own destiny and those who declare the behavior of men is merely the product of natural forces, blind and impersonal. In looking back over the propositions of this book, it appears that neither of these positions is tenable in their extreme forms. We have argued that definable principles exist which account for the development of systems from simple to complex. We have affirmed that in this development emergent characteristics appear which cannot be found in systems of simpler structure and organization. Moreover, as complexity increases, so does uncertainty. Furthermore, uncertainty in Heisenberg's sense is at the very base of even the simplest systems. These propositions, we submit, are mechanistic only in the sense that they are rational, understandable, and interrelated. Within their framework there remains an element of "chance": the accidental meshing of one system with another, the inability to predict the emergent characteristic from a complete prior knowledge of the unintegrated components.

We have proposed that the organization of components into a system in the simplest case is the consequence of accidental coupling of two components. Moreover, if we follow the implications of Heisenberg's uncertainty, it is clear, as Back, Hood, Orne, and others have shown, that the observers of social systems, no less than the dead instruments in microphysical systems, disturb what is being observed. Even the decision by the observer of what he is to examine becomes a constraint on the coupled observer-object system. "And in the last analysis the interpretation given to it all, the very meaning of the observation is peculiarly his responsibility" (Matson, 1964, p. 144). For the physical scientist this has been underscored by no less a prestigious physicist than Max Born (1956), when he says, "For if an experiment must be set up in a definite way to investigate one or the other of a conjugate pair of quantities, it is impossible to obtain information of the system considered as such; the observer has to decide beforehand which kind of answer he wants to obtain. The subjective decisions are inseparably mixed with objective observations."

The consequence of this deduction is that just as the law is what judges say it is, so the principles and theories of science are based on what scientists—fallible human beings—choose to examine and interpret. If this is true for the semiexact physical systems, it is true with a vengeance for social systems where the values, social norms, and total cultural milieu may be the objects of investigation and the inescapable disturbing influences on the observer.

The dependence of scientific discovery upon the predilections of the scientist has been put in dramatic terms by van den Berg in his *Introduction to a Historical Psychology* (1964), in which he proposes that the seminal ideas of the field are not so much revelations of what has always been true of human nature, but formulations which carried the elements of a self-fulfilling prophesy. One example will suffice. Prior to the mid-nineteenth century, the psychological phenomena of adolescence were largely unknown. The turn of the century witnessed a burgeoning of research and speculation in this area, emphasizing the problems, stresses, and anxieties which seemed to be the inescapable accomplishments of growing up. Prior to this time the tutelage of children was a tradition-bound process to which adults gave little thought. They did what came naturally. During the past sixty years, parents, alerted to their children's storm and stress, found what the psychologists had discovered and, in the finding, unwittingly created a widening gulf between themselves and their offspring, which further confirmed the discovery. Of course, the growing complexity of family life, the social conditions requiring mobility, and the specialization of occupations van den Berg recognizes as contributing as well to the disparities between parents and children.

In a more subtle way, van den Berg's thesis fits within the general systems theory. Stated bluntly, it is that the societal circumstances of an era influence what we find in human nature. Were it not for Victorian sexual taboos, Freud would never have discovered the unconscious, because, says van den Berg, it did not exist before that time, or certainly was not a needed concept to account for any significant portion of general behavior. It is the suprasystem that creates certain requirements for its member systems which are changed in the process. Hence what may be true of human beings in one culture at one time may not be their nature in another, or at another time.

The root concept of the mechanistic view of science is cause and effect, stimulus and response. Assuming the validity of the interactive character of the scientist and his subject matter we have just set forth, it becomes clear that cause and effect are not distinguishable except by some arbitrary division of the circular flow of events. It has long been an ignored conundrum in psychology that neither stimulus nor response can be distinguished independently of the other. What is stimulus may simultaneously be response. Yet this impossible distinction has been the shaky basis for a superstructure of psychological experimentation and theory that had as its goal a Newtonian mechanistic view abandoned by the most advanced contemporary physical scientists whom the laboratory psychologists wished to emulate! It is one of the ironies of current theoretical developments that it was the physicists, not the psychologists, who rediscovered the significance of the observer.[2] Eddington expressed the interdependence of person and thing in a compelling metaphor: "We have found that where science has progressed the farthest, the mind has but regained from nature that which the mind has put into nature. We have found a strange footprint on the shores of the unknown. We have devised profound theories, one after another, to account for its origin. At last we have succeeded in reconstructing the creature that made the footprint. And lo! it is our own" (quoted in Heisenberg, 1958, p. 153).

The essential point of this discussion has been to emphasize that the earlier mechanistic conception of the universe, including mankind and his culture operating on a cause-and-effect basis, is no longer tenable. Rather, our empirical data and interpretations currently compel us to view the subject matter of all science as consisting of interdependent circular transactions among linked systems in which cause cannot be distinguished from effect except by doing violence to the phenomena themselves. Moreover the probabilistic nature of the transactions in principle denies the possibility of viewing the universe as a giant clockwork grinding its inexorable way through eternity. Given the variability of systems and Garner's contingent probabilities, there is considerable room for indeterminacy and choice. The feedback propositions permit of system self-control, self-direction, whether the system is living or non-living. In these latter respects one could hardly think of a less mechanistic

[2] We emphasize *re*discovered because, as every psychologist knows, in 1796 the Greenwich astronomer, Maskelyne, dismissed his assistant because the latter persisted in recording stellar transits later than his master. Thus arose an interest in the "personal equation," which came to be limited to reaction-time studies.

theory. We have not proposed that the universe of systems is a mere machine. At the level of living systems—particularly at the human level—self-direction becomes the freedom to choose among the alternative lines of action, recognizing that the environment may restrict these alternatives and render some more attractive than others. Our propositions instead represent a set of broad relationships transcending, but giving sense to the particulars at various levels of analysis.

THE UNIFICATION OF SCIENCE?

It has been argued by Ackoff and others (1964) that the boast of general systems theory to unify science is doomed to failure and may lead to just the opposite result—further separation. One immediate response—and this is a defensive one—is to declare that general systems theory has not yet been given a chance. A product of only a few brief years, the approach has barely become known except to a small, widely scattered collection of people whose basic intellectual capital is rooted in their respective specialties. No program of graduate study labeled General Systems yet exists. A distantly related movement called General Education, spearheaded by Harvard University, did not develop the momentum to carry a graduate program of study. If unification should occur among sciences, are we not overly optimistic to expect the millennium this soon?

What degree of unification may be desirable is of course a matter for the future to decide. We have made it a proposition in this formulation that in any system the components must maintain a degree of identity, and so we would expect that, no matter how far science progresses toward unity, the specialties will remain viable. Indeed, one wonders whether the current objections against general systems theory or other tendencies toward interdisciplinary collaboration are not expressions of this very proposition; namely, that the subsystems (the various disciplines) tend to oppose actions which would otherwise destroy their boundaries.

Although there may have been overly enthusiastic hopes for a unity of science expressed by some of the early proponents, a sober assessment even at close range would suggest that the chief value of this approach is in suggesting significant areas for research *within each specialty*. The cognitive value of any theory—broad scale or narrow—lies in its power to uncover the critical issues which currently block understanding. General systems theory, as we have elaborated it and attempted to apply it to social systems, has demonstrated its value in this respect. We have repeatedly pointed to gaps in our knowledge, gaps which would be less obvious and of less apparent significance without the theoretical framework. For instance, growth and adaptation have been seen as critical issues in the development of any system, but especially living systems. Relatively little research pertaining to social systems has addressed itself to these questions. Through the logical development of some general propositions about growth and adaptation (along with the reverse of adaptation, conflict), a vast program of researchable topics unfolds before us. The search for, and development of, isomorphic principles may not unify science in the sense that all scientists will eventually speak the same language. On the other hand, such isomorphisms may encourage the forward movement of the knowledge frontier along a broad front rather than in limited salients.

The need for such conceptual unification within psychology is particularly acute. Perhaps other disciplines are equally prone to invent terms and constructs without particular reference to simpler or more fundamental ones, but the disease appears particularly acute among the behavioral sciences. Concepts such as libido, self-actualization, level of aspiration, synergy, ends-means-readiness, interstructurance counterdependence are no doubt valuable in designating particular phenomena or labeling certain intervening variables. However, these and other terms are for the most part unconnected to any common set of fundamental concepts. It is not possible to construct a hierarchy of psychological concepts that will arrive at something like the periodic table of chemical elements or the nucleus-proton-neutron-atom-molecule series of physics. If someone can write persuasively and voluminously around a term like subception, and persuade a corps of graduate students to conduct a program of research on problems related to the topic, the term gets into the literature even though it floats unrelated to any other concept or theoretical formulation. Such conceptual inventions are like rainbows; they are "real," but their anchors are shifting and uncertain.

This is not a plea for anchors just to satisfy a compulsive need for conceptual tidiness. Anchors, or conceptual connectedness, are necessary in order to discover the ways in which the systems at one level may be in fact related with other levels. Sanford (1965) argued for a holistic conceptual organization in psychology, pointing out that the field is accenting the production of knowledge rather than discovering how all the bits and pieces add up. He made the telling point that "just as complex phenomena are to be explained in part in terms of the activities of constituent processes, so simple processes have to be understood as partly determined by the larger structures in which they have place." In our discussion of social systems, it was impossible to translate many of the empirical findings into our terms or indeed into any common language.

One psychologist who shall remain nameless, when asked how he was able to integrate a mass of several hundred empirical studies pertaining to small groups into a simplified theoretical scheme, confessed that it took courage and prayer. While recognizing the virtues of both, I would suggest that the progress of science needs also a considerable measure of intellectual self-control to avoid the proliferation of disconnected descriptive concepts, however beautiful their etymological roots may be.

I am by no means supremely confident that the propositions provided in this book will be an improvement on the current situation, or that they will provide the needed anchors. Their chief virtue, as I see them, is in their relevance not alone to social systems but to other levels of system analysis. Their parenthood can be traced and I think will be found legitimate. Unification of science in this sense may be possible. This is not, however, a plea for the reductionism espoused by the logical positivists, whose effort was to identify the source of all concepts as "physical-thing predicates." Our emergent characteristics proposition, founded on the further assumption that outputs are different in some identifiable way from inputs, denies the possibility of simple reductions.

Somewhat the same point has been made by Rapoport (1962) when he argues that the demonstration of some isomorphic principles extending across levels of systems suggests that others may be discovered. In the meantime, the biologist (or psychologist), for instance, may continue to study biological events with specific biological (or psychological) concepts; but if he is alert to the possible conceptual connections with physical or chemical principles, he does not invent his biological (or psychological) concepts *ad hoc*. Instead, his lines of communication are open so that both the biological and chemophysical concepts may be enriched.

We can do no better in closing this book than to quote another of Rapoport's thoughts: "It is axiomatic in science that every opportunity for generalization is an opportunity for progress. . . . Every model is of course an analogy. What makes a model heuristically valuable is that it is treated as a point of departure, not arrival."

BIBLIOGRAPHY

CHAPTER I

Ackoff, R. L., "Systems, Organizations and Interdisciplinary Research," *General Systems Yearbook*, 1960, *5*, p. 6.

Ashby, W. R., "General Systems Theory as a New Discipline," *General Systems Yearbook*, 1958, *3*, pp. 1–6.

Boulding, K. E., "Toward a General Theory of Growth," *General Systems Yearbook*, 1956, *1*, pp. 66–75.

Bronowski, J., *Science and Human Values*, New York, Harper & Row, 1959, pp. 23ff.

Fields, W. S., and Abbott, W. (eds.), *Information Storage and Neural Control*, Springfield, Ill., Charles C. Thomas, 1963, p. 358.

Gerard, R. W., "Summary and General Discussion," in W. S. Fields and W. Abbott (eds.), *Information Storage and Neural Control*, Springfield, Ill., Charles C. Thomas, 1963, Chap. 15.

Levy, M. J., Jr., *Modernization and the Structure of Societies: A Setting for International Affairs*, Princeton, N.J., Princeton University Press, 1966.

Lwoff, A., "Interaction among Virus, Cell and Organism," *Science*, 1966, *152*, p. 1216; or *Nobel Foundation Lectures*, Amsterdam and New York, Elsevier Publishing Co.

McClelland, C. A., "System Theory and Human Conflict," in E. B. McNeil (ed.), *The Nature of Human Conflict*, Englewood Cliffs, N.J., Prentice-Hall, 1965, p. 271.

Miller, A., "The Role of P.E.N.," *Saturday Review*, June 4, 1966, p. 16.

Miller, J. G., "Living Systems: Basic Concepts," *Behavioral Science*, 1965, *10*, pp. 193–237, 380–411.

Miller, J. G., "Toward a General Theory for the Behavioral Sciences," *American Psychologist*, 1955, *10*, pp. 513–531.

Nagel, E., *The Structure of Science,* New York, Harcourt, Brace, 1961, pp. 108–109.
Rapoport, A., "The Diffusion Problem in Mass Behavior," *General Systems Yearbook,* 1956, I, p. 6.
Sui, R. G. H., *The Tao of Science,* Cambridge, Mass., M.I.T. Press, 1957.
Von Bertalanffy, L., "An Outline of General System Theory," *British Journal of Philosophical Science,* 1950, *1,* pp. 134–165.
Von Neumann, J., "The General and Logical Theory of Automata," in L. A. Jeffress (ed.), *Cerebral Mechanisms in Behavior,* New York, Wiley, 1951, pp. 22ff.
Whitehead, A. N., *Science and the Modern World,* New York, Macmillan, 1926, p. 26.

CHAPTER II

Ashby, W. R., "What Is an Intelligent Machine?," *General Systems Yearbook,* 1963, 8, p. 214.
Ashby, W. R., *Design for a Brain,* New York, Wiley, 1960, Chap. 8.
Ashby, W. R., "General Systems Theory as a New Discipline," *General Systems Yearbook,* 1958, *3,* 3ff.
Baldwin, E., *The Nature of Biochemistry,* London, Cambridge University Press, 1962, p. 21.
Beer, S., *Cybernetics of Management,* London, English Universities Press, 1959, Chap. VI.
Bird, C., "Maturation and Practice: Their Effects upon the Feeding and Reaction of Chicks," *Journal of Comparative Psychology,* 1933, *16,* pp. 343–366.
Blum, H. F., *Time's Arrow and Evolution,* 2nd ed., New York, Harper, 1962, Chap. VIII, pp. 130–132.
Bunge, M., "A General Black Box Theory," *Philosophy of Science,* 1963, *3,* pp. 346–358.
Clark, R. K., and McFarland, R. L., "Systems Concept of Stimulus," *Perceptual and Motor Skills,* 1963, *17,* pp. 99–102.
Gibson, J. J., "The Concept of Stimulus in Psychology," *American Psychologist,* 1960, *15,* pp. 694–703.
Grinker, R. R. (ed.), *Toward a Unified Theory of Human Behavior,* New York, Basic Books, 1956, p. 5.
Henderson, L. J., *The Fitness of the Environment,* New York, Macmillan, 1913.
Herbst, P. G., "Measurement of Behavior Structures by Means of Input-Output Data," *Human Relations,* 1957, *10,* pp. 335–346.
Lashley, K. S., "The Problems of Serial Order in Behavior," in L. A. Jeffress (ed.), *Cerebral Mechanisms in Behavior,* New York, Wiley, 1951, p. 112.
Lehinger, A. L., "How Cells Transform Energy," *Scientific American,* 1961, *205,* No. 3, pp. 62–73.

Miller, J. G., "Living Systems: Basic Concepts," *Behavioral Science*, 1965, *10*, pp. 193–237, 380–411.

Miller, J. G., "Toward a General Theory for the Behavioral Sciences," *American Psychologist*, 1955, *18*, pp. 513–531.

Shannon, C., and Weaver, W., *The Mathematical Theory of Communication*, Urbana, Ill., University of Illinois Press, 1949.

Simon, H., "The Architecture of Complexity," *Proceedings of the American Philosophical Society*, 1962, *106*, No. 6; reprinted in *General Systems Yearbook*, 1965, *10*, pp. 63–76.

Von Bertalanffy, L., *Theoretische Biologie*, Berlin, I, Gebrüder Borntraeger, 1932.

Von Neumann, J., "The General and Logical Theory of Automata," in L. A. Jeffress (ed.), *Cerebral Mechanisms in Behavior*, New York, Wiley, 1951.

Whittesey, C. R., *Principles and Practices of Money and Banking*, New York, Macmillan, 1949, p. 3.

Wiener, N., *Cybernetics*, New York, Wiley, 1948.

Zadek, L. A., "The Concept of State in System Theory," in M. D. Mesarovic (ed.), *Views on General Systems Theory*, New York, Wiley, 1964, pp. 39–50.

CHAPTER III

Ashby, W. R., *Design for a Brain*, New York, Wiley, 1960, Chap. 8.

Beer, S. *Cybernetics of Management*, London, English Universities Press, 1959, Chap. XVI.

Cannon, W. B., *The Way of an Investigator*, New York, Norton, 1945, pp. 113–114.

Davis, R. C., "The Domain of Homeostasis," *Psychological Review*, 1958, *65*, pp. 11–13.

Davis, R. C., and Buchwald, A. M., "An Exploration of Somatic Response Patterns: Stimulus and Sex Patterns," *Journal of Comparative and Physiological Psychology*, 1957, *50*, pp. 44–52.

Davis, R. C.; Lundervold, A.; and Miller, J. D., "The Pattern of Somatic Response during a Repetitive Motor Task and Its Modification of Visual Stimuli," *Journal of Comparative and Physiological Psychology*, 1957, *50*, pp. 53–60.

Gerard, R. W., "Symposium: Theoretical-Experimental Approaches to Memory," *Journal of Verbal Learning and Verbal Behavior*, 1963, *2*, pp. 22–33.

Gerard, R. W., "What Is Memory?," *Scientific American*, 1953, *77*, p. 119.

Grinker, R. R. (ed.), *Toward a Unified Theory of Human Behavior*, New York, Basic Books, 1956, p. 5.

Gutherie, E. R., *The Psychology of Learning*, New York, Harper, 1952.

Kempf, E. J., "Basic Biodynamics," *Annals of the New York Academy of Science*, 1958, *73*, pp. 869–910.

Koell, W. R., and Ferry, A., "Cortico-Subcortical Homeostasis in the Cat's Brain," *Science,* 1963, *142,* pp. 586–589.

Le Châtelier, H., "Recherches expérimentales et théoriques sur les équilibres chimiques," *Annales des Mines,* Huitième Série, Memoires, XIII, Paris, Dumond, 1888.

Lehninger, A. L., "How Cells Transform Energy," *Scientific American,* 1961, *205,* pp. 62–73.

Lorente de No, R., "Analysis of the Activity of the Chains of Internuncial Neuroses," *Journal of Neuro-physiology,* 1938, *1,* pp. 207–244.

Pareto, V., *The Mind and Society,* Vol. IV, New York, Harcourt, Brace, 1935.

Von Foerster, H., "Quantum Theory of Memory," in *Transactions of Sixth American Conference on Cybernetics,* New York, Josiah Macy, Jr., Foundation, 1950.

Weiss, P., "Animal Behavior as System Reaction," originally published in *Biologia Generalis,* 1925, *1,* pp. 167–248; translated and republished in *General Systems,* 1959, *4,* pp. 1–44.

Wiener, N., and Schade, J. P., (eds.), *Nerve, Brain and Memory Models,* Amsterdam, Elsevier, 1963, p. 2.

CHAPTER IV

Ashby, W. R., "Principles of Self-Organizing Systems," in H. von Foerster, *Principles of Self Organization,* New York, Macmillan, 1962, pp. 262ff.

Bronowski, J., in M. Banton, *Darwinism and the Study of Society,* Chicago, Quadrangle, 1961, p. xvii.

Brower, L. P.; Brower, J. V. Z.; and Wescott, P. W., "Experimental Studies of Mimicry," *American Naturalist,* 1960, *64,* pp. 343–355.

Campbell, D. T., "Blind Variation and Selective Retention in Creative Thought as in Other Knowledge Processes," *Psychological Review,* 1960, 7, pp. 380–400.

Cannon, W. B., *The Way of an Investigator,* New York, W. W. Norton, 1945, pp. 113–114.

Coleman, J. C., *Personality Dynamics and Effective Behavior,* Chicago, Scott, Foresman, 1960, p. 69.

Cott, H. B., *Protective Coloration in Animals,* New York, Oxford, 1940, pp. 281–289.

Garner, W. R., *Uncertainty and Structure as Psychological Concepts,* New York, Wiley, 1962.

Gerard, R. W., "Symposium: Theoretical-Experimental Approaches to Memory," *Journal of Verbal Learning and Verbal Behavior,* 1963, 2, pp. 22–33.

Grant, V., *The Origin of Adaptations,* New York, Columbia, 1963, Part I.

Hall, C. S., and Lindsey, G., *Theories of Personality,* New York, Wiley, 1957, p. 468.

Harada, K., and Fox, S. W., "The Thermal Synthesis of Amino-Acids from a Hypothetically Primitive Terrestrial Atmosphere," in S. W. Fox (ed.), *The Origins of Prebiological Systems and Their Molecular Matrices,* New York, Academic Press, 1965, pp. 187–201.

Harada, K., and Fox, S. W., "Thermal Synthesis of Natural Amino-Acids from Postulated Terrestrial Atmosphere," *Nature,* 1964, *201,* pp. 335–336.

Harlow, H. F., and Harlow, M. K., "Social Deprivation in Monkeys," *Scientific American,* 1962, *207,* pp. 137–146.

Heisenberg, W., *The Physical Principles of the Quantum Theory* (trans. by C. Eckart and F. C. Hoyt), New York, Dover, 1930.

Henderson, L. J., *Fitness of the Environment,* New York, Macmillan, 1913.

Hersey, J., *Hiroshima,* New York, Knopf, 1946, p. 49.

London, I. D., "The Concept of the Behavioral Spectrum," *Journal of Genetic Psychology,* 1949, *74,* pp. 177–184.

Marney, M. C., and Smith, N. M., "The Domain of Adaptive Systems: A Rudimentary Taxonomy," *General Systems Yearbook,* 1964, *9,* p. 113.

Minsky, M., "Steps Toward Artificial Intelligence," in E. A. Feigenbaum and J. Feldman, *Computers and Thought,* New York, McGraw-Hill, 1963, pp. 406–450.

National Research Council, Committee on Disaster Studies, 1952–61.

Norris, K. S., "Trained Porpoise Released in an Open Sea," *Science,* 1965, *147,* pp. 1048–1050.

Powell, J. W., *An Introduction to the Natural History of Disaster,* Baltimore, Psychiatric Institute of the University of Maryland, 1954.

Rogers, C. R., *Client-Centered Therapy,* Boston, Houghton Mifflin, 1951, pp. 509ff.

Rosenblatt, J. S., and Lehrman, D. S., "Maternal Behavior of the Laboratory Rat," in H. L. Rheingold (ed.), *Maternal Behavior in Mammals,* New York, Wiley, 1963, Chap. 1.

Russell, W. M. S., "Evolutionary Concepts in Behavioral Science: IV, The Analogy Between Organic and Individual Behavioral Evolution, the Evolution of Intelligence," *General Systems Yearbook,* 1962, *7,* pp. 157–193.

Selye, H., *The Physiology and Pathology of Exposure to Stress,* Montreal, Acta, 1950.

Sherif, M., and Cantril, H., *The Psychology of Ego-Involvements,* New York, Wiley, 1947.

Skinner, B. F., *Science and Human Behavior,* New York, Macmillan, 1953, p. 282.

Snygg, D., and Coombs, A. W., *Individual Behavior,* New York, Harper, 1949.

Wertheimer, M., "Experimentelle Studien uber des sehen von bewegung," *Zeitschrift für Psychologie,* 1912, *61,* pp. 161–265.

Whyte, W. J., Jr., *The Organization Man,* New York, Simon & Schuster, 1956.

Wolfenstein, M., *Disaster, a Psychological Essay,* Glencoe, Ill., Free Press, 1957.

Zadek, L. A., "The Concept of a State in Systems Theory," in M. D. Mesarovic (ed.), *Views on General Systems Theory,* New York, Wiley, 1964.

CHAPTER V

Allee, W. C., and Evans, G., "Further Studies on the Effect of Numbers on the Rate of Cleavage in Eggs of Arbacia," *Journal of Cell and Comparative Psychology,* 1937, *10,* pp. 15–28.

Berlyne, D. E., "The Arousal and Satiation of Perceptual Curiosity in the Rat," *Journal of Comparative and Physiological Psychology,* 1955, *48,* pp. 328–346.

Best, J. B., and Marschak, J., "Round Table Discussion of Behavior Theory," *Behavioral Science,* 1956, *1,* pp. 69–78.

Boulding, K. E., "Toward a General Theory of Growth," *General Systems Yearbook,* 1956, *1,* pp. 66–75.

Butler, R. A., "Discrimination Learning by Rhesus Monkeys to Visual-exploration Motivation," *Journal of Comparative and Physiological Psychology,* 1953, *46,* pp. 95–98.

Coghill, G. E., "Correlated Anatomical and Physiological Studies of the Nervous System of Amphibia," *Journal of Comparative Neurology,* 1926, *40,* pp. 127–141.

Dember, W. N.; Earl, R. W.; and Paradise, N., "Response by Rats to Differential Stimulus Complexity," *Journal of Comparative and Physiological Psychology,* 1957, *50,* pp. 514–518.

Detwiler, S. R., "Further Experiments upon the Transplantation of Embryonic Spinal-Cord Segments," *Journal of Experimental Zoology,* 1929, *52,* pp. 351–366.

Dingman, W., and Sporn, M. B., "Molecular Theories of Memory," *Science,* 1964, *144,* pp. 26–29.

Garner, W. R., *Uncertainty and Structures as Psychological Concepts,* New York, Wiley, 1962.

Grinker, R. R. (ed.), *Toward a Unified Theory of Human Behavior,* New York, Basic Books, 1956, p. 120.

Harlow, H. F.; Harlow, M. K.; and Meyer, D. R., "Learning Motivated by a Manipulation Drive," *Journal of Experimental Psychology,* 1950, *40,* pp. 228–234.

Luckwill, L. C., "Fruit Growth in Relation to Internal and External Chemical Stimuli," in D. Rudnick (ed.), *Cell, Organism and Milieu,* New York, Ronald, 1959, p. 225.

Merwin, R., "Some Group Effects on the Rate of Cleavage and Early Development of Frog Eggs," *Physiological Zoology,* 1945, *18,* pp. 16–34.

Miller, J. G., "Living Systems: Basic Concepts," *Behavioral Science,* 1965, *10,* pp. 193–237, 380–411.

Russell, W. M. S., "Evolutionary Concepts in Behavioral Science," *General Systems,* 1958, *3,* pp. 18–28.

Thibaut, J. W., and Kelley, H. H., *The Social Psychology of Groups,* New York, Wiley, 1959.

Torrey, J. G., "Experimental Modification of Development in the Root," in D. Rudnick (ed.), *Cell, Organism and Milieu,* New York, Ronald, 1958, pp. 203–204.

CHAPTER VI

Adams, S. N., "Status Congruency as a Variable in Small Group Performance," *Social Forces,* 1953, *32,* p. 17.

Allport, F. H., *Theories of Perception and the Concept of Structure,* New York, Wiley, 1955, pp. 522ff.

Argyris, C., *Personality and Organization,* New York, Harper, 1957.

Asch, S. E., *Social Psychology,* New York, Prentice-Hall, 1952, p. 484.

Back, K. W., "Can Subjects Be Human and Humans Be Subjects?," in J. H. Criswell, H. Solomon, and P. Suppes, *Mathematical Methods in Small Group Processes,* Palo Alto, Stanford, 1962, p. 35.

Back, K. W.; Hood, T. C.; and Brehm, M. L., "The Subject Role in Small Group Experiments," *Social Forces,* 1964, *43,* pp. 181–187.

Bales, R. F., *Interaction Process; A Method for the Study of Small Groups,* Cambridge, Mass., Addison-Wesley, 1950.

Barker, R. G. (ed.), *The Stream of Behavior,* New York, Appleton-Century-Crofts, 1963.

Bauer, R. A., "The Obstinate Audience: The Influence Process from the Point of View of Social Communication," *American Psychologist,* 1964, *19,* pp. 319–328.

Berrien, F. K., "Homeostasis of Small Groups," *General Systems Yearbook,* 1964, 9, pp. 205–217.

Berrien, F. K., *Democracy in Village Japan,* New Brunswick, N.J., Rutgers, The State University, Technical Report 12, Contract Nonr-404(10), 1963.

Berrien, F. K., and Angoff, W. H., *Homeostasis Theory of Small Groups V: Case Study,* New Brunswick, N.J., Rutgers, The State University, Technical Report 7, Contract Nonr-404(10), 1960.

Biddle, B. J., and Thomas, E. J. (eds.), *Role Theory,* New York, Wiley, 1966.

Bunge, M. A., "A General Black Box Theory," *Philosophy of Science,* 1963, *30,* pp. 346–358.

Cartwright, D., and Zander, A. F. (eds.), *Group Dynamics,* Evanston, Ill., Row, Peterson, 1959, Chap. 3.

Cattell, R. B.; Saunders, D. R.; and Stice, G. F., "Dimensions of Syntality in Small Groups," *Human Relations,* 1953, *6,* pp. 331–356.

Davison, W. P., "On the Effects of Communication," *Public Opinion Quarterly,* 1959, *23,* p. 360.

Du Brul, E. L., *Evolution of the Speech Apparatus,* Springfield, Ill., Thomas, 1958, p. 90.

Durkin, J., "Groups in Loops," unpublished Ph.D. dissertation, New Brunswick, N.J., Rutgers, The State University, 1965.

Edwards, W., "The Theory of Decision Making," *Psychological Bulletin,* 1954, *51,* pp. 380–417.

Festinger, L., *A Theory of Cognitive Dissonance,* Evanston, Ill., Row, Peterson, 1957.

Festinger, L., "A Theory of Social Comparison Processes," *Human Relations,* 1954, *7,* pp. 117–140.

Garner, W. R., *Uncertainty and Structures as Psychological Concepts,* New York, Wiley, 1962.

Getzels, J. W., and Guba, E. G., "Role Conflict and Personality," *Journal of Personality,* 1955, *24,* pp. 74–85.

Goldman, R. M., "Conflict, Cooperation and Choice: An Exploration of Conceptual Relationships," in N. F. Washburn (ed.), *Decisions, Values and Groups,* New York, Macmillan, 1962, pp. 410–439.

Gross, E., "Symbiosis and Consensus as Integrating Factors in Small Groups," *American Sociological Review,* 1956, *21,* pp. 174–179.

Guetzkow, H., "Differentiation of Roles in Task-Oriented Groups," in D. Cartwright, and A. Zander (eds.), *Group Dynamics,* Evanston, Ill., Row, Peterson, 1960, pp. 283–704.

Harbison, F. H., and Coleman, J. R., *Goals and Strategy in Collective Bargaining,* New York, Harper, 1951.

Hare, A. P., *Handbook of Small Group Research,* New York, Free Press, 1962, p. 74.

Heider, F., *The Psychology of Interpersonal Relations,* New York, Wiley, 1958.

Helson, H., "Adaptation Level Theory," in S. Koch (ed.), *Psychology, a Study of a Science,* Vol. 1, New York, McGraw-Hill, 1959, pp. 565–621.

Heyns, R. W., "Effects of Variation in Leadership on Participant Behavior in Discussion Groups," unpublished dissertation, Ann Arbor, University of Michigan, 1948.

Hood, T., *The Decision to Participate in Small Group Experiments: Patterns of Self-Disclosure and the Volunteer,* Durham, N.C., Duke University, Technical Report 14, Contract Nonr-1181-11, 1964.

Hughes, E. C., "The Knitting of Racial Groups in Industry," *American Sociological Review,* 1946, *11,* pp. 512–519.

Indik, B. P., *Homeostasis Theory of Small Groups VIII: Longitudinal Study,* New Brunswick, N.J., Rutgers, The State University, Technical Report 11, Contract Nonr-404(10), 1963.

Klein, J., *The Study of Groups,* London, Routledge & Kegan Paul, 1956, p. 114.

Leavitt, H. J., "Some Effects of Certain Communication Nets upon Organization and Performance in Task-Oriented Groups," *Journal of Abnormal and Social Psychology,* 1951, *46,* pp. 38–50.

Leavitt, H. J., and Bass, B. M., "Organizational Psychology," in *Annual Review of Psychology,* Palo Alto: Annual Reviews, 1964, *15,* p. 381.

Lodahl, T. M., and Porter, L. W., "Psychometric Score Patterns, Social Characteristics and Productivity of Small Industrial Work Groups," *Journal of Applied Psychology,* 1961, *45,* pp. 73–79.

Maccoby, N., and Maccoby, E. E., "Homeostatic Theory in Attitude Change," *Public Opinion Quarterly,* 1961, *28,* pp. 538–545.

Maier, N. R. F., and Hoffman, L. R., "Organization and Creative Problem Solving," *Journal of Applied Psychology,* 1961, *45,* pp. 277–280.

Mason, E. S., *The Corporation in Modern Society,* Cambridge, Mass., Harvard, 1960.

Miles, M. B., *Innovation in Education,* New York, Teachers College, 1964, Chap. 19.

Miller, J. G., "The Organization of Life," *Perspectives in Biology and Medicine,* 1965, *9,* pp. 107–125.

Mills, T. M., "A Sleeper Variable in Small Group Research: The Experimenter," *Pacific Sociological Review,* 1962, *5,* pp. 21–28.

Murchison, C., "The Formation of Social Hierarchies in Gallus Domesticus," *Journal of Social Psychology,* 1935, *6,* pp. 3–30; and *Journal of General Psychology,* 1935, *12,* pp. 3–39.

Newcomb, T., *The Acquaintanceship Process,* New York, Holt, Rinehart and Winston, 1961.

Newcomb, T., *Social Psychology,* New York, Dryden, 1950.

Ora, J. P., Jr., *Charactcristics of the Volunteer for Psychological Investigations,* Nashville, Tenn., Vanderbilt University, Contract Nonr-2149(0), Technical Report 27, 1965.

Orne, M. T., "On the Social Psychology of the Psychological Experiment," *American Psychologist,* 1962, *17,* pp. 776–783.

Osgood, C., and Tannenbaum, H., "The Principle of Congruity in the Prediction of Attitude Change," *Psychological Review,* 1953, *60,* pp. 393–404.

Parsons, T., and Shils, E. A., *Toward a General Theory of Action,* Cambridge, Mass., Harvard, 1951.

Pepitone, A., *Attraction and Hostility,* New York, Atherton, 1964.

Ramsöy, O., *Social Groups as System and Sub-system,* New York, Free Press, 1963.

Ronken, H. O., and Lawrence, P. R., *Administering Change,* Boston, Harvard University Graduate School of Business Administration, 1952.

Schelling, T. C., *The Strategy of Conflict,* Cambridge, Mass., Harvard, 1963, Chap. 4.

Schulman, C. A., "Some Properties of Thurstone Scales," unpublished Ph.D. dissertation, New Brunswick, N.J., Rutgers, The State University, 1964.

Schutz, W. C., *FIRO,* New York, Rinehart, 1958.

Sells, S. B., *Ecology and the Science of Psychology,* Fort Worth, Texas Christian University, Special Report, Contract Nonr-3436(00), 1965.

Sherif, M., "An Experimental Approach to the Study of Attitudes," *Sociometry,* 1937, *1,* pp. 90–98.

Sherif, M.; Harvey, O. J.; White, B. J.; Hood, W. R.; and Sherif, C. E., *Intergroup Conflict and Cooperation,* Norman, Okla., Institute of Group Relations, 1961.

Sherif, M.; White, B. J.; and Harvey, O. J., "Status in Experimentally Induced Group," *American Journal of Sociology,* 1955, *60,* pp. 370–379.

Simon, H. A., *Models of Man: Social and Rational,* New York, Wiley, 1957, pp. 200–206.

Steinzor, B., "The Development and Evaluation of a Measure of Social Interaction," *Human Relations,* 1949, *2,* pp. 103–121, 319–347.

Talland, G. A., "Task and Interaction Process: Some Characteristics of Therapeutic Group Discussion," *Journal of Abnormal and Social Psychology,* 1955, *50,* pp. 105–109.

Thibaut, J. W., and Kelley, H. H., *The Social Psychology of Groups,* New York, Wiley, 1959.

Thomas, E. J., "Effects of Role Interdependence on Group Functioning," *Human Relations,* 1957, *10,* pp. 347–366.

Thrasher, F., *The Gang,* Chicago, University of Chicago Press, 1927.

Trow, D., and Herschdorfer, G., *An Experiment on the Status Incongruence Phenomenon,* Binghamton, N.Y., State University of New York, Technical Report 3, Contract Nonr-3679(00), 1965.

Tuddenham, R. D., *Studies in Conformity and Yielding,* Berkeley, Calif., University of California, Contract Nonr-NR-170-159, 1961.

Von Neumann, J., "The General and Logical Theory of Automata," in L. A. Jeffress (ed.), *Cerebral Mechanisms in Behavior,* New York, Wiley, 1951, pp. 1–41.

Webb, E. J., and others, *Unobtrusive Measures,* New York, Rand McNally, 1966.

Wolfe, D. M., and Snoek, J. D., "A Study of Tension and Adjustment under Role Conflict," *Journal of Social Issues,* 1962, *18, 3,* pp. 102–121.

Zaleznik, A., *Worker Satisfaction and Development,* Boston, Harvard University Graduate School of Business Administration, 1956, pp. 75ff.

CHAPTER VII

Benne, K.; Bradford, L. P.; and Lippitt, R. O., "The Laboratory Method," in L. P. Bradford, J. R. Gibb, and K. D. Benne (eds.), *T-Group Theory and Laboratory Method,* New York, Wiley, 1964.

Berrien, F. K., "Homeostasis of Groups," *General Systems Yearbook,* 1964, *9,* pp. 205–217.

Bradford, L. P.; Gibb, J. R.; and Benne, K. D. (eds.), *T-Group Theory and Laboratory Method,* New York, Wiley, 1964.

Bunker, D. R., "Individual Applications of Laboratory Training," *Journal of Applied and Behavioral Science,* 1965, *1,* pp. 131–148.

Caplow, T., "A Theory of Coalitions in the Triad," *American Sociological Review,* 1956, *21,* pp. 489–493.

Day, R. C., and Hamblin, R. L., *Some Effects of Close and Punitive Styles of Supervision,* St. Louis, Mo., Washington University, Technical Report 8, Contract Nonr-816(11), 1961.

DeCharms, R., and Bridgeman, W., *Leadership Compliance and Group Behavior,* St. Louis, Mo., Washington University, Technical Report 9, Contract Nonr-816(11), 1961.

Etzioni, A., "Two Approaches to Organizational Analysis: A Critique and a Suggestion," *Administrative Science Quarterly,* 1960, *5,* p. 264.

Festinger, L., "The Psychological Effects of Insufficient Rewards," *American Psychologist,* 1961, *16,* pp. 1–11.

Fleishman, E. J.; Harris, E. F.; and Burtt, H. E., *Leadership and Supervision in Industry,* Columbus, Bureau of Educational Research, Ohio State University, 1955.

Frost, R., "Mending Wall," in G. D. Sanders and J. H. Nelson, *Chief Modern Poets,* New York, Macmillan, 1938.

Gardner, J. W., "Renewal in Societies and Men," *Annual Report,* New York, Carnegie Corporation, 1962, p. 4.

Gerard, R. W.; Kluckhohn, C.; and Rapoport, A., "Biological and Cultural Evolution: Some Analogies and Explorations," *Behavioral Science,* 1956, *1,* pp. 6–34.

Gibb, C. A., "The Sociometry of Leadership in Temporary Groups," *Sociometry,* 1950, *30,* pp. 226–243.

Gross, B. M., "The State of the Nation: Social Systems Accounting," in R. A. Bauer, *Social Indicators,* Cambridge, Mass., M.I.T., 1966.

Gross, B. M., *The Managing of Organizations,* New York, Free Press, 1964.

Guetzkow, H., and Bowes, A., "The Development of Organization in a Laboratory," *Management Science,* 1957, *3,* pp. 380–402.

Haire, M., "Biological Models and Empirical Histories of the Growth of Organizations," in M. Haire (ed.), *Modern Organizational Theory,* New York, Wiley, 1959.

Indik, B. P., "Organization Size and Member Participation: Some Empirical Tests of Alternative Explanations," *Human Relations,* 1965, *18,* pp. 339–350.

Indik, B. P., "The Relation between Organization Size and Supervision Ratio," *Administrative Science Quarterly,* 1964, *9,* pp. 301–312.

Klein, J., *The Study of Groups,* London, Routledge and Kegan Paul, 1956, p. 179.

March, J. G., and Simon, H. A., *Organizations,* New York, Wiley, 1958.

McNulty, J. E., "Organizational Change in Growing Enterprises," *Administrative Science Quarterly,* 1962, *7,* pp. 1–21.

Miller, J. G., "Living Systems: Basic Concepts," *Behavioral Science,* 1965, *10,* pp. 193–237.

Roethlisberger, F. J., and Dickson, W. J., *Management and the Worker,* Cambridge, Mass., Harvard, 1949, Part IV.

Seashore, S., and Yuchtman, E., "The Elements of Organizational Performance," in B. P. Indik and F. K. Berrien (eds.), *People, Groups and Organizations,* New York, Teachers College, 1968.

Stock, D. A., "A Survey of Research on T-Groups," in L. P. Bradford, J. R. Gibb, and K. D. Benne (eds.), *T-Group Theory and Laboratory Method,* New York, Wiley, 1964, pp. 395–441.

Trow, D., *An Experiment on the Status Incongruence Phenomena,* Columbus, O., Ohio State University, Contract Nonr-3679, Technical Report 3, 1965.

Vinacke, W. E., and Arkoff, A., "An Experimental Study of Coalitions in the Triad," *American Sociological Review,* 1957, *22,* pp. 406–414.

Vinacke, W. E., and Gullickson, G. R., *Age and Sex Differences in the Formation of Coalitions,* Honolulu, University of Hawaii, Contract Nonr-3748(02), Technical Report 3, 1963.

Yinger, J. M., *Toward a Field Theory of Behavior,* New York, McGraw-Hill, 1965.

Youngberg, C. F. X.; Hedberg, R.; and Baxter, B., "Management Action Recommendations Based on One versus Two Dimensions of a Job Satisfaction Questionnaire," *Personnel Psychology,* 1962, *15,* pp. 145–150.

Zaleznik, A.; Christensen, C. R.; and Roethlisberger, F. J., *Motivation, Productivity, and Satisfaction of Workers,* Boston, Harvard Graduate School of Business Administration, 1958, pp. 324 ff.

CHAPTER VIII

Abelson, R. P., "Mathematical Models of the Distribution of Attitudes under Controversy," in N. Fredericksen and H. Gulliksen (eds.), *Contributions to Mathematical Psychology,* New York, Holt, Rinehart and Winston, 1964, Chap. 6.

Adams, S., "Social Climate and Productivity in Small Military Groups," *American Sociological Review,* 1954, *19,* pp. 421–425.

Ashby, W. R., *An Introduction to Cybernetics,* London, Chapman and Hall, 1956.

Bales, R. F., "Small-Group Theory and Research," in R. K. Merton, L. Brown, and L. S. Cottrell (eds.), *Sociology Today: Problems and Prospects,* New York, Basic Books, 1959, pp. 303–305.

Bales, R. F., "The Equilibrium Problem in Small Groups," in P. Hare, E. F. Borgatta, and R. F. Bales (eds.), *Small Groups: Studies in Social Interaction,* New York, Knopf, 1955, pp. 424–463.

Bales, R. F., "The Equilibrium Problem in Small Groups," in T. Parsons, R. F. Bales, and E. A. Shils, *Working Papers in the Theory of Action,* New York, Free Press, 1953, pp. 111–161.

Barnard, C. I., *Functions of the Executive,* Cambridge, Mass., Harvard University Press, 1938.

Bennis, W. G., "Organizational Developments and the Fate of Bureaucracy," *Industrial and Management Review,* 1966, 7, No. 2, pp. 41–56.

Berrien, F. K., "Homeostasis of Groups," Ann Arbor, *General Systems Yearbook,* 1964, 9, pp. 205–217.

Berrien, F. K., and Angoff, W. H., *Homeostasis Theory of Small Groups V,* New Brunswick, N.J., Rutgers, The State University, Technical Report 7, Contract Nonr-404(10), 1960.

Berrien, F. K., and Angoff, W. H., *Homeostasis Theory of Small Groups II,* New Brunswick, N.J., Rutgers, The State University, Technical Report 3, Contract Nonr-404(10), 1958.

Berrien, F. K., and Indik, B. P., *Homeostasis Theory of Small Groups VI: Voluntary Organizations,* New Brunswick, N.J., Rutgers, The State University, Technical Report 8, Contract Nonr-404(10), 1961.

Boulding, K. E., "The Economics of Human Conflict," in E. B. McNeil, *The Nature of Human Conflict,* Englewood Cliffs, N.J.: Prentice-Hall, 1965.

Cannon, W. B., *The Way of an Investigator,* New York, Norton, 1945, p. 113.

Forrester, J. W., *Industrial Dynamics,* New York, Wiley, 1961.

Guetzkow, H. (ed.), *Simulation in Social Science: Readings,* Englewood Cliffs, N.J., Prentice-Hall, 1962.

Guetzkow, H., and Gyr, J., "An Analysis of Conflict in Decision-Making Groups," *Human Relations,* 1954, 7, pp. 367–382.

Gullahorn, J. T., and Gullahorn, J. E., "A Computer Model of Elementary Social Behavior," in E. A. Feigenbaum and J. Feldman, *Computers and Thought,* New York, McGraw-Hill, 1963, pp. 375–388.

Haire, M. (ed.), *Modern Oragnization Theory,* New York, Wiley, 1959.

Hare, A. P., *Handbook of Small Group Research,* New York, Free Press, 1962, pp. 339–363.

Holsti, O. R., "East-West Conflict and Sino-Soviet Relations," *Journal of Applied and Behavioral Science,* 1965, *1,* pp. 115–130.

Homans, G. C., *Social Behavior: Its Elementary Forms,* New York, Harcourt, Brace & World, 1961.

Indik, B. P., *Homeostasis Theory of Small Groups VII: Longitudinal Studies,* New Brunswick, N.J., Rutgers, The State University, Technical Report 10, Contract Nonr-404(10), 1962.

Indik, B. P.; Georgopoulos, B. S.; and Seashore, S. E., "Superior-Subordinate Relationships and Performance," *Personnel Psychology,* 1961, *14,* pp. 357–374.

Indik, B. P., and Tyler, J., *Homeostasis Theory of Small Groups VIII,* New Brunswick, N.J., Rutgers, The State University, Technical Report 11, Contract Nonr-404(10), 1963.

Katz, D.; Maccoby, N.; Gurin, G.; and Floor, L. G., *Productivity, Supervision, and Morale among Railroad Workers,* Ann Arbor, Survey Research Center, University of Michigan, 1951, pp. 33–34.

Lewin, K., "Frontiers in Group Dynamics," *Human Relations,* 1947, *1,* pp. 2–38.

Likert, R., *New Patterns of Management,* New York, McGraw-Hill, 1961, pp. 102–103.

March, J. G., and Simon, H. A., *Organizations,* New York, Wiley, 1958.

Meier, R. L., "Explorations in the Realm of Organization Theory IV: The Simulation of Social Organization," *Behavioral Science,* 1961, *6,* pp. 232–248.

Miller, J. G., "Living Systems: Basic Concepts," *Behavioral Science,* 1965, *10,* pp. 193–237, 380–411.

Noel, R. C., *Theory and Procedures for a Simulation of International Relations,* Englewood Cliffs, N.J., Prentice-Hall, 1963.

Parsons, T., *Essays in Sociological Theory, Pure and Applied,* Glencoe, Ill., Free Press, 1949, p. 35.

Pfiffner, J. M.; Comrey, A. L.; Beem, H. P.; High, W. S.; Wilson, R. C.; and others, "Factors Influencing Organizational Effectiveness, I-VIII," *Personnel Psychology,* 1952, *5,* to 1955, *8.*

Psathas, G., "Phase Movement and Equilibrium Tendencies in Interaction Process in Psychotherapy Groups," *Sociometry,* 1960, *23,* pp. 177–194.

Roethlisberger, F. J., *Management and Morale,* Cambridge, Mass., Harvard, 1944, p. 112.

Rome, S. C., and Rome, B. K., "Computer Simulation toward a Theory of Large Organizations," in H. Borko (ed.), *Computer Applications in the Behavioral Sciences,"* Englewood Cliffs, N.J., Prentice-Hall, 1962, Chap. 22.

Ronken, H. O., and Lawrence, P. R., *Administering Changes: A Case Study,* Cambridge, Mass., Harvard, 1952.

Simon, H. A., *Administrative Behavior,* New York, Macmillan, 1947.

Stewart, L., "Management Games Today," in J. M. Kibbee, C. J. Craft, and B. Nanus (eds.), *Management Games,* New York, Reinhold, 1961, Chap. 11.

Whyte, W. F., and others, *Money and Motivation,* New York, Harper, 1955, Part 1.

Zaleznik, A.; Christensen, C. R.; and Roethlisberger, F. J., *Motivation, Productivity, and Satisfaction of Workers,* Boston, Harvard Graduate School of Business Administration, 1958, p. 327.

CHAPTER IX

Ardrey, R., *The Territorial Imperative,* New York, Atheneum, 1966.

Ash, M. A., "An Analysis of Power, with Special Reference to International Politics," *World Politics,* 1951, *3,* pp. 218–237.

Berkowitz, L., *Aggression: A Social Psychological Analysis,* New York, McGraw-Hill, 1962, pp. 27–29.

Boulding, K. E., *Conflict and Defense: A General Theory,* New York, Harper, 1962, Chap. 1.

Brehm, J. W., *A Theory of Psychological Reactance,* New York, Academic Press, 1966.

Brody, R. A., "Systematic Effects of the Spread of Nuclear Weapons Technology," *Journal of Conflict Resolution,* 1963, *7,* pp. 675–676, 699–712.

Brown, J. S., and Farber, I. E., "Emotions Conceptualized as Intervening Variables—with Suggestions toward a Theory of Frustration," *Psychological Bulletin,* 1951, *48,* pp. 465–495.

Buss, A. H., *The Psychology of Aggression,* New York, Wiley, 1961, pp. 28–29.

Campbell, D. T. (a), "Perception as a Substitute Trial and Error," *Psychological Review,* 1956, *63,* pp. 330–432.

Campbell, D. T. (b), "Adaptive Behavior from Random Response," *Behavioral Science,* 1956, *1,* pp. 105–110.

Coe, R. M., *Conflict, Interference and Aggression: Computer Simulation of a Social Process,* St. Louis, Mo., Washington University, Technical Report 17, Contract Nonr-816(11), 1963.

Davies, J. C., "Toward a Theory of Revolution," *American Sociological Review,* 1962, *27,* pp. 5–10.

Day, R. C., and Hamblin, R. L., *Some Effects of Close and Punitive Styles of Supervision,* St. Louis, Mo., Washington University, Technical Report 8, Contract Nonr-816(11), 1961.

Dollard, J., and others, *Frustration and Aggression,* New Haven, Yale, 1939.

Driver, M. J., *A Structural Analysis of Aggression, Stress, and Personality in Internation Simulation,* Lafayette, Ind., Purdue University, Institute for Research in Behavioral, Economic, and Management Sciences, Paper 97, 1965.

Feierabend, I. K., and Feierabend, R. L., "The Relationship of Systemic Frustration, Political Coercion, International Tension and Political Stability: A Cross-National Study," paper presented at American Psychological Association Meetings, New York, 1966.

Guetzkow, H. (ed.), *Simulation in Social Science: Readings,* Englewood Cliffs, N.J., Prentice-Hall, 1962.

Hamilton, G. V., "A Study of Perseverance Reactions in Primates and Rodents," *Journal of Comparative Psychology,* 1933, *16,* pp. 237–253.

Harvey, O. J.; Hunt, D. E.; and Schroeder, H. M., *Conceptual Systems and Personality Organization,* New York, Wiley, 1961.

Holsti, O. R., "Perceptual and Action Data, July 1956," in R. A. Brody, O. R. Holsti, and others, *Internation Conflict, Dyadic and Mediated: Case Studies of Egypt, Israel, and the United Nations at Five Points in Time,* Stanford, Calif., Stanford University, Technical Report 1, Contract Nonr-225(82), 1965.

Holsti, O. R., and North, R. C., "The 1914 Case," *American Political Science Review*, 1965, *59*, pp. 365–378.

Katona, G., *The Mass Consumption Society*, New York, McGraw-Hill, 1964, p. 343.

Lewin, K., *Field Theory in Social Science*, New York, Harper, 1951, Chap. III.

Loomis, S., *Paris in the Terror: June 1793–July 1794*, Philadelphia, Lippincott, 1964, pp. 11–12.

Mack, R. W., and Snyder, R. C., "The Analysis of Social Conflict—Toward an Overview and Synthesis," *Journal of Conflict Resolution*, 1957, *3*, pp. 312ff.

Maier, N. R. F., *Frustration: A Study of Behavior Without a Goal*, New York, McGraw-Hill, 1949.

Maier, N. R. F., "The Role of Frustration in Social Movements," *Psychological Review*, 1942, *49*, pp. 586–599.

Maier, N. R. F.; Glaser, N. M.; and Klee, J. B., "Studies of Abnormal Behavior in the Rat, III. The Development of Behavior Fixations Through Frustration," *Journal of Experimental Psychology*, 1940, *26*, pp. 521–546.

McClelland, C., *A World Politics Game*, San Francisco State College, 1959 (mimeographed).

McNeil, E. B., "Personal Hostility and International Aggression," *Journal of Conflict Resolution*, 1961, *5*, pp. 279–290.

McNeil, E. B. (ed.), *The Nature of Human Conflict*, Englewood Cliffs, N.J., Prentice-Hall, 1965, Chap. 2.

Merritt, R. L., "Systems and the Disintegration of Empires," *General Systems Yearbook*, 1963, *8*, pp. 91–103.

Miller, N. E., "The Frustration-Aggression Hypothesis," *Psychological Review*, 1941, *48*, pp. 337–342.

Murray, H. A., *Explorations in Personality*, New York, Oxford, 1938.

Noel, R. C., *Theory and Procedure for a Simulation of International Relations*, Englewood Cliffs, N.J., Prentice-Hall, 1963.

Patrick, J. R., "Studies in Rational Behavior and Emotional Excitement, II. The Effect of Emotional on Rational Behavior in Human Subjects," *Journal of Comparative Psychology*, 1934, *18*, pp. 153–195.

Pruitt, D. G., *Reaction Systems and Instability in Interpersonal and International Affairs*, Buffalo, State University of New York, Technical Report 2, Contract Nonr-00014-67, 1967.

Rank, O., *Truth and Reality*, New York, Knopf, 1936.

Richardson, L. F., *Arms and Insecurity*, London, Stevens, 1960.

Richardson, L. F., *Statistics of Deadly Quarrels*, London, Stevens, 1960.

Rogers, C. R., "The Actualizing Tendency in Relation to 'Motive' and to Consciousness," *Nebraska Symposium on Motivation*, Lincoln, University of Nebraska Press, 1963, pp. 6–8.

Rummel, R. J., "Dimensions of Conflict Behavior within and between Nations," *General Systems Yearbook*, 1963, *8*, pp. 1–49.

Singer, J. D., *Studies in Deterrence VII: Soviet and American Foreign Policy Attitudes, a Content Analysis of Elite Articulations,* China Lake, Calif., U.S. Naval Ordnance Test Station, TP 3226, 1964.

Stagner, R., *The Psychology of Industrial Conflict,* New York, Wiley, 1956.

Thibaut, J. W., and Riecken, H. W., "Authoritarian Status and the Communication of Aggression," *Human Relations,* 1955, *8,* pp. 95–120.

Wilkins, E. J., and DeCharms, R., *Authoritarianism and Power Cues,* St. Louis, Mo., Washington University, Technical Report 12, Contract Nonr-816(11), 1961.

CHAPTER X

Ackoff, R. L., "General Systems Theory and Systems Research: Contrasting Conceptions of Systems Science," in M. D. Mesarovic (ed.), *Views of General Systems Theory,* New York, Wiley, 1964.

Asch, S. E., "Opinions and Social Pressure," *Scientific American,* 1955, *193,* pp. 31–35.

Born, M., *Physics in My Generation,* New York, Pergamon, 1956, p. 128.

Boulding, K. E., "General Systems Theory—the Skeleton of Science," *Management Science,* 1956, *2,* pp. 198–199.

Brayfield, A. H., and Crockett, W. H., "Employee Attitudes and Employee Performance," *Psychological Bulletin,* 1955, *52,* pp. 396–424.

Cofer, C. N., "Motivation," *Annual Review of Psychology,* Palo Alto, Calif., Annual Reviews, 1959, pp. 173–202.

Durkheim, É., *Les Formes élémentaires de la vie réligieuse,* Paris, Alcan, 1912.

French, J. R. P., Jr., and Raven, B., "The Basis of Social Power," in D. Cartwright (ed.), *Studies in Social Power,* Ann Arbor, Institute for Social Research, 1959.

Gerard, R. W.; Kluckhohn, C.; and Rapoport, A., "Biological and Cultural Evolution," *Behavioral Science,* 1956, *1,* pp. 6–43.

Heisenberg, W., *The Physicist's Conception of Nature,* New York, Harcourt, Brace, 1958, p. 153.

Homans, G. C., *Social Behavior,* New York, Harcourt, Brace & World, 1961.

Homans, G. C., *The Human Group,* New York, Harcourt, Brace, 1950.

Kelly, G. A., "Europe's Matrix of Decision," *Nebraska Symposium on Motivation,* Lincoln, University of Nebraska Press, 1962, pp. 82–123.

March, J. C., and Simon, H. A., *Organization,* New York, Wiley, 1958.

Matson, F. W., *The Broken Image,* New York, Braziller, 1964.

Mesarovic, M. D. (ed.), *Views of General Systems Theory,* New York, Wiley, 1964.

Morse, N. C., *Satisfactions in the White Collar Job,* Ann Arbor, Survey Research Center, 1953.

Newcomb, T., "The Pigeon Reveals the Man," *Contemporary Psychology,* 1961, *6,* pp. 441–442.

O'Kelly, L. I., "Psychophysiology of Motivation," *Annual Review of Psychology,* Palo Alto, Calif., Annual Reviews, 1963, pp. 57–92.

Pitts, J. R., "Introduction," in T. Parsons, E. Shils, K. D. Naegele, and J. R. Pitts (eds.), *Theories of Society,* New York, Free Press, 1961, II, 685–686.

Rapoport, A., "An Essay on Mind," *General Systems Yearbook,* 1962, *7,* pp. 85–101.

Raven, B., "Social Influence and Power," in I. D. Steiner and M. Fishbein (eds.), *Readings in Contemporary Social Psychology,* New York, Holt, Rinehart and Winston, 1965.

Rogers, C. R., "Actualizing Tendency in Relation to 'Motives' and to Consciousness," *Nebraska Symposium on Motivation,* Lincoln, University of Nebraska Press, 1963, pp. 1–24.

Rosenblatt, F., *Principles of Neurodynamics,* Washington, D.C., Spartan Books, 1962.

Sanford, N., "Will Psychologists Study Human Problems?," *American Psychologist,* 1965, *20,* pp. 192–202.

Seashore, S. E.; Indik, B. P.; and Georgopoulos, B. S., "Relationships among Criteria of Job Performance," *Journal of Applied Psychology,* 1960, *44,* pp. 195–202.

Stagner, R., *Psychology of Personality,* 3rd ed., New York, McGraw-Hill, 1961.

Van den Berg, J. H., *The Changing Nature of Man: Introduction to a Historical Psychology,* New York, Dell, 1964, p. 252.

Zaleznik, A.; Christensen, C. R.; and Roethlisberger, F. J., *Motivation, Productivity, and Satisfaction of Workers,* Boston, Harvard University Graduate School of Business Administration, 1958.

AUTHOR INDEX

SUBJECT INDEX